Professional Integrity

Professional Integrity

Thinking Ethically

Michael S. Pritchard

University Press of Kansas

Published by the
University Press of
Kansas (Lawrence,
Kansas 66045),
which was organized
by the Kansas Board
of Regents and is
operated and funded
by Emporia State
University, Fort Hays
State University,
Kansas State
University, Pittsburg
State University, the
University of Kansas,
and Wichita State
University

© 2006 by the University Press of Kansas

Library of Congress Cataloging-in-Publication Data

Pritchard, Michael S.
    Professional integrity : thinking ethically /
Michael S. Pritchard.
            p. cm.
Includes bibliographical references and index.
    ISBN 0-7006-1446-x (cloth : alk. paper)
    1. Professional ethics.   i. Title.
    BJ1725.P752   2006
    174—dc22   2005032813

British Library Cataloguing in Publication Data is available.

Printed in the United States of America

10 9 8 7 6 5 4 3 2 1

The paper used in this publication meets the minimum
requirements of the American National Standard for
Permanence of Paper for Printed Library Materials z39.48-1984.

For James A. Jaksa, good friend and colleague

Contents

Preface, *ix*

1   Introduction, *1*

2   Practical Ethics, *14*

3   Trust and Truthfulness, *32*

4   Good Judgment, *51*

5   Professional Integrity, *67*

6   Basic Duties and Codes of Ethics, *85*

7   Good Works, *100*

8   Working Together, *113*

9   Dispositions, Perception, and Imagination, *133*

10   Moral Development, *151*

Notes, *165*

Selected Bibliography, *183*

Index, *187*

Preface

During the more than twenty-five years that I have been teaching courses in professional ethics, I have wrestled with the question of what role my own discipline, philosophy, should play. This book represents my current thinking on this matter. Initially, like so many others, I thought that such courses should begin with a general introduction to major ethical theories, particularly those, like utilitarianism, that attempt to organize our thinking around one grounding principle. The basic idea was that these theories would then somehow be applied to the practical context of the professions.

For me, this approach was short-lived, for several reasons. First, I found that it consumed much more time than I anticipated — it was often only after we were several weeks into a course that I began addressing the practical context of the professions to any significant degree. Understandably, students grew somewhat impatient with all this theorizing.

Second, the more I learned about the practical context of professional life, the harder I found it to apply major ethical theories in ways that illuminate the actual ethical problems professionals face. I worried that attempting to fit their problems within the standard ethical theories was placing them in a Procrustean bed that, unfortunately, seemed to cut off, or at least squash, many of their most interesting features.

Third, early on, I had the good fortune of meeting with a group of faculty from engineering and philosophy for two weeks at a workshop held at the Illinois Institute of Technology. Essentially, the engineers and philosophers had to learn how to talk with one another about ethics. Especially eye-opening for me was the response of a very thoughtful engineer to what I thought was a brilliant philosophical lecture on ethical relativism. "What *were* you talking about?" he asked. "With all those 'isms,' I didn't understand a word you said." This was, no doubt, an overstatement, but one with a powerful point: the lecturer had made no attempt to connect his talk with engineering practice.

How this connection might best be made is, indeed, an interesting and important question. However, connecting philosophical concerns about relativism with professional practice should not be that difficult. It is easy to imagine, for example, that engineers working in an international setting might wonder what they should do when confronted with a particular moral demand that seems contrary to what is regarded as acceptable in their home country. But, ethical relativism is a comprehensive theory about *all* of morality; and whether casting a practical problem in such broad terms is helpful is something that itself must be shown rather than taken for granted. Furthermore, bearing the burden of explaining what the theory of ethical relativism amounts to also carries the risk of using practical examples primarily to clarify and test the theory, rather than using the theory to illuminate the practical problems.

Philosophers are well advised to keep this risk in mind as they join with others in talking about the practical, ethical problems that professionals face. My initial foray into engineering ethics at the Illinois Institute of Technology workshop has served me well in this regard. It led me, with my colleague James A. Jaksa (Communication), to take the time to interview dozens of practicing engineers about the ethical challenges they meet in their work. It also led me to collaborate with my Texas A&M colleagues, Charles E. Harris Jr. (Philosophy) and Michael Rabins (Mechanical Engineering), in writing *Engineering Ethics: Concepts and Cases* (3rd ed., Wadsworth, 2005). Throughout our work together we have striven to write with a steady eye on the needs of students preparing themselves to become professionals. This book is written in that spirit as well.

I make no attempt to deal comprehensively with professional ethics. Instead, I concentrate on particular aspects of professional ethics to help us understand what is required if one is to become a responsible professional. The first and second chapters focus on professional ethics as a kind of practical ethics and discuss the implications this has for teaching professional ethics and for the kinds of contributions we might expect philosophical reflection to make to this endeavor. Chapters 3 and 4 explore the importance of trustworthiness and reliable judgment for professional practice. Implicit in these chapters is an appeal to professional integrity, a topic that receives more detailed attention in chapter 5.

Chapter 6 examines the idea of codes of ethics for professions, considering their grounding, possible uses, and limitations. Understandably, codes of ethics emphasize basic duties, the violation of which constitutes wrongdoing. They contain aspirational statements, as well; but these statements are typically brief and undeveloped. Chapter 7 addresses this more aspirational side of professional responsibility, shifting attention from wrongdoing and its prevention or avoidance to the more positive idea of "good works." Chapter 8 emphasizes the fact that professionals typically work with others, not alone. Rather than considering ethical problems as exclusively "mine" or "yours," the notion that many problems are best viewed as "ours" is explored. Chapter 9 develops the idea that dispositions of character and imagination are basic to professional responsibility, thus making it important to consider the sorts of virtues that are needed for responsible practice.

Chapter 10, "Moral Development," ends the book where some might think it should begin. When I give talks on professional responsibility to groups of professionals, it is quite common for someone in the audience to suggest that preparation for professional responsibility should begin with the moral education of children. I agree, and this is what I discuss in chapter 10. However, it seems to me that this is best discussed after considering what responsible professional practice may require. Still, readers anxious to see what I have to say about the relevance of the moral development of children can begin with this chapter—and then read the preceding chapters to see why I say what I do.

It is impossible for me to identify all those who, over my many years of thinking and writing about professional ethics, have helped me in developing my ideas in this book. My colleagues at Western Michigan University, most especially Shirley Bach, the late Sylvia Culp, John Dilworth, Joseph Ellin, Insoo Hyun (now at Case Western Reserve), and James Jaksa, were always available to respond constructively to my half-formed thoughts. Colleagues around the country have been similarly helpful, most especially C. E. Harris and Michael Rabins in our collaborative work in engineering ethics and Vivian Weil, Deborah Johnson, and Michael Davis in our many discussions of conflicts of interest and other topics in professional ethics.

Mike Martin and Martin Benjamin read and commented most helpfully on an earlier draft of the book. Elaine Englehardt did the same with the penultimate draft. I am greatly indebted to all three for their thoughtful suggestions and encouragement.

I also thank Nancy Jackson and others at the University Press of Kansas for their constant encouragement, support, and patience as I worked on this book.

Finally, I must offer special thanks to my now-retired colleague and good friend, James Jaksa, to whom I dedicate this book. Jim and I began teaching an interdisciplinary course on ethics in communication in 1980 and kept this up for fifteen years, when he retired from Western Michigan University's Department of Communication. We also worked together several years, with support from the National Science Foundation, interviewing engineers about ethics in their work. More than anyone else, Jim pressed me to try to clarify what philosophy can contribute to ethical reflection on practical matters. Our joint publications include the now out-of-print *Communication Ethics: Methods of Analysis,* 2nd ed. (Wadsworth, 1994), from which a few passages have been adapted for this book. It has been an honor and a privilege to work closely for so many years with Jim. The tennis and golf have been good, too. One could not hope for a better colleague and friend.

CHAPTER ONE

Introduction

This book is a philosophical examination of some of the contours of profes-sional responsibility. As such, it is a book in practical ethics. To believe that phi-losophy, proceeding alone, can shed much light on professional responsibility is naive. Still, philosophical reflection should be able to contribute something useful. That, at least, is an underlying assumption of this endeavor.

What sorts of philosophical ambitions should guide this inquiry? It is wise to proceed with some caution. On the one hand, as Henry Sidgwick pointed out more than a century ago, insofar as we try to "get to the bottom of things" philo-sophically, we risk falling into interminable disagreement over foundations while failing to shed any light on the practical issues at hand.[1] On the other hand, if we concentrate our attention solely on the specific contexts in which practical issues arise, we risk falling into interminable disagreement about the particulars while at the same time failing to shed any light on the more general aspects of practical and professional ethics.

These are not the concerns of philosophers alone. Since the early 1970s, there has been a rapid rise in the number and variety of courses in ethics in our col-leges and universities, especially regarding the professions. Traditionally, courses in ethics have resided in departments of philosophy or religion. However, fol-lowing the lead of medical ethics, there has been a mushrooming of courses in accountancy, business, communication, computer science, education, engi-neering, journalism, law, nursing, psychology, public administration, and social work, as well as many other professional areas. In the mid-1970s a *Doonesbury* comic strip suggested that the rise of interest in ethics would be a passing fad like "streaking" and that it is simply "Watergate fallout."[2] This forecast has proven false. In short, what we have witnessed over the last several decades is the development of a broad range of inquiry that is commonly referred to as *practical ethics*.[3] Although philosophers have played a leading role in this devel-opment, the issues demanding attention have their origins in the practical realm; and the discussants are not just philosophers.

Had philosophers not joined others in discussing ethical issues in the pro-fessions, conversations would have gone on anyway. How those conversations might have differed is an interesting question. In any case, it seems fair to ask, what is it reasonable to expect philosophical reflection (whether by philosophers or others) to add to these conversations? Serious interest in practical ethics has historical precedence in philosophy; and, as I hope to show throughout this text, much can be learned from these earlier reflections. Among others, prominent philosophers such as Thomas Reid in the eighteenth century and William Whewell and Henry Sidgwick in the nineteenth century devoted a great deal of attention to the question of what role philosophy might play in exploring issues in practical ethics.[4]

Although ethics, like logic, metaphysics, epistemology, and aesthetics, is a major branch of philosophical study, reflection on ethical issues in, say, engineering, law, or medicine requires some familiarity with the kinds of problems that actually arise in practice, as distinct from simply relying on the imagination of philosophers, who may have little acquaintance with those settings. So, it seems essential to include practitioners from a broad range of disciplines in discussions of practical ethics as an area of inquiry in higher education.

This is precisely what the Hastings Center did in the late 1970s, as courses in ethics began to show up across the curriculum.[5] A large gathering of educators from various disciplines convened periodically at the Hastings Center to discuss what, if any, common goals there should be in teaching ethics in higher education. The result was a series of publications on ethics in a wide range of disciplines. Consensus was reached on five goals, regardless of the disciplinary area. Students should be given assistance in

- Stimulating their moral imagination
- Recognizing moral issues
- Analyzing key concepts and principles
- Eliciting their sense of responsibility
- Dealing constructively with ambiguity and disagreement[6]

These are appropriate goals for courses in practical ethics, regardless of their specific focus (e.g., accountancy, engineering, law, medicine, or the professions generally); and they will be borne in mind in the chapters that follow.

Actually, it is the fourth goal — engaging one's sense of responsibility — that is most central to this book. When I first used the Hastings Center goals in my own courses in ethics, I was puzzled by this goal. What was being commended? Simply that students be urged to "be responsible"? Concerned that this might seem to be a bit "preachy," I decided to concentrate on the other four goals and let the matter of the students' sense of responsibility take care of itself. If the course successfully promoted the other four goals, I thought, wouldn't their sense of responsibility be engaged, as well? The answer is yes.

However, eventually I realized that each of these goals is important in helping students come to grips with what it takes to be a responsible professional. Furthermore, inviting students to reflect on what they might do if faced with certain ethical problems in professional life is, in effect, attempting to engage their sense of responsibility. I also realized that there is more than one way to look at one's responsibilities. Some seem satisfied to do what is minimally required of them by their clients, employers, or the general public. Others regularly demand much more of themselves than others would be warranted in expecting from them; they go "above and beyond the call of duty." Most reside somewhere in between these two extremes. For reasons that I hope will become apparent in subsequent chapters, reflecting on these possibilities can contribute significantly to becoming the sort of responsible professional one aspires to be.

More than anything else, what has helped me realize the importance of reflecting explicitly on one's sense of responsibility is a striking statement by William F. May. Noting our increased dependence on professionals to provide us with the services we need, the complex institutional settings within which most professionals work, and the increased specialization that goes with this, May concludes:[7]

> Few others — whether lay people or other professionals — know what any given expert is up to. [They] had better be virtuous. Few may be in a position to discredit [them]. The knowledge explosion is also an ignorance explosion; if knowledge is power, then ignorance is powerlessness. Although it is possible to devise structures that limit the opportunities for the abuse of specialized knowledge, ultimately one needs to cultivate virtue in those who wield that relatively inaccessible power. One test of character and virtue is what a person does when no one else is watching. A society that rests on expertise needs more people who can pass that test.

The thrust of May's statement will be examined at several junctures in this book. Here I note only that, if May is right, it is quite possible that some can appear to pass this test when, actually, they do not. Equally important, passing this test, but only minimally, may ensure that individual professionals avoid serious wrongdoing, but it does not ensure that, either individually or collectively, members of a profession will succeed in providing society with the services it needs. For example, a serious shortage of medical professionals in a given area means that medical needs in that area are unlikely to be well met.

Although there is a need for more medical professionals in that area, it would be difficult, if not impossible, to identify any specific medical professionals as having an obligation to work there — especially if they are already employed elsewhere.

This book will focus on different conceptions of the responsibilities of individual professionals rather than on the collective responsibilities of different professions, or even the collective responsibilities of smaller groups of professionals who work together either on the same tasks or for the same employer. Collective responsibilities will be considered, but primarily in relation to how this affects the responsibilities of individuals. This is not intended to slight the importance of group or collective responsibility; nor is it intended to suggest that collective responsibility is somehow "reducible" to individual responsibility. The topic of collective responsibility is important and complex; but, however the issues get sorted out, questions remain regarding what this might mean for individuals who are members of a profession or who work with others on the same tasks or for the same employer. These questions will be the primary focus of this book.

There are no generally accepted definitions of "profession" or "professional," but this should not present a barrier to fruitful inquiry. Michael Bayles's approach should suffice.[8] He identifies three central features of virtually all professions and several other features that are common to many professions. First, professions require extensive training, most commonly acquired in higher education and internships. Second, as implied by the acquiring of an advanced academic degree, this training involves a significant intellectual component. This contributes to the role of professions in providing advice to those who have little, if any, knowledge or understanding of certain matters. Third, the training of professionals enables them to provide important services to society. As Bayles puts it, "Physicians, lawyers, teachers, accountants, engineers, and architects provide services vital to the organized functioning of society — which chess experts do not."[9] Common features include credentialing or licensing, professional organizations along with codes of ethics, a monopoly of the kinds of services provided, and some degree of autonomy, or discretionary judgment, on the part of professionals.

This emphasis on the employment of expertise in service to others should not obscure the fact that a profession also can be expected to support the self-interest of its members; one's profession is a means of livelihood. Nevertheless, professionals do not stand alone. They are members of professions that themselves avow certain ethical standards. They are employed by others, whether individual clients or institutions, who have ethical (and other) expectations of them, as well. All of this gives rise to serious questions about how individual professionals should conduct themselves in their professional lives.

A SET OF ASSUMPTIONS

It is a noteworthy feature of the Hastings Center goals in teaching ethics that they focus primarily on the possible perspectives of individuals rather than professions, or institutions, as such. By focusing attention on those who are preparing to become professionals, they make a number of assumptions about students in courses in practical ethics. First, they assume that students are already somewhat sophisticated morally. Exercising one's moral imagination, recognizing moral issues, analyzing key concepts and principles, engaging one's sense of responsibility, and dealing with ambiguity and disagreement are not entirely new to students. Rather than initiating such capacities and abilities, the aim is to enhance them. Conspicuously absent from this list is the suggestion that students are to be indoctrinated with the "right" answers to the ethical questions that are posed. This does not mean that there are no right or wrong answers, better or worse answers, or the like; rather, it is assumed that, given a suitable educational environment for inquiry, students will be able to make these determinations themselves — and that they should be encouraged to do so. This, in turn, suggests that students should be regarded as co-inquirers rather than simply as recipients of instruction as they undertake the study of practical ethics.

Second, they assume that there is a practical context to which the study of ethics is tethered. Each of these goals is to be pursued in the context of, say, family relations, friendship, political life, or professional practice, not simply in the abstract, where the specific practical context plays no role. This does not mean that there are no general concepts or principles that cut across the various areas of concern. Issues of harm, trust, honesty, fairness, confidentiality, respect and care for others, rights, responsibilities, conflicts of interest, and so on, can be found in all areas of practical ethics. However, there may be nuances within various practices that mark significant differences; and it is important, in any case, to examine with care just how these issues arise and play themselves out in these different settings.[10]

Third, it is assumed that reflection of some sort can, and should, make a moral difference to what we notice and take into account, how we understand the relevance and importance of what we notice, how (or whether) we deliberate about moral issues, how we address moral issues with others, and how we finally attempt to resolve these issues.[11]

Fourth, all of the Hastings Center goals seem to share the aim of shedding light on moral issues that can be expected to arise in practice. These issues are not the special creation of philosophers; they are issues facing doctors, lawyers, engineers, consumers, and ordinary persons in their daily lives. These issues are there, either explicitly or latently, before philosophers arrive on the scene; and the question for philosophers should be what, if any, light they can help shed on the practical problems at hand. In short, whatever place ethics should have within the academic discipline of philosophy, the problems of practical ethics have their own life; and, whatever role philosophers might play, they should not assume that it is up to them, all on their own, to determine either what these problems are or how they might best be addressed.

REASONABLENESS AS A GOAL

A strength of the Hastings Center goals is that they reinforce the virtue of reasonableness in practical ethics. In *Reasonable Children* I argued that the schools can and should promote the reasonableness of students.[12] This applies to the teaching of ethics in higher education as well. It is important to distinguish reasonableness from those forms of rationality that are highly individualistic and self-centered. An individual might regularly attempt to impose his or her way of thinking on others and simply ignore what others have to say. In some circumstances this might be regarded as irrational behavior, but in general it is not. It may be egocentric, or self-centered; it may often be selfish, domineering, or boorish. Still, as a strategy for getting what one wants, it may often work. So, in this respect, at least in the short run, it may be rational behavior — or, in any case, not irrational behavior. However, it is unreasonable behavior. Its demands are excessive, unfair, and skewed in ways that others justifiably find unacceptable — and in ways the person behaving in this way would probably find unacceptable if he or she were on the receiving end of such behavior.

In contrast, reasonableness is a social disposition. As Lawrence Splitter and Ann Margaret Sharp put it: "The reasonable person respects others and is prepared to take into account their views and their feelings, to the extent of changing her own mind about issues of significance, and consciously allowing her own perspective to be changed by others. She is, in other words, willing to be reasoned with."[13] This does not mean that a reasonable person simply gives in to the views of others. It does mean that one accepts a burden of giving reasons for one's actions and beliefs that can be subjected to public scrutiny, not simply private confirmation.

W. H. Sibley best sums up what reasonableness in morality requires of us as individuals, whether deliberating alone or with others:

> If I desire that my conduct shall be deemed *reasonable* by someone taking the standpoint of moral judgment, I must exhibit something more than mere rationality or intelligence. To be reasonable here is to see the matter — as we

commonly put it — from the other person's point of view, to discover how each will be affected by the possible alternative actions; and, moreover, not merely to "see" this (for any merely prudent person would do as much) but also to be prepared to be disinterestedly *influenced,* in reaching a decision, by the estimate of these possible results. I must justify my conduct in terms of some principle capable of being appealed to by all parties concerned, some principle from which we can reason in common.[14]

A second feature of reasonableness is its acceptance of some degree of uncertainty. This may be uncertainty about whether one's own views are necessarily right, or even uncertainty that anyone's views are. This is not to be confused with skepticism. As Max Black says, we may be able to show that some actions or judgments are more reasonable than others; still, "we are very seldom able to choose a single action as uniquely reasonable."[15] What this means is that it is quite possible for two people to come to different judgments on some matters, without either being unreasonable. Further discussion might reasonably convince one or the other to modify or even abandon a previously held position, but it might not — the final verdict may still be out.

The hope is that by the time one begins to prepare for a particular profession, he or she will have already developed the virtue of reasonableness. The task then is not so much that of acquiring a new virtue, but of discovering what it requires of one as a professional.

PHILOSOPHICAL CONTRIBUTIONS

As a course of study, practical ethics is concerned with ways in which practical, ethical questions might be best understood and addressed. A topic of considerable interest and controversy recently has been the relevance of ethical theory to resolving these questions. In their book, *Abuse of Casuistry,* Albert Jonsen and Stephen Toulmin describe and criticize what they call a "top-down" approach to moral reasoning and decision making.[16] This approach begins with general principles, looks for possible applications to practice, and then attempts to derive an appropriate conclusion. For this to work, we must make sure we have defensible moral principles. This is something to which philosophers devote a lot of their time. However, if defensible principles are to do their work well, we must also ascertain that the range of available principles adequately covers the practical arena to which they are to be applied. This requires having more than a set of moral principles; it also requires detailed attention to the situations in which practical problems arise.

However, when we attend to those details, not everything we might observe is relevant to the ethical problem at hand. For example, the number of blades of grass under the left shoe of someone deliberating about whether to break a promise is not relevant to whether breaking the promise might be justifiable, whereas the fact that a promise was made is. Whose job is it to determine criteria of relevance? Certainly philosophers will want to say something about this, too; but so will others, as they should.

Once defensible moral principles and criteria of relevance are in hand, there remains the problem of appropriate application to actual circumstances. Philosophers can try their hand at this, too. However, there is little reason to believe that philosophers are more qualified to do this than other thoughtful persons, or that they can do it alone. In fact, Sidgwick, who ironically is Jonsen and Toulmin's favorite example of a "top-down" philosopher, explicitly acknowledges the limitations of philosophers in this regard.[17]

Sidgwick's *Methods of Ethics* articulates and defends utilitarianism as the most adequate theoretical framework within which to understand our moral lives.[18] However, in *Practical Ethics,* Sidgwick says, "A moral philosopher, in my opinion, should always study with reverent care and patience what I am accustomed to call the Morality of Common Sense."[19] The Morality of Common Sense consists of "middle axioms" (concerning, for example, truthfulness and promise-keeping) that through time have proven themselves to be invaluable in addressing and resolving the practical problems of ethics. These are not exceptionless rules, but they are quite serviceable and normally place a burden of proof on those who would take exception to them.

In *Practical Ethics,* Sidgwick urges members of his Cambridge Ethical Society, with its emphasis on reaching "results of value for practical guidance and life," to try to restrict themselves to "the region of middle axioms," about which there is virtual consensus, despite deep differences regarding first principles and the ultimate grounds of morality.[20] For practical purposes, he advises, "we should give up altogether the idea of getting to the bottom of things, arriving at agreement on the first principles or the Summum Bonum."[21]

Thus, however sympathetic *in principle* Sidgwick might be to the "top-down" approach described by Jonsen and Toulmin, it seems that *in practice,* particularly when engaging in practical moral inquiry with others, he is prepared to seriously modify this approach. The "top" will be, for the most part, "middle axioms," or rules, about which there is consensus. The actual problems of the day provide the context within which inquiry will proceed; and the everyday experiences of thoughtful people from all walks of life will be taken as an essential resource for, and check on, the reflections of those who are joined in inquiry — including philosophers. So, our reflection should begin, it seems, in "the thick of things," where we can draw on practical experience and shared moral understanding. Departures from this starting point get their warrant from the light these departures shed on the practical problems with which we begin.

Sidgwick is convinced that much of the Morality of Common Sense can be fully vindicated on utilitarian grounds. At the same time, he insists that its "middle axioms" are not always adequate for resolving moral problems. They sometimes conflict with each other and, by themselves, are unable to resolve these conflicts. Although he does not press hard for this in *Practical Ethics*, the principle of utility ("the greatest good for the greatest number") is Sidgwick's candidate for mediation. Yet, even in his more theoretically ambitious *Methods of Ethics*, Sidgwick takes a modest stance in regard to what utilitarian philosophers can accomplish alone:

> I hold that the utilitarian, in the existing state of our knowledge, cannot possibly construct a morality *de novo* either for man as he is (abstracting his morality), or for man as he ought to be and will be. He must start, speaking broadly, with the existing social order, and the existing morality as a part of that order; and in deciding the question whether any divergence from this code is to be recommended, must consider chiefly the immediate consequences of such divergence, upon a society in which such a code is conceived generally to subsist.[22]

Nevertheless, Sidgwick apparently agreed with members of the ethical societies in Cambridge and London that it might still be reasonable for them to try to construct a "Science or Theory of Right" that attempts to "eliminate error and contradiction from current morality, reduce all valid moral perceptions and judgments to their elements or principles, and present them as connected in a logical system of thought."[23] Philosophers could be expected to play a major role in such an enterprise. However, Sidgwick insists that philosophers cannot proceed alone, for several reasons:

- Philosophers cannot be expected to have access to all the facts that inform good judgment. A "Science or Theory of Right" seeks to provide a theory for "humanity as a whole, and not only for some particular section; and to do this satisfactorily and completely we must have adequate knowledge of the conditions of this life in all the bewildering complexity and variety in which it is actually being lived."[24]
- Philosophers' judgments need to be "aided, checked, and controlled by the moral judgment of persons with less philosophy but more special experience."[25]
- The judgments of ordinary persons regarding "what ought to be done in particular circumstances are often much sounder than the reasons they

give for them; the judgments represent the result of experience unconsciously as well as consciously imbibed."[26]

Although constructing a "Science or Theory of Right" is a more modest undertaking than trying to "get to the bottom of things," it is nevertheless a very ambitious one. We should pause to ask what a successful outcome might look like. What Sidgwick is talking about seems to be what, one hundred years earlier, Thomas Reid referred to as a "moral system," a systematic taxonomy of moral rules and ideas that apply to moral practice.[27] Reid distinguishes a moral system of this sort from theories of the mind that explain our capacities for moral sentiments, beliefs, and reasoning. Although, according to Reid, the latter is as difficult an area of philosophy as any, articulating an adequate moral system is much more manageable.

However, the mistake philosophers must avoid, Reid insists, is thinking that "in order to understand his duty, a man must needs be a philosopher and a metaphysician."[28] Furthermore, although moral systems "swell to great magnitude," this is not because there is a large number of general moral principles. Reid says that, actually, they are "few and simple." Moral systems swell because applications of these principles "extend to every part of human conduct, in every condition, every relation, and every transaction of life."[29]

What would a good moral system look like? Reid says:

A system of morals is not like a system of geometry, where the subsequent parts derive their evidence from the preceding, and one chain of reasoning is carried on from the beginning; so that, if the arrangement is changed the chain is broken, and the evidence is lost. It resembles more a system of botany, or mineralogy, where the subsequent parts depend not for their evidence upon the preceding, and the arrangement is made to facilitate apprehension and memory, and not to give evidence.[30]

Reid and Sidgwick would probably agree that a system of morality based solely on the Morality of Common Sense is more like a system of botany or mineralogy than a system of geometry. However, it is also likely that Sidgwick's ambition would be to show that, at the level of principles and maxims, the best system of morality would be more like a system of geometry. A thorough examination of the Morality of Common Sense, he thinks, will show its inability to deal with problems that bring the "middle axioms" into conflict. The principle of utility could (and, Sidgwick thinks, should) serve as the mediator, a master principle from which all other principles or maxims can be derived, and which can be used to resolve conflicts among "middle axioms."

Reid is unwilling to grant the principle of utility this status. For him, an adequate moral system will contain a plurality of basic principles that cannot be derived from one another or placed in a general hierarchy of priority. Justice and utility, for example, may be equally basic, although in some instances one overrides the other, whereas in other instances the priority is reversed — without there being an overarching principle that determines when one takes priority over the other.

In regard to the views of ordinary, but reflective, persons (such as members of the Cambridge and London ethical societies), it would seem that Reid and Sidgwick agree that there is no consensus about what might serve as a master principle of the sort Sidgwick desires. In *Practical Ethics,* Sidgwick is willing to forgo explicit reliance on a master principle. He does not want progress in addressing the practical problems of the day to get bogged down in endless controversy.

Reid has another point to make. He places an important restriction on the proper role of theory in ethics: "There is in Ethicks as in most Sciences a Speculative and a practical Part, the first is subservient to the last."[31] Bearing this in mind, it should be noted that "Mens private Interests, their Passions, and vicious inclinations & habits" are the primary culprits in prompting the bias and prejudice that often infect our judgment.[32] So, it is these sources of misperception, as well as ignorance of relevant facts, rather than the absence of an overriding master principle that get in the way of good judgment.

In any case, it seems that both Reid and Sidgwick accept as their starting point for philosophical reflection the Morality of Common Sense, and their aim is to proceed as far as possible in arranging our moral understanding systematically. Since it is not assumed that the Morality of Common Sense constitutes a geometric-like system, but that it should be regarded with utmost respect, there should be a fair amount of space for shared understanding and the possibility of some give-and-take at least in the initial stages of inquiry. Whether, in the end, consensus will result in a more-or-less geometric system rather than a botanical or mineralogical one can be left open.

What this means, in practice, is that the process of practical inquiry should begin more like a botanical or mineralogical quest than a geometric one. That is, it should begin piecemeal, with many of the parts and their relationships to one another left to be determined — and with no insistence that nothing significant can be known until the final structure of the system is itself known. But what this implies, as Sidgwick seems to concede, is that the inquiry is best undertaken as a joint one involving philosophers and nonphilosophers alike.

In characterizing what is needed, Sidgwick says that we need to use the method of casuistry, which involves testing the applicability of "middle axioms" to new and unresolved problems, comparing and contrasting these problems with thus far well-established precedents, and then suggesting reasonable resolutions. This appeal to casuistry is ironic in two respects. First, this is what Jonsen and Toulmin offer as an alternative to what they take to be Sidgwick's "top-down" approach. Second, Sidgwick acknowledges that his *Methods of Ethics* is partly a product of his dissatisfaction with William Whewell's *Elements of Morality*, the casuistic text that introduced Sidgwick and his contemporaries to systematic moral thinking. Sidgwick's complaint is that Whewell's text is filled with endless qualifications and superficiality, because it lacks a comprehensive, coherent foundation.[33]

In the preface to the first edition of *Elements of Morality*, Whewell goes to great pains to distinguish his practical aims from those of what he called a "Philosophy of Morality." The distinction he has in mind resembles Reid's distinction between a philosophical theory that attempts to explain the origin and nature of our moral capacities, on the one hand, and a "system of morality," on the other. Like Reid's *Practical Ethics*, Whewell's *Elements of Morality* seeks to construct a "system of morality." Whewell suggests that the distinction between a philosophy of morality and a moral system is comparable in some respects to the distinction between a philosophy of geometry and a system of geometry. Euclid's system of geometry can be well understood and put to practical use without anyone having a philosophy of geometry (a metaphysical concern about the nature and foundations of geometry). Similarly, we can understand and put to practical use a system of morality without having a philosophy of morality. In fact, Whewell claims, it is only because there is a system of geometry available to consider that metaphysicians can undertake constructing a philosophy of geometry. The same, he holds, is the case with morality. However, Whewell does not think that we have a system of morality anywhere nearly as well-developed and coherent as Euclidean geometry. Thus, like Reid, he no doubt would agree that a system of morality is more like a system of botany or mineralogy than a system of geometry. In fact, Whewell himself was a mineralogist as well as a philosopher.[34]

Despite the disclaimer that he does not see his *Elements of Morality* as a work in Philosophy of Morality, Whewell does not shy away from asserting that it is, nevertheless, a philosophical endeavor: "I am desirous that [the reader] should understand that, though I do not speak of my work as a Philosophy of Morality, I have tried to make it a work of rigorous reasoning, and therefore, so far at least, philosophical."[35] As for how successful he thinks *The Elements of Morality* is in providing an adequate moral system, Whewell is quite modest. He seems content to say that, at least in some areas, he has made some progress in organizing our thinking — but in ways that do not require the completion of an entire system in order to be of practical use.

Despite their philosophical differences, Reid, Whewell, and Sidgwick's shared approach to practical ethics is roughly this. Beginning with the practical problems that face us, drawing on the experience and ordinary moral sensibilities of philosophers and nonphilosophers alike, careful inquiry can be expected to yield practical assistance in dealing reasonably with these problems. This inquiry can be fairly characterized as philosophical insofar as the reasoning employed is as rigorous and systematic as the subject allows.[36] Whether this might result in anything like a comprehensive, orderly system need not be settled in advance any more than it is in botany or mineralogy. More importantly, there is no reason to concede in the meantime that nothing useful can be discovered.

CHAPTER TWO

Practical Ethics

PRACTICAL FOCUS

Some years ago a *New Yorker* cartoon featured the pilot of a large commercial flight announcing to his stunned passengers, "Hello, folks. This is Captain Holroyd, here to tell you that I'm finally beginning to get hold of my life." The captain may reason, "If I can't get hold of my life, it doesn't matter whether I live or die." The passengers worry that if he loses his grip on life mid-flight, it may not matter to him whether *they* live or die either.

We find it easy to imagine someone so despondent that he fails to attend properly to his professional duties. What takes the passengers by surprise is not only that their pilot may be in such a state of mind, but that he has announced this over the loudspeaker — as a note of assurance that their lives are safely in his hands, an assurance that they would normally take for granted, but now no doubt question. What is humorous in a cartoon would be terrifying in reality. Captain Holroyd's internal logic may be hard to assail, but his willingness to pilot a commercial flight in full awareness of his continuing struggle is not.

What this example suggests is that a professional's personal and philosophical struggles can be radically out of step with his or her professional responsibilities. Whatever internal logic those struggles may have for the personal lives of professionals, that logic does not necessarily shed light on what their responsibilities as professionals are. Captain Holroyd's personal struggles are, indeed, meaningful and important, but they should not be allowed to interfere with his responsibilities *as a pilot*. In fact, it is just because his personal struggles are so meaningful and important to him that he should probably not be flying. A responsible pilot, we think, should know better.

There are, of course, dangers in staying away from certain philosophical questions in order to remain focused on the practical problems at hand. There is a risk of overlooking something that, in the end, would prove to be practically

Portions of this chapter are based on parts of my "Practical Ethics and Philosophical Reflection," in *Teaching Ethics* 1, no. 1 (March 2001): 19–46.

relevant. A litmus test might be this: What sorts of philosophical questions show some promise of shedding light on the particular problem at hand? It may be difficult to apply this test fully and fairly in many cases. Yet, as the above instance of philosophical humor suggests, sometimes it is not.

Three of Plato's early dialogues, *Euthyphro, Crito,* and *Apology,* are instructive exercises in practical ethics. Each begins with an important practical issue that, thoughtfully considered, requires raising philosophical questions. However, two fare much better than the other in addressing the practical matters at hand. Plato's *Euthyphro* fails to make substantial inroads into the practical problem with which it begins and digresses, instead, into philosophical issues that, fascinating as they are in their own right, show little promise of shedding any light on the practical problem at hand. At the heart of this failure is Euthyphro's acceptance of a philosophical challenge posed by Socrates — to define "piety," or "righteousness." It seems clear that Euthyphro is not up to the task. Furthermore, a point not noted explicitly by Socrates, even if a satisfactory definition were produced, it seems that the practical issue with which they began would remain as unresolved as before. In contrast, Plato's *Crito* and *Apology* thoughtfully address and keep a steady eye on the original practical issues without getting bogged down in failed attempts to define key ideas. Yet, all three dialogues clearly qualify as philosophical. So, a brief comparison of these dialogues may help us better understand both the promise of and limitations of philosophical reflection in practical ethics.

SOCRATES AND EUTHYPHRO

Plato's *Euthyphro* begins with an encounter between Socrates and Euthyphro as they are on their way to court. Socrates is on his way to face those who have accused him of corrupting the youth and believing in false gods. He is surprised to learn that Euthyphro is on his way to court to prosecute his own father for murder. Given the unusual role that Euthyphro has taken on, Socrates suggests that it must be that the person his father killed is also a relative. Euthyphro quickly replies:

> It is ridiculous, Socrates, for you to think that it makes any difference whether the victim is a stranger or a relative. One should only watch whether the killer acted justly or not; if he acted justly, let him go, but if not, one should prosecute, even if the killer shares your hearth and table. The pollution is the same if you knowingly keep company with such a man and do not cleanse yourself and him by bringing him to justice.[1]

Euthyphro then explains the circumstance in more detail. While in a drunken rage, one of his father's household slaves killed a former family servant. His father bound and gagged the slave and left him unattended in a ditch for several days while a messenger was sent off to consult with a priest about what should be done. Unfortunately, the slave died before the messenger returned.

Euthyphro says that his father and other relatives are angry with him. On the one hand, they claim, his father did not actually kill the slave; he simply ignored him for several days while waiting for advice about what to do. The slave, on the other hand, did unjustly take the life of someone, albeit while drunk. "They say," continues Euthyphro, "that such a victim does not deserve a thought and that it is impious for a son to prosecute his father for murder."[2] To this, Euthyphro objects that his detractors have mistaken ideas about piety and impiety.

Socrates takes this as an invitation to press Euthyphro to clarify his general grasp of piety and impiety.[3] Euthyphro eagerly accepts Socrates' invitation, thus shifting their attention away from the specific ways in which Euthyphro seemingly has departed from common opinion to the more general question concerning the nature of piety, or righteousness.

Euthyphro's first inclination is to favor the view that what makes something pious is that it is loved by the gods. But this raises the question of how he knows that what he is proposing to do would be loved by them. After all, Euthyphro acknowledges Socrates' observation that the gods frequently quarrel about "the just and the unjust, the beautiful and the ugly, the good and the bad."[4] Even if the gods agree on some such matters, the case at hand is complicated by a number of factors.

Euthyphro replies: "I think, Socrates, that on this subject no gods would differ from one another, that whosoever has killed anyone unjustly should pay the penalty."[5] Socrates agrees that it is appropriate to punish those who kill unjustly. But he presses Euthyphro to show how this principle applies in the present case. Socrates is actually posing two questions here. The first is about whether the gods would agree that Euthyphro's father *is* guilty of murder. The second is about whether they would agree that it is appropriate for a *son* to play the role of prosecutor in such a case.

But rather than pressing Euthyphro on either of these questions, Socrates shifts their attention back to the question of definition. To resolve the problem of the gods quarreling over issues of right and wrong, is Euthyphro simply going to settle for unanimity among the gods as the mark of the pious and the impious? Euthyphro's answer is affirmative. He seems quite satisfied to reiterate his claim that "the pious is what all the gods love, and the opposite, which all the gods hate, is the impious."[6] At this point, Socrates completely drops his effort to get Euthyphro to discuss the specifics of what he is proposing to do. Instead, he asks, "Is the pious loved by the gods because it is pious, or is it pious because it is loved by the gods?" As readers of the dialogue know, Euthyphro fumbles this question badly. Eventually, he answers affirmatively to both alternatives; and Socrates proceeds to demonstrate the incoherence that follows.

In the end, Euthyphro complains that their discussion has only gone in circles. Socrates agrees but points out that they have only followed Euthyphro's own words where they lead. He continues, "But now I know well that you believe you have clear knowledge of piety and impiety. So tell me, my good Euthyphro, and do not hide what you believe."[7] Euthyphro replies, "Some other time, Socrates, for I am in a hurry now, and it is time for me to go."[8] The implication is that Euthyphro is in a hurry to get on with the business of prosecuting his father for murder, but without being able to provide any justification for doing so. So, the dialogue ends on a decidedly negative note.

There is much to be learned from following the dialogue to its negative conclusion. Modern readers convert Socrates' question about piety and what is loved by the gods into the monotheistic question, "Are things right because God says they are, or does God say things are right because they are right?" This, in turn, launches vigorous discussions of the divine command theory of right and wrong.

However, the request for an essential definition is a daunting one in almost any area of inquiry, but it is especially daunting to have to come up with one that covers the entire breadth of morality. The thought that we cannot properly begin to discuss particular cases until we have such a definition threatens to paralyze discussion. For example, consider "lying," a morally important, but less comprehensive, concept than piety. In order to explain what is wrong with lying in a particular case, is it reasonable to demand a definition of lying that identifies what it is about *all* lies that makes them lies (as distinct from, say, acts of deception or keeping one's beliefs to oneself)? Or, consider "fairness." Must one know what *all* instances of fairness have in common in order to know that this or that is fair (or unfair)? So, if one of the lessons of *Euthyphro* is that proper inquiry must begin with definitions of this sort, this is an invitation to failure and paralysis.

There are many questions Socrates could have asked instead. Even if Euthyphro's father should be prosecuted, why does this responsibility fall on Euthyphro? Can a son be expected to proceed in the impartial manner that justice requires and that Euthyphro himself seems to value? Has Euthyphro considered whether his father should be prosecuted for negligent homicide, deliberate murder, or under some other designation? Is Euthyphro qualified to make such discriminations and apply them in such a case? And so on.

The rigorous pursuit of questions like these seems as likely to raise doubts in an inquirer's mind about whether what Euthyphro is doing is right as would the pursuit of a definition of piety. At the same time, these doubts can be expected to shed light on what the best course of action might be. It might be objected that this would not be a truly Socratic way of going about things — that the quest for the essence of morality (here, piety) is the true mark of Socratic inquiry — that it is here that philosophical inquiry must begin, and stay. However, the passages in *Euthyphro* in which Socrates asks about the details of Euthyphro's case suggest otherwise; and this is further confirmed by Plato's *Crito*.

SOCRATES AND CRITO

Crito, too, opens with a practical question: Should Socrates accept the offer of Crito and his friends to help him escape from prison and avoid his execution? In a close vote by the citizens of Athens, Socrates has been found guilty of corrupting the youth and believing in false gods. His penalty is death — he is to drink a cup of hemlock. Socrates and his friends all agree that he should not have been found guilty; but, at least initially, they disagree about what should happen next.

Nowhere in *Crito* is there a request for essential definitions. Yet, it is filled with arguments about obligations to parents, children, friends, and the state. There are discussions of the bindingness of promises, the principle of not returning evil for evil, the distinction between just procedures and just results, the importance of remaining true to one's own principles, and the likely consequences of escaping. Throughout the dialogue, however abstract a point may be, it is brought directly to bear on the practical question at hand: Should Socrates accept the offer of help in escaping?

No overall theory of the right or the good is offered. This does not mean that no general principles are invoked in Socrates' defense of not escaping. In fact, as just noted, several are. But they are not derived from a master principle (such as the principle of utility); nor are they arranged hierarchically. Combined with the particular facts of this case, they are used to resolve the question of whether Socrates should escape. However, this is a matter for careful judgment, not the application of an algorithm. For example, although Socrates firmly argues for accepting his sentence, he does not advocate a view that always opposes disobedience.[9]

Regardless of whether those who examine Socrates' exchange with Crito are persuaded by the arguments presented, much light is shed on the ethical issues at stake. Furthermore, as in all good discussions of particular cases, much can be learned about other cases as well. Even if one takes issue with some of the arguments, rigorous reasoning is employed in addressing central topics in moral, social, and political philosophy, but without digressing from the particular question about what action should be taken.

Finally, although *Crito* is a philosophical dialogue, one does not need to be a philosopher to follow the reasoning and enter the discussion. So, although Crito might have needed such a discussion in order to see that he and his friends need not help Socrates escape in order to do the right thing, Crito and his friends did not themselves need to be philosophers or metaphysicians to understand what is at stake and why Socrates believed he should not escape. Nevertheless, engaging in such a philosophical discussion might have been necessary for them to understand Socrates' position. So, philosophical reflection is helpful in this case. We might also add that having a philosopher of Socrates' caliber lead the discussion no doubt gives it a needed philosophical boost — suggesting that at least some philosophers may have much to offer practical ethics.

SOCRATES' APOLOGY

Euthyphro and *Crito* are commonly presented as part of a trilogy, with Plato's *Apology* wedged in between. Given the contrast I have drawn between *Euthyphro* and *Crito,* it is helpful if *Apology* can serve as a bridge; and I believe it can. *Euthyphro* provides a detailed illustration of someone who believes he possesses a kind of wisdom that Socrates seeks but claims never to find. His apology to the court says as much. Accused of regarding himself as possessing wisdom, Socrates famously replies that he has never claimed to possess the sort of wisdom that Euthyphro and many others claim they have. Nevertheless, he says, he may be wiser than they are, because he knows that he lacks this wisdom, whereas they do not know that they lack it, too.

The sort of wisdom (worthwhile knowledge) that Socrates has counsels modesty, not skepticism, about how to conduct oneself in practical affairs. That Socrates is not advocating practical skepticism can be seen in his comment about those who are reputed to be the wisest and those thought to be the least so: "I found that those who had the highest reputation were nearly the most deficient, while those who were thought to be inferior were more knowledgeable."[10] He claimed to find this to be the case among politicians, poets, and craftsmen alike. Although each could fairly claim to have special talents, none possessed the wisdom they were reputed to have. Socrates' comments about craftsmen are especially instructive:

I knew that they had knowledge of many fine things. In this I was not mistaken; they knew things I did not know, and to that extent they were wiser than I. But, gentlemen of the jury, the good craftsmen seemed to me to have the same fault as the poets; each of them, because of his success at his craft, thought himself very wise in other most important pursuits, and this error of theirs overshadowed the wisdom they had, so that I asked myself, on behalf of the oracle, whether I should prefer to be as I am, with neither their wisdom nor their ignorance, or to have both. The answer I gave myself and the oracle was that it was to my advantage to be as I am.[11]

Given the choice posed by Socrates, his conclusion seems appropriate. However, another option to consider is that a craftsman could retain wisdom regarding his craft but share the Socratic wisdom that craft wisdom does not extend to other areas; and it may not even extend to all appropriate uses of that craft. This, it seems, would be especially appropriate today regarding the professions. That professionals have special expertise is undeniable. It is to be hoped that they recognize that they have a responsibility to exercise that expertise wisely. But it is also to be hoped that they, like Socrates, recognize the limitations of their expertise and that they do not attempt to extend it beyond their range of competence. Accountants, attorneys, engineers, and physicians have expertise that we depend on, but it needs to be exercised in ways that respect the values of their clients, customers, employers, and the general public as well. In this broader domain, "expertise" seems to be in short supply. It should be noted that the examined life Socrates is talking about is not an internal monologue. It involves dialogue with others. Insofar as this dialogue is marked by reasonableness, it can be expected to feature the sort of reasoning with others that is open both to correction and modest gain.

THEORY AND PRACTICE

Plato's *Euthyphro* and *Crito* both begin with a particular problem and quickly move to a more general, philosophical level. *Crito* does this without losing sight of the original problem, whereas *Euthyphro* ascends to philosophical heights from which its original problem cannot be illuminated. Both provide practical lessons. *Crito* illustrates how philosophical analysis can help us thoughtfully address particular issues. *Euthyphro* illustrates how philosophical ambition can distract us from the particular issues at hand.

A combined lesson from these two dialogues is Sidgwick's view, noted in the Introduction, that when trying to resolve issues of practical ethics with others, it may be best not to try to "get to the bottom of things" — or at least not in the way

Socrates and Euthyphro attempt. It is better to remain within those regions that connect particular issues with what Sidgwick calls "middle-level axioms," or rules.

COMMON MORALITY

Sidgwick recommends that in practical ethics we should begin with what he calls the Morality of Common Sense, and we should retain great respect for it even when embarking on the deepest quests in moral philosophy.[12] If we are to follow Sidgwick's advice, something should be said about the content, scope, and supportability of what he has in mind. From the outset it is important to acknowledge that his Morality of Common Sense concentrates on those aspects of morality that have had some success in attaining broad consensus. Since there is no consensus about the ultimate foundations of morality, we should expect the primary focus of the Morality of Common Sense to lie elsewhere — on moral values we share, despite possibly deep differences in the grounding we give them. This means that, for many, there is much more to morality than the Morality of Common Sense represents. The important point here, however, is that there not be less. That is, whatever else can be said about morality, the Morality of Common Sense has solid footing in our lives and can do a lot of work for us.

What Sidgwick refers to as the Morality of Common Sense, contemporary philosopher Bernard Gert calls *common morality*.[13] Gert's account of common morality provides ample room for unresolved disagreement among well-informed reasonable persons. Whereas Sidgwick thinks that the conflicts found within common morality call for a higher principle (the principle of utility) to resolve them, Gert rejects the idea that, for every moral question, there must be one and only one rationally supportable answer. Nevertheless, Gert holds, common morality provides us with a structure within which we must operate if we are to be moral, and it is sufficiently detailed and restrictive to enable those who agree on the relevant facts to come to moral agreement in the overwhelming majority of cases.[14]

Common morality, Gert says, "is the moral system that thoughtful people use, usually implicitly, when they make moral decisions and judgments."[15] It is based on universal features of human nature such as our fallibility, rationality, and vulnerability. He points out that common morality is not a system derived from his, or any other, moral theory. Common morality comes first. Its existence does not depend on the theorizing of moral philosophers. In fact, like Whewell, Gert says that common morality is accepted in all philosophical theories of morality.[16] Given this, a preliminary task is to try to determine how common morality functions in the lives of thoughtful people who may never attempt to construct a philosophical theory of morality.

GERT'S MORAL RULES

Gert says that thoughtful people usually make implicit rather than explicit use of the system of common morality he describes. A central feature of Gert's explicit account is a list of ten moral rules and ten moral ideals. Acknowledging that it is likely that his presentation still has unclarities, or even mistakes, he says he is confident that his description comes close to adequately capturing what common morality is.[17] Philosophers will undoubtedly find something about which to quarrel. But a close approximation may be the best that one can reasonably hope for. In any case, the purpose of discussing Gert here is not to challenge his description in any serious way. Rather, it is to emphasize a strength of his account — namely, that it directs our attention to common morality as a fundamental moral resource available to all thoughtful people, not just philosophers. This is not something philosophers should deny. Something very much like Gert's conception of common morality is central to discussions of issues in practical ethics, including professional ethics.

Although philosophical theories of morality acknowledge the importance of common morality, Gert believes that, thus far, moral philosophers (including Sidgwick) have not given an adequate description of it before presenting their moral theories. Gert regards the task of providing an adequate description as an essential first step. Each of his rules and ideals captures something of central moral importance, and collectively they are intended to be comprehensive. At the same time, conceding this does not rule out alternative descriptions of various aspects of common morality. After all, it is not a part of the moral education of children that they learn and employ Gert's ten moral rules and ten moral ideals per se. His rules and ideals are a rational reconstruction of central features of our moral lives — albeit, a reconstruction that attempts to represent faithfully something implicit in our lives rather than to reform or otherwise alter what is there.

Gert's first five rules are:

- Do not kill
- Do not cause pain
- Do not disable
- Do not deprive of freedom
- Do not deprive of pleasure

None of these rules is "absolute," in the sense of having no exceptions; there are occasions when they conflict with one another, the second set of five moral rules, or the moral ideals. However, violations of these rules require a justification that can be accepted by all rational, moral agents.

The second five rules are:

- Do not deceive
- Keep your promises
- Do not cheat
- Obey the law
- Do your duty

Again, none of these rules is "absolute," but violations require a justification. That there can be justified departures from a moral rule is a central feature of common morality, which, although providing a framework for making moral decisions, also allows, within limits, "divergent answers to most controversial questions."[18]

All moral agents, says Gert, agree that killing, causing others pain or disability, and depriving others of freedom or pleasure are morally wrong without some justification. This is in contrast to, for example, taking a walk or not taking a walk, neither of which normally requires any justification. Likewise, all moral agents agree that deceiving, breaking promises, cheating, breaking the law, and neglecting duties are in need of moral justification. Gert concludes: "The claim that there are moral rules prohibiting such actions as killing and deceiving means only that these kinds of actions are immoral unless they can be justified. Given this understanding, all moral agents agree that there are moral rules prohibiting such actions as killing and deceiving."[19] However, since common morality is only implicit in the lives of most moral agents, it should not be supposed that ordinary moral agents would, if asked, produce Gert's specific list of moral rules. Instead, what should be expected is that ordinary moral agents are sensitive to the immorality of, as he puts it, certain *kinds* of actions. The moral rules are offered as articulations of those kinds of actions.

Gert allows for the possibility that other formulations of moral rules might also do this, "but the present formulation is both natural and has less serious problems than other commonly proposed formulations."[20] Some alternatives are too broad to capture important distinctions. Gert acknowledges that "Do not cause harm" could include all of the first five rules, but it fails to differentiate basic kinds of harm. "Do not violate trust" could include all of the second five, but promise breaking, cheating, deceiving, disobeying the law, and failing to do one's duty are importantly different ways of violating trust.[21]

It is noteworthy that Gert does not include a rule about fairness or unfairness. This is not because he thinks fairness and unfairness are unimportant. He associates unfairness with cheating, commenting: "In the basic sense of the word 'unfair,' only the violation of this moral rule ['Don't cheat'] counts as unfair. Unfortunately, 'unfair' is now commonly used simply as a synonym for 'immoral.'"[22] Insofar as "unfair" is used as a synonym for "immoral," Gert has a point. However, it seems that we have something more specific in mind when we object to the unfairness of punishing the innocent, to not considering all the readily available relevant facts when assessing someone's guilt or innocence, to not hiring someone because she is not a white male, to grading someone's paper without reading it carefully (or at all), and so on. None of these is an example of cheating in any straightforward sense. Gert might reply that these kinds of cases can be handled under some other moral rule (such as "Do not deprive of freedom" or "Do not disable"). But this does not undermine the point that, from the perspective of ordinary moral agents, these are standard illustrations of unfairness and not simply instances of immorality.

Gert does say that "it is more important that every immoral act be covered by some moral rule than it is to determine which particular rule is violated."[23] This is reasonable. But, by the same token, the suggestion that cheating is the only basic kind of unfairness seems off the mark; and recasting a complaint of unfairness in terms of one of his other moral rules risks losing sight of the fact that it is, say, the unfairness of punishing the innocent rather than simply depriving them of freedom that bothers us.

However, in regard to the importance of common morality for professional ethics, there is no need to press these issues. If Gert's system of morality is only implicit in the lives of ordinary moral agents, including professionals, we should be able to begin the task of describing common morality without relying explicitly on the precise list of moral rules and ideals that are central to his account. We could, instead, begin with, say, the virtues and vices that he says go along with his moral rules. The question of whether his ten moral rules, or some modification or emendation of his list, best depicts common morality as a system can be left open here. Gert compares learning a moral system with learning a grammatical system: "People don't explicitly use the moral system when making their moral decisions and judgments. People also do not explicitly use a grammatical system when speaking and when interpreting the speech of others."[24] Children learn to make the right moral decisions and judgments by listening to and watching adults do this, and they learn from being praised and corrected. Assuming this goes well, eventually they can be expected to develop moral virtues.

Although these moral virtues are distinct from Gert's moral rules, there are connections, especially with the second five rules. Because there is no special moral credit for not violating the first five rules, Gert says, there are no moral virtues corresponding to them, only a moral vice, cruelty.[25] However, each of the rules in Gert's second set of five has a corresponding virtue and vice: truthfulness and deceitfulness go with "do not deceive"; dependability and undependability go with "keep your promises"; fairness and unfairness go with "do not cheat"; honesty and dishonesty go with "obey the law"; and conscientiousness and neglectfulness go with "do your duty." Again, we might fuss over some of the details, for example, objecting that dependability and undependability seem to go as much with "do your duty" as conscientiousness and neglectfulness do. Or we might wonder why honesty and dishonesty are associated only with "obey the law" rather than, say, making and keeping promises.

More important, however, is the fact that the virtues operate much as Gert's moral rules do. In general, one should be honest, but not always. For a basically honest person not to undermine his or her virtue of honesty, it is important to have a justification for acting dishonestly on some occasions. Turning in someone else's term paper as one's own detracts from the virtue of honesty, whereas lying in order to save an innocent person from an assailant does not. So, Gert says, having the appropriate virtue does not mean one never violates the corresponding moral rule. Nevertheless, the virtues

all require knowing (but do not require being able to articulate) when it is justified to break the moral rule. There are no precise rules for attributing these virtues and vices to a person. Making moral judgments about people, rather than actions, is related to an appraisal of how much the person exceeds or falls below what rational persons would expect of people.[26]

Given this characterization of the virtues, including their centrality in common morality, it can be seen that those who acquire the sorts of virtues associated with Gert's moral rules and ideals bring a powerful moral resource with them into professional life. Admittedly, there is much about ethics in a given profession that the neophyte must learn (all too often, the hard way). But the basic elements of common morality, with its accompanying virtues, should already be in place.

It is clear that Gert's moral rules and ideals, or any approximations of them, do not provide us with a system that can be expected to give us algorithmic solutions to problems in practical ethics. No doubt many cases will be straightforwardly analyzable as morally acceptable or unacceptable. However, more challenging cases require the exercise of interpretative and critical skills. So, one of the tasks of moral education is to prepare children for the tasks of moral reflection that will be required of them as adults, if not already as children. This applies especially to those children who will become professionals, on whose expertise and discretionary judgment we depend.

DEALING WITH DISAGREEMENT

People often disagree about moral issues. However, it is important to get as clear as we can about the source and significance of these disagreements when they occur. Frequently, disagreements can be traced to differences in our grasp of factual matters rather than differences in moral values. If, for example, we are relying on different sets of data in discussing whether we think an experimental drug is now safe enough to be approved by the Food and Drug Administration, it should not surprise us when we come to different conclusions, despite the fact that we are committed to the same standards of safety. Of course, we may also disagree about what an appropriate level of risk is in certain areas, making it less clear to what extent we actually are committed to the same standards of safety. Or, even if we agree that certain moral values are relevant in deciding what to do, we may disagree about the relative weight of those values in a given situation. Finally, we may find that, at some fundamental level, we have very different moral orientations; and we wonder to what extent it is possible to find points of agreement from which we might proceed.

In the face of such disagreements, we may experience doubt and uncertainty. However, even if we conclude that moral certainty is often unobtainable, efforts can be made to make our reasoning about moral choices more precise in order to become clearer about points of both agreement and difference. Seeking exact points of difference can help resolve disagreements by exposing false distinctions and evasions. Tolerating differences that survive is an option when there is no need for agreement. When there is a need for agreement, as in the case of joint action, opportunities for compromise can be sought.[27]

A common way of responding to those with whom one has moral differences is to say something like, "Everyone's entitled to an opinion," "It's really just a matter of opinion," or "Value judgments are subjective." Such statements tend to bring discussion quickly to an end. Although they seem to express an attitude of tolerance, they also suggest that we do not have much to learn from one another's "opinions." But, quite apart from the question of whether our beliefs about moral matters can be "true" or "correct," we can evaluate their internal consistency and coherence, their comprehensiveness, their clarity, their supporting reasons, the extent to which they exhibit careful reflection, and so on.

JUSTIFICATION

An important feature of common morality is that justification requires more than private confirmation. To attempt to justify a principle, belief, attitude, decision, policy, or action is to seek good reasons in support of it. Good reasons are reasons one is willing to commend to others. This means that justificatory processes are essentially public, not private.

This public requirement does not mean that one is never justified in engaging in deceptive practices or in withholding information from others. For example, consider the question of whether doctors are ever justified in withholding diagnostic information from their patients. Most would concede that although information ordinarily should not be withheld, exceptional cases do occur. If, in such an exceptional case, Dr. Jones is justified in not telling Mr. Adams about his condition, this does not mean that Dr. Jones should be willing to announce publicly that she is doing this. Such an announcement would obviously be self-defeating. Rather, Dr. Jones must be willing to defend publicly the idea that in certain kinds of situations withholding information of this sort can be justified. That is, she should be willing to acknowledge and defend her acceptance of this kind of practice, but she is not required to announce to all the world that Mr. Adams's circumstance is a case in point.

If justificatory processes are essentially public rather than private, this means that one's reasons must be generalizable to similar situations. More formally, moral judgments must be *universalizable:* Whatever is right (or wrong) in one situation is right (or wrong) in any relevantly similar situation.[28] Thomas Reid holds that having a basic understanding of this idea is essential to being a moral agent, for, he says, this principle "comprehends every rule of justice without exception." As he puts it: *"In every case, we ought to act that part towards another, which we would judge to be right in him to act toward us, if we were in his circumstances and he in ours; or more generally — What we approve in others, that we ought to practise in like circumstances and what we condemn in others we ought not to do."*[29] By itself, this principle of universalizability does not determine what is right or wrong, but before satisfying ourselves that something is right (or wrong) in a particular case, we need to ask whether we would regard it as right (or wrong) in all cases that are relevantly similar — including those in which we might be on the receiving end of the action taken.

Although universalizability requires a kind of impartiality, some care must be taken in explaining what this means. Impartiality comes into play at two levels in morality. First, in the process of justification, impartiality requires determining what kinds of actions, practices, rules, or principles are morally acceptable. Identification of particular, actual people or groups is excluded. This prevents particular persons or groups from making unfair exceptions of themselves. This is the sort of impartiality universalizability requires.

However, this requirement of impartiality should not be confused with impartiality at a second level. Some practices or rules can be impartially approved even though they themselves allow for partiality in the treatment of individuals.

Family members and friends show partiality to one another. The father who insists on paying as much attention to all children as to his own would be trying to be impartial at this second level; and he is unlikely to succeed without neglecting some of the needs of his own children (including the need for a good father). Partiality toward one's own children is both expected and morally justified. At the same time, the kinds of partiality toward others that we find desirable should be consistent with practices or rules that themselves can be justified impartially.

In some cases, partiality toward loved ones is morally objectionable. For example, if a father's daughter is a member of a class he is teaching, partiality toward her would be inappropriate. If he is either lenient or severe with her, a moral complaint would be in order; he will either be unfair to the other students or unfair to his daughter.

So, the question of the extent to which we should treat others impartially in particular situations is complicated. However, this concerns impartiality only at the second level. First level impartiality, the kind required by moral justification, asks of partiality at the second level: Can we impartially support an action, practice, rule, or principle that permits (or even requires) some persons to be given preferential treatment because of the special relationships they have to someone? The answer is, sometimes, yes — subject to certain limitations.[30] This is no less true in professional relationships than in family relationships, although just what the limitations are may vary significantly.

Universalizability is a requirement of consistency in judgment. If Dr. Jones is justified in delaying information to Mr. Adams, she is justified in doing the same in any relevantly similar situation. So are other doctors. To discourage doctors from arbitrarily insulating medical practice from other practices or situations, it is also important for Dr. Jones to consider whether withholding information in this particular situation is relevantly similar to nonmedical situations in which one might be inclined to withhold information from others.

The requirement that our judgments be universalizable does not itself provide us with the criteria for relevance that we are expected to bear in mind as we look beyond the particular situation at hand to other circumstances that may be similar. It also cannot dictate how conflicts in values should be resolved. So, although the principle of universalizability places important constraints on moral judgment, what this means in practice can be understood only in the context of practice itself.

THE GOLDEN RULE

The idea of universalizability is closely related to what is perhaps the most widely accepted moral maxim, the Golden Rule:[31] "Do unto others as you would have them do unto you." Some form of the Golden Rule is embraced by virtually all of the major religious and moral systems. At the same time, it is also one of the most widely criticized moral maxims. Bernard Gert, for example, includes it among a set of moral slogans that distort our natural understanding of morality.[32] However, the maxim's longevity and near-universal acceptance suggests that it has considerable natural appeal of its own. So, it may be helpful to see if there are better and worse ways of understanding and employing it, rather than simply dismissing it.

The Golden Rule is sometimes interpreted as a maxim of prudence, a guide to self-interest. Thus, we might say, "If you don't want others to do that to you, don't do it to them," or "If you want others to treat you well, you should treat them well." Although this can be good practical advice, it does not seem to capture the moral spirit of the Golden Rule. This is because, interpreted in this way, if it can be shown that one can get away with harming or exploiting others, the Golden Rule would have no effective reply. Certainly in most religious and moral systems, the Golden Rule demands more from us than this. However, stating just what that something more is has proven to be quite challenging.

A century and a half ago, Richard Whately outlined three fundamental objections that have been leveled against the Golden Rule.[33] The first objection is that certain applications of the Golden Rule lead to *absurd* results. For example, farmers renting land would prefer to have their land rent-free. So, it might be contended, if those who rent their land to farmers are concerned to do unto others as they would have others do unto them, they should provide the land rent-free. After all, were they renting land from someone, this would be their preference as well. The second objection is that Golden Rule reasoning can lead to *immoral* results. For example, jailers should release their prisoners, since that is what prisoners want; and this is what jailers would want if they were prisoners. The third objection is that the Golden Rule can lead to *impossible* results because it provides no means for mediating between two contesting parties.

Such objections suggest that the Golden Rule is deeply flawed, however firmly entrenched it might be in our traditional religious and moral thinking. Are there any effective responses to these objections? Marcus G. Singer makes a strong case that there is a plausible reading of the Golden Rule that can withstand them.[34] He discusses four possible interpretations of the maxim, concluding that only the fourth does justice to its spirit.

1. *Do unto others what they would do unto you.* This is a rather straightforward form of reciprocity. As such, it has some natural appeal. But, although it encourages mutuality (for example, returning favors and mutual kindness, consideration, and respect), it can also lead to more problematic behavior

(such as, lying to those who lie to us, cheating those who cheat us, stealing from those who steal from us). Since this view simply commends returning in kind, it uncritically assumes the appropriateness of such responses. It neither urges us to try to understand the perspectives of others nor to weigh the likely short- or long-term consequences of simply returning in kind. Furthermore, this view overlooks the possibility that one might not want to return in kind (for example, to deceive, hit back, punish, or return evil for evil). However natural it might seem to do to others what they do to us, it does not follow that it is either acceptable or desirable to do so.

2. *Do unto others what they would have you do to them.* This reading promises more benign treatment of others, since most of us wish to have our well-being supported, or at least not undermined, by others. In addition, it encourages us to make a serious effort to understand what the interests of other are, thereby challenging our egocentric tendency to assume that others have the same values we do. But this reading of the Golden Rule requires too much from us. As Whately's first objection points out, always doing unto others what they would have us do for them will leave too little for ourselves. Ironically, if everyone followed this maxim, none of us would keep what we receive from others because someone else would, in turn, want us to give them our newly acquired goods. So, taken literally, this reading of the Golden Rule would likely result in a chaotic altruism that would not really benefit anyone.

3. *Do unto others what you would have them do unto you.* This reading has the unfortunate consequence of tolerating egocentric thinking. For example, suppose that John is the sort of person who, in certain circumstances, would prefer being lied to rather than receive bad news. So, he lies to Jane in order to keep bad news from her. However, Jane may be the sort of person who appreciates the truth, however upsetting it might be to her. This reading of the Golden Rule does not encourage John to be sensitive to this possibility.

4. *Do unto others as you would have them do unto you.* This reading differs from the second and third versions by replacing "what" with "as." As Singer points out, this is not merely a verbal shift. Rather it marks a substantial shift of focus. Instead of focusing on the particular likes, dislikes, preferences, or interests of those involved, we are now to consider matters from a more general perspective. That is, the directive is not to do what (in particular) others want for themselves (the second version) or what we want for ourselves (the third version). Instead, we might say, it is to treat others in accordance with sharable principles, rules, or considerations that require us to imagine ourselves on both the giving and the receiving end.

So, although farmers might want rent-free land, it is doubtful that they would accept a similar requirement that they give away their crops to those who wish to have them at no cost. This more inclusive perspective requires us to take into account the full variety of situations in which we might find ourselves. Prisoners must ask what else would be implied by a rule or principle that approves their release. (For example, would this require that they voluntarily return to jail, since this is what their jailers would like?) Or, John must ask whether he would object to having *his* basic interests slighted or ignored simply because others are too egocentric to notice that his interests are different from theirs.

Admittedly, the Golden Rule does not by itself supply the more general considerations that should be addressed. Instead, it tells us that we must not only try to understand the specific context calling for a moral decision, but we must also move our reflections to a more general level. As anyone who has taken this seriously knows, this can place real constraints on what we find it acceptable to do; and it can press us to try to understand and take properly into account the stake that others have in what we do.

Sissela Bok points out the dizzying effect Golden Rule thinking can have on us:

> We need to learn to shift back and forth between the two perspectives, and even to focus on both at once, as in straining to see both aspects of an optical illusion. In ethics, such a double focus leads to applying the Golden Rule: to strain to experience one's acts not only as subject and agent but as recipient, and sometimes victim. And while it is not always easy to put oneself in the place of someone affected by a fate one will never share, there is no such difficulty with lying. We all know what it is to lie, to be told lies, to be correctly or falsely suspected of having lied. In principle, we can all readily share both perspectives.[35]

It might be objected that this shifting back and forth invites perpetual confusion. As Singer observes, first one decides in favor of the liar, then the lied-to. One's choice fluctuates back and forth as one's perspective changes. Singer's way out of this problem is to urge us to resist fixing on just one perspective at a time. Instead, we must focus on a more general perspective that can be acceptable to everyone at once. This seems to be what Bok has in mind when she insists that we "focus on both at once, as in straining to see both aspects of an optical illusion."

CHAPTER THREE

Trust and Truthfulness

WHAT WE EXPECT

We all rely on professionals. I go to a dentist to have my teeth examined, cavities filled, or a bridge installed. I go to a lawyer for help composing my will, planning my estate, or dealing with some legal difficulty. I go to a doctor for a checkup, diagnosis of some particular ailment, or needed medical procedure. I go to an accountant for help filing my income tax or straightening out my financial affairs, and so on.

These are all instances of an individual seeking out the assistance of a particular professional or group of professionals. Of course, professionals affect our lives in many other ways as well. When we enter the elevator, we assume that it will operate safely and efficiently. Although we will never meet them, we rely on the work of those engineers involved in the design, manufacture, and installation of the elevator. In fact, our society is filled with professionals we will never meet or even see but on whose reliable work we heavily depend in our ordinary, daily living.

Given our extensive dependence on professionals, we expect them to conduct themselves responsibly. This is not to say that we can simply assume that they will (like one expects rain when observing storm clouds moving in), for they may not. This expectation, then, is normative, implying standards of accountability. Specific standards vary widely among, and even within, professions. Speaking at a very general level, however, we can say that, at a minimum, we expect professionals to be trustworthy. This requires that they be both competent in and committed to their work. Of course, extending our trust to professionals with whom we interact or on whom we otherwise depend does not guarantee that they actually are trustworthy — i.e., worthy of our trust. Whether they are can be difficult to determine. But much is at stake regarding whether they are.

Professionals attempt to assure us that they are trustworthy simply by letting us know that they are professionals. In some instances they may do this by becoming formally licensed or registered to practice. However, this is not uniformly required of professionals. Still, whether or not professionals have official "credentials," they present themselves as professionals to their employers, their clients, and the public in general. Evidence of competence is provided by their actual record of performance and may be documented in their résumés. This, plus their acceptance of employment or their availability for providing services, is taken as an implicit pledge, or promise, that reliable service can be expected from them. The extent to which they take that pledge seriously is a mark of their trustworthiness.

A NEED FOR TRUST

We regard professionals as having made a commitment to provide competent services appropriate to their professions of choice. Whether made explicitly or implicitly, this commitment is understood to extend to employers, colleagues, clients, and others who have a right to count on them to exercise their expertise responsibly. But, as Adam Smith reminds us, in return for their services, professionals expect to make a living at what they do.[1] This does not preclude some pro bono work, but we should not routinely count on this from professionals any more than from anyone else who provides us with goods or services. However, we can call on the "natural propensity to barter, truck, and exchange" that Smith brings to our attention. This propensity lies at the heart of our ability to make and keep promises, whether we are professionals offering our services or employers, colleagues, clients, or others who pay for them.

Thus far, this account depicts the professional as acquiring responsibilities through voluntary arrangements with others. This seems to fall in line with Annette Baier's observation that modern moral philosophy has tended to focus on what she calls "fairly cool relationships" among those who see themselves as agents capable of entering into voluntary agreements.[2] Accordingly, she says, insofar as trust has been given explicit attention, it is in regard to such relationships. From this vantage point, she says, we regard paying for goods we want to own, doing what we are employed to do, returning what we have borrowed, and supporting our spouses as instances of fulfilling voluntary agreements, or contracts. But, we might reply, although these arrangements all do involve voluntary agreements, they need not be simply, or even primarily, that. Supporting one's spouse, for example, may be based in part on the fact of marriage (as a voluntary arrangement), but it may be based on love as well.

However, Baier responds with a more radical break from voluntary agreements. Consider, she replies, the trust she has in the plumber sent by the municipal drainage authority after she has reported that her drains are clogged. This is not simply trust that he will fulfill contractual obligations to her or his employer:

When I trust him to do whatever is necessary and safe to clear my drains, I take his expertise and his lack of ill will for granted. Should he plant explosives to satisfy some unsuspected private or social grudge against me, what I might try to sue him for (if I escaped alive) would not be damages for breach of contract. His wrong, if wrong it were, is not breach of contract, and the trust he would have disappointed would not have been that particular form of trust.[3]

This is surely right; trusting that the plumber will not plant explosives in one's drains is not based on any voluntary agreement. If caught planting such explosives, it will hardly do for the plumber to reply, "But I never promised I wouldn't do this." Trusting that the plumber will do a competent job, however, does seem to be based on voluntary agreements, in this case, at least two. The first is the agreement the plumber has with his employer that he will competently do the work assigned to him. The second is with the customer, an implicit agreement when he is invited into one's home to do the work.

However, Baier apparently thinks that this still overworks the idea of voluntary agreement, or contract. Noting that we count on others in many ways even in the absence of contracts, she says: "For these cases of trust in people to do their job conscientiously and not to take the opportunity to do us harm once we put things we value into their hands are different from trust in people to keep their promises in part because of the very indefiniteness of what we are counting on them to do or not to do."[4] This seems more problematic. Certainly there are limits to what one promises. However, it is not clear that promises necessarily have the degree of definiteness to them that Baier supposes. In the case of providing professional services, not only is the customer typically not well positioned to know in advance precisely what is called for, but the professional may not be either.

The plumber, for example, will not know until he has had a look just what is causing the drains to plug and, therefore, what remedy is needed. To make either determination, he needs to be permitted entry into the home. Assuming that there is not a standing invitation for virtually anyone to enter at their whim, either the plumber will be greeted at the door, or other arrangements will explicitly be made. It seems plausible to construe the agreement as including that the plumber will stick to his business, not snoop around the house, not steal items, and the like. Of course, this would not be specified in the agreement, mentioned by the plumber, or demanded by the customer as a condition of entry. However, it is understood as included in professional behavior. We may trust, in general, that those invited into our homes will not do such things. But if an uninvited stranger were to enter our house and snoop around, we would not say that this is unprofessional, whereas we would say this of the plumber. Such snooping in either case would be inappropriate, but there is an additional objection to the plumber's conduct.

Baier seems to come close to conceding this in her discussion of vulnerability and trust. An advantage of contracts, she says, is the additional security they can provide:

> They make it possible not merely for us to trust at will but to trust with minimal vulnerability. They are a device for trusting others enough for mutually profitable future-involving exchanges without taking the risks trusters usually do take. They are designed for cooperation between mutually suspicious risk-averse strangers, and the vulnerability they involve is at the other extreme from that incurred by trusting infants.[5]

I would not invite just anyone to enter my home to inspect and fix my plugged drains. I invite in a total stranger — but someone who presents himself as a licensed professional plumber. This I take as including commitment, not only to attend to my drains but also to respect my property and privacy. I may expect the latter from other strangers invited into my home; but, as Baier points out, the plumber provides me with additional assurance, precisely by presenting himself as a plumber.

A professional possesses expertise on which others need to rely. To exercise that expertise, the professional may need to have access to things to which he or she ordinarily would not. As a condition for being permitted such access, it is understood that the professional will not abuse that privilege, by, for example, stealing from the client. Although no one may have the right to steal something from me, professionals in my service provide me special assurance that I can trust them not to do this. They do this, not by explicitly saying so, but by presenting themselves to me as professionals.

HONESTY: POLICY OR PRINCIPLE?

Nevertheless, what professionals say does matter. We regard truthfulness in professionals as a fundamental feature of their trustworthiness. Why this should be so is worth exploring in some detail. A *New Yorker* cartoon depicts a boardroom meeting at which someone proclaims: "Of course, honesty is one of the better policies."[6] We find it wryly amusing that honesty is acknowledged to be merely a practical option rather than a moral principle. Presented as a matter of business policy, honesty loses its moral luster and has to fight it out on even terms with other practical policies. Intuitively, we seem to grasp an important difference between moral norms and prudential rules of thumb, or useful guides to self-interest. Nowhere is this more evident than in our concerns about honesty, or truthfulness. Our amusement at the *New Yorker* cartoon suggests that we are not taken in by the nostrum "Honesty is the best policy" and that we are somewhat cynical about the level of honesty we can realistically expect from those in business and the professions. Given the central importance we attach to honesty, we should not be surprised to find that this is part of a more general cynicism about ethics in business and the professions.

In fact, Gallup Polls taken every year since the mid-1970s consistently show that the level of public confidence in the moral integrity of professionals is strikingly low.[7] The polls ask: "How would you rate the honesty and ethical standards of people in these different fields — very high, high, average, low, or very low?" For most professional areas, fewer than 60 percent of the respondents give rankings of "very high" or "high." There has been relatively little change in these rankings over the past three decades. Recently, nurses, grade school teachers, pharmacists, and military officers have distanced themselves somewhat from the others, receiving high rankings from over 70 percent of the respondents.[8] Engineers, clergy, college teachers, medical doctors, bankers, and accountants remain consistently lower. Lawyers, auto mechanics, news reporters, politicians, and nursing home operators receive high rankings from, at most, about 25 percent — not that much higher than advertisers and used car salespersons, traditionally ranked at the bottom.

Polls only reflect people's perceptions, not necessarily the realities. How trustworthy professionals actually are may be another matter entirely. Nevertheless, the trust extended to professionals is determined by perceptions. Professionals need to be trusted in order to perform well; and, since we are so dependent on professionals, we would certainly like to be able to place our trust in them — if only we can be convinced that they merit it.

Of course, to merit our trust professionals need to be more than honest, or truthful. They also need to be competent and committed to serving us fairly and well. However, as Sissela Bok makes clear, truthfulness occupies center stage:

> I can have different kinds of trust: that you will treat me fairly, that you will have my interests at heart, that you will do me no harm. But if I do not trust your word, can I have genuine trust in the first three? If there is no confidence in the truthfulness of others, is there any way to assess their fairness, their intentions to help or to harm? How, then, can they be trusted? *Whatever* matters to human beings, trust is the atmosphere in which it thrives.[9]

What Bok says here seems to apply as much to our lives in general as to the professions. Given its pivotal role in all social life, we might ask how truthfulness can bear such a burden.

VERACITY AND CREDULITY

Thomas Reid's view is that, as inherently social creatures, we begin with trust in the word of others. He comments: "The wise and beneficent Author of Nature, who intended that we should be social creatures, and that we should receive the greatest and most important part of our knowledge by the information of others, hath, for these purposes, implanted in our natures two principles that tally with each other."[10] The first principle, the "principle of veracity," is "a propensity to speak truth, and to use the signs of language, so as to convey our real sentiments."[11] The second, "the principle of credulity," counterpart to the first, is "a disposition to confide in the veracity of others, and to believe what they tell us."[12]

Whatever their origin, these two principles do seem to play the sort of role in human development that Reid suggests. These propensities, says Reid, suit our social nature. Asked what time it is, we naturally say what we believe the time to be; and others take us at our word. The principle of veracity, says Reid, "has a powerful operation, even in the greatest liars; for where they lie once, they speak truth a hundred times. Truth is always uppermost, and is the natural issue of the mind. It requires no art or training, no inducement or temptation, but only that we yield to a natural impulse."[13] So, if we lie, we act contrary to this natural impulse; and we do sometimes lie. However, adds Reid, "I find, that truth is always at the door of my lips, and goes forth spontaneously, if not held back. It requires neither good nor bad intention to bring it forth, but only that I be artless and undesigning."[14] This is especially true in early childhood. Although eventually we come to lie and to distrust others, this is something learned through experience. The principles of veracity and credulity, however, are not the result of learning; they are what make learning possible.

As natural propensities that are operative in us prior to the development of our moral sensitivities, the principles of veracity and credulity are not themselves moral principles. However, a principle of nature does not need to be a moral principle in order to have obvious moral importance. We also have a natural aversion to pain and suffering. Just as deliberately inflicting pain or suffering on others ordinarily is morally objectionable, taking advantage of the natural credulity of others through deceit ordinarily is morally objectionable. Furthermore, the principles of veracity and credulity play an essential role in establishing and sustaining communities of people whose well-being depends on not betraying those principles. The principle of credulity, says Reid, "is unlimited in children, until they meet with instances of deceit and falsehood: and it retains a very considerable degree of strength through life."[15] If it did not have this staying power, "no proposition that is uttered in discourse would be believed, until it was examined and tried by reason; and most men would be unable to find reasons for believing the thousandth part of what is told them." The resulting distrust would, says Reid, "deprive us of the greatest benefits of society."[16]

For young children, Reid's principles of veracity and credulity help pave the way to eventual commitment to truthfulness as moral norm. The staying power of those principles ensures that truthfulness as a norm cannot easily be unseated from its central position in morality, and certainly not without tremendous social cost. It also ensures that it cannot easily be unseated from its central position in the professions, as is evidenced in virtually all codes of professional ethics.

MORAL NORMS

If something like Reid's view is right, our social nature plays an important role in the acquisition of truthfulness as a moral norm, and perhaps other moral norms as well. However, since his principles of veracity and credulity are not themselves moral principles, they need to be supplemented with an account of how distinctively moral norms come to have significance in our lives.

James Wallace's account of moral norms and the virtues with which they are associated is helpful in this regard.[17] "Morality," says Wallace, "refers to practical considerations, principles, norms that apply to more than one practical domain — considerations that are important in many activities."[18] This is what gives morality its generality. At the same time, Wallace says, the point of moral norms comes from the various particular activities to which they belong. The salient features of morality, he says, are these. Morality is a social artifact, with a history that is bound up with human activities and practices. These activities and practices involve attempts to satisfy human needs and interests, as well as attempts to resolve problems and conflicts. Those norms we call moral, or ethical, are nothing apart from these activities and practices; but they have proven somewhat useful in resolving problems and conflicts that recur across many practical domains. As activities and practices change, so might the moral norms associated with them. Even though moral norms are embedded in existing activities and practices, they can also be used to evaluate those activities and practices — sorting out appropriate from inappropriate forms of conduct, arbitrary or capricious conduct from reasonable conduct.

Although inseparable from activities and practices, Wallace says, moral norms are also instruments for helping us navigate our way through those activities and practices. They help us address a broad range of concerns: agreements, cooperation, reciprocity, trust, property, role responsibilities, authority, truthfulness, compassion, honor, loyalty, friendship, and justice.[19] Disparate as these concerns may be, they center around the social character of human life, and they address questions about "how to live."

Wallace notes that our earliest learning of moral norms is in domestic and educational settings. Even in these settings children must begin to learn how to balance tensions between various moral norms. For example, like adults, children are sensitive to the fact that justice requires treating people equally — *and* according to their needs, *and* according to their abilities, *and* according to their merit, *and* according to their efforts, *and* according to their contributions.[20]

It is Wallace's view that harm can come from presenting children with moral norms in an absolutist form, such as "Never be untruthful." But if norms are not presented as absolute, exceptionless rules, then they are going to be somewhat incomplete. There can still be paradigms of appropriate applications of norms, but the paradigms do not lend themselves to exceptionless generalizations. However, a crucial matter is how children understand the incompleteness of the norms they learn. Are they to be encouraged to learn to think for themselves in dealing with situations not definitively settled by the norms as they currently understand them? Or are they simply to wait until someone else tells them how to go on? Both views are compatible with the idea that norms are not presented as absolute, exceptionless rules. Let me illustrate.

I recall from my early lessons in Latin that the inflections of nouns and adjectives are highly regular — to a point. Our teacher had us memorize lists of first declension nouns and adjectives. But all along we were told that this was only a part of what we would eventually learn about the declension of nouns and adjectives. Initially, we had to learn what can be neatly organized. First declension nouns and adjectives, second declension nouns and adjectives, and so on. Eventually we got to the really messy, unsystematic bits. Nevertheless, we knew there were answers, even if the taxonomic approach could not provide them. When ready, we would be told what the answers were. And our's was not to question why, but to repeat the right reply.

In contrast, Ronald Dworkin suggests another way of going on, one that encourages children to think for themselves:

Suppose I tell my children simply that I expect them not to treat others unfairly. I no doubt have in mind examples of the conduct I mean to discourage, but I would not accept that my "meaning" was limited to these examples, for two reasons. First, I would expect my children to apply my instructions to situations I had not and could not have thought about. Second, I stand ready to admit that some particular act I had thought was fair when I spoke was in fact unfair, or vice-versa, if one of my children is able to convince me of that later; in that case I should want to say that my instructions covered the case he cited, not that I had changed my instructions. I might say that I meant the family to be guided by the *concept* of fairness, not by any specific *conception* of fairness.[21]

Dworkin's instruction to his children about fairness comes much closer to what Wallace might favor in moral education than the Latin learning approach I have outlined. Still, much more needs to be said.

Wallace cites with approval John Dewey's urging that we "transfer the attention of theory from preoccupation with general conceptions to the problem of developing effective methods of inquiry."[22] Given the open-ended features of moral norms, the conflicts that arise among them, the absence of algorithms for resolving these conflicts, and the changing contexts within which our deliberations take place, Dewey's urging seems well taken. At the same time, the methods of inquiry Dewey favors need to be consistent with serious moral commitment, and they should not pose a threat to the trust we need to extend to others. A child who has few, if any, qualms about lying is not trustworthy. However, a child who is basically honest, even though not "absolutely" so, is morally serious about truthfulness and to that extent trustworthy.[23]

PREPARATION FOR THE PROFESSIONS

Wallace contrasts Violet, a young child, with Vincent, an attorney. Violet is a truthful child; she knows when she should be truthful in the familiar domains of the home, the school, and the playground. This will serve her well later, perhaps when she becomes an attorney. But she has much more to learn in the meantime. Vincent, the attorney, is generally truthful, but he sometimes says things in court in behalf of his client that he does not believe. Sometimes he even builds on what he knows to be false testimony by his client. He might even lie to a judge who asks him an improper question if this is necessary to protect his client's rights. Are these departures from truthfulness wrong?

Wallace takes up the debate between Kenneth Kipnis and Sissela Bok about such matters. Bok says that attorneys go too far in protecting client confidentiality, claiming that this is a practice they have adopted for their own purposes;

protection of client confidentiality as a justification for complicity in perjury could not stand up to public scrutiny. Kipnis thinks that sometimes it can. Both appeal to their understanding of current legal practice and the larger purposes of law; but it is essential to both of their defenses that they accept the burden of convincing an imagined public — a public that is also well informed about current legal practices and the larger purposes of law. This cannot be a debate for attorneys only.

What might prepare Vincent to enter into such a debate? He, too, needs a good understanding of current legal practice and the larger purposes of law. As a generally truthful person, Vincent has a basic understanding of the importance of honesty; and neither this nor the understanding that goes with his other virtues (for example, his sense of fairness) were first acquired in his legal training. This is essential to his being able to sift his way through the moral challenges of the profession he has entered.

So, there are four kinds of resources that are vital for Vincent as he practices law: (1) knowledge of the law and its purposes; (2) knowledge of the Model Code of the American Bar Association and related, enforced regulations where he is practicing; (3) knowledge of the particular case at hand; and (4) his own moral skills and sensibilities. Assuming Vincent is well qualified in regard to (1), (2), and (3), we still need to know what his capabilities are in regard to (4). His beginnings may have been like those of truthful Violet. We need to know, more specifically, what sorts of moral skills and sensibilities Vincent has acquired since those earlier years that have prepared him to join in the debate between Bok and Kipnis.

If moral norms are regarded by Vincent as general but not exceptionless rules, he will see them as somewhat open-ended and sometimes in conflict with one another. According to Wallace, from this level of generality Vincent needs to move "downward" and immerse himself in the context of legal practice, rather than attempt to move "upward" to an even higher level of generality; and he needs to do this with intelligence, sensitivity, and imagination. All of this requires the sort of critical inquiry skills to which Dewey alludes.

It can be expected that norms will conflict in particular situations, but this need not threaten to undermine their usefulness. I may have to choose between truthfulness and fairness in a particular situation, but this need not upset paradigm, or clear-cut, examples of when truthfulness or fairness is called for. In fact, paradigms help us to understand why there is a conflict in this situation. Ideally, we want to be truthful and fair. Although norms might be talked about in the abstract, their intelligent use is in particular activities. We may wish for some sort of prioritizing; but, Wallace says, ordered structures are available only for particular practical domains "where a learned activity is pursued in accordance with its particular group of norms, including relevant moral norms."[24] He continues:

> It is not surprising that there are no algorithms for harmonizing moral norms in the abstract. The absence of algorithms for harmonizing the moral norms that pertain in a particular practical domain is no more remarkable than the absence of mechanical decision procedures for medical practice, scientific research, or family life. The world in which we practice changes, and our knowledge and interests change in response. The life we share through our shared practical knowledge and interests continually encounters problems, some of them unprecedented. We must create ways of coping. . . . This is perhaps the supreme test of intelligence.[25]

CRITIQUING NORMS

The norms that are adopted by a profession at any given time may be flawed to some extent. Those norms cannot be understood without having some grasp of the practice. Still, once they are understood, they may need to be evaluated. Some basis for developing a critical perspective can be found among members of the profession who are already dissenting. What resources might new professionals bring with them that will enable them to engage in this sort of critical reflection?

Wallace says of the individual who undertakes to participate in a practice: "Normally, the person will develop a cultivated concern with the purposes of the practice, and will accept the guidance of the norms of the practice, the standards by which the person's pursuit of the practice is judged to be good or bad."[26] However, this acceptance need not imply passive or "blind" conformity. It can be more open-ended. The purposes of the practice themselves may be somewhat open-ended — with some widespread consensus at a minimal level, but with room for a fair amount of diversity that is compatible with that consensus. For example, protecting public health, safety, and welfare is commonly accepted as an engineer's paramount duty. Nevertheless, this operates more as a side-constraint than as the main goal of an engineering project (for example, developing a golf course). This side-constraint can be viewed as a shared minimum standard, whereas improving the environment is not. Yet, for many engineers, protecting and improving the environment shade into one another in ways that can put them in conflict with others who accept only the more modest protective standard. Or, all engineers might see themselves as committed to maintaining the dignity of the profession but may not agree that this requires placing restrictions on advertising. Yet, until the Supreme Court ruled against it, engineering codes of ethics did place severe restrictions on advertising. At the same time, the Supreme Court ruling does not require advertising; so, individual engineers and firms may continue to restrict their own ways of advertising as a way of trying to maintain the dignity of the profession.

As changes occur in society, norms may change as well. So, it seems that someone who is well prepared to enter a practice or profession needs to be prepared to deal with this open-endedness. However, one of the problems Wallace has to face is that of explaining how, if norms can be understood only within practices and activities, they can be used to evaluate critically those very same practices and activities. The value of moral norms in this regard is that, by cutting across a broad range of practices, they transcend any particular practice or activity. Furthermore, as we have seen, for Wallace, individual moral norms are not "absolutes" — that is none can be stated in terms of "always" or "never." So, moral norms must be understood in relation to each other as well as in relation to the practices and activities that give them their life.

Wallace's general observations about the overall importance of truthfulness for practices and activities can help us see how this might work. Truthfulness, he insists, is not the only important value that cuts across a broad range of practices and activities that are important to us. Other values include: loyalty, unselfishness, trustworthiness, compassion, justice, and restraint, particularly as they apply to agreements, cooperation, reciprocity, property, role responsibilities, authority, and so on.[27]

Of course, all of these values have to be understood within particular practices and activities in order to grasp their nuanced meanings and importance. But this does not require understanding how they might work their way through *all* particular activities. A child may not understand the nuances of legal or scientific practices and, therefore, not understand how truthfulness, for example, should be played out in those practices. However, the moral education of children can help prepare them to understand many of the moral values underlying professional practices prior to their acquiring a detailed understanding of those practices.

TRUTHFULNESS IN THE PROFESSIONS

While agreeing that truthfulness is a virtue in a wide range of activities, Wallace's account of the norm of truthfulness ties it more concretely to actual practice. Nearly everyone can think of circumstances in which lying does not seem wrong. This indicates that, although we might regard truthfulness to be very important, it is not our only important moral value. What we must come to understand, Wallace says, is "the importance of truth *in various areas of life*, why it is important, and how it is to be compared in importance with other considerations that pertain in these areas."[28] From this it follows that one cannot understand the importance of truthfulness in isolation from other values or independently of particular activities or practices. So, an "absolute" maxim such as "Always tell the truth" is unworkable, as it does not take into account the variety of contexts in which truthfulness is only one practical consideration among many that matter to us. Just how important truthfulness is cannot be understood in the abstract; its importance depends on the particular contexts within which it and other values operate as norms.

According to Wallace, it is because truthfulness is important for such a wide range of activities and practices that it takes on moral significance for us. Thus, he says of truthfulness:

> Truthfulness is a virtue that is exhibited in a variety of activities, including productive activities. It is a virtue of (moral) character because it promotes important human purposes in a wide variety of undertakings. It is a tendency to act well in accordance with certain norms that pertain widely across a broad range of human activities, but those norms themselves are important in those various activities because they tend to promote the purposes that people have in engaging in these and other particular activities.[29]

So, Wallace apparently does see truthfulness as one virtue (among many others), even though the moral value it has may vary across different practices, which themselves serve different purposes.

Some professions, however, place special emphasis on truthfulness as an essential feature of the work that is done. Journalism, for example, purports to provide the public with information on which it can rely both for understanding what has happened and for making future plans. In light of this, Stephen Klaidman and Thomas Beauchamp suggest a "reasonable reader" standard for journalists:

> The reasonable reader, then, is a person with needs for information about matters such as the risks, alternatives, and consequences of what is being reported. Using this general model, we argue for standards of completeness, accuracy, understanding, and objectivity that are designed to yield fair and responsible journalism that is, within attainable limits, impartial and objective.[30]

Meeting this standard can be challenging, and it is not always clear what specifically should count as "completeness, accuracy, understanding, and objectivity." Nevertheless, failure to take this standard seriously is to abandon journalism as it is commonly understood. As for all professions, public trust is essential. While acknowledging that the trustworthiness of journalists rests on more than truthfulness, Klaidman and Beauchamp say that it does provide the foundation for trust in journalism.[31]

Accountancy is another profession whose services are essentially bound up with truthfulness. Accountants are expected, as a matter of course, to make honest reports on and assessments of the financial status of clients and employers. The Code of Professional Conduct of the American Institute of Certified Public Accountants (AICPA), for example, stresses the importance of professional integrity, "the quality from which the public trust derives and the benchmark against which a member must ultimately test all decisions."[32] This integrity requires honesty and candor in reporting: "Service and the public trust should not be subordinated to personal gain and advantage. Integrity can accommodate the inadvertent error and the honest difference of opinion; it cannot accommodate deceit or subordination of principle."[33] Accountants are expected to be objective, which requires impartiality and intellectual honesty and being free from conflicts of interest.[34] In this regard, an accountant "shall not knowingly misrepresent facts or subordinate his or her judgment to others."[35] Regarding providing others with information, an accountant is expected to gather "sufficient relevant data to afford a reasonable basis for conclusions or recommendations in relation to any professional services performed."[36] In providing services, an accountant exercises special expertise in analyzing data and in making recommendations. A norm of truthfulness is tied to the specific techniques that are to be employed.

Employers, clients, and the general public depend on accountants to respect truthfulness as a norm while exercising their expertise. However, once the principles and techniques of accounting are learned, they can be abused, as evidenced in the recent Enron, Arthur Anderson, and WorldCom fiascos.[37] In these cases the harms to the public were widespread and devastating. However, when disclosed, even smaller-scale departures from accepted standards of accounting can seriously damage trust in accountancy as a profession.

SCIENCE AND TRUTHFULNESS

Wallace focuses on science to illustrate his views on the relationship between truthfulness and specific kinds of activities and practices. Central to caring about science, says Wallace, is that scientists accurately report the results of their work: "The *understanding* of the importance of truthfulness in research will be, in a person who cares about research, an *appreciation* of its value in research. Practical knowledge normally involves appreciating the importance of certain things, valuing things."[38] Curiously, however, Wallace now asks whether we have two norms operating: one technical, the other moral. He says of scientific fraud: "A moral standard is violated and so, too, is a technical norm."[39] One might think that he would opt for a single standard. However, he does not; there is a "technical," scientific standard, *and* a moral one.

What does it mean to view the norm as "technical"? "The requirement of truthfulness in science can be viewed as a technical norm, a directive that gets its authority from the character of the practice of scientific inquiry and the concerns peculiar to this activity."[40] The wrongness of a researcher's contemplated fraud does not depend on his or her particular purposes: "It depends, rather, upon the activity of science and the concerns and interests that this activity serves."[41] In this case, there is contemplation of a departure from standard scientific practice — say, a falsification rather than an objective presentation of data. Falsification of data, we say, is not real science, however much one might try to make it look like it is. So far, however, this sounds like just the sort of thing Wallace says about moral norms. Moral norms, he insists, do not stand apart from the particular activities in which they serve as norms. It is just that moral norms cut across a wide range of particular activities (unlike, say, specific norms for specific crafts); lying can be about data, what we have or have not done, what our names are, where we are from, or whatever.

However, Wallace goes on to contrast the technical norm of truthfulness in science with truthfulness as a moral norm — a moral norm that also applies to science. As a moral norm, Wallace says, "its authority has a different source from the authority of the technical norms of science. Presumably its source is to be found outside of the practice of scientific inquiry. Truthfulness as a moral norm belongs to a different realm of practical knowledge that somehow applies to scientific inquiry and many other activities."[42] Still, Wallace acknowledges that we do not have to embrace the view that the source of the authority of the moral norm is radically different from that of the technical norm:

> The source that is external to the activity of scientific inquiry, upon which the moral requirement of truthfulness depends for its authority, is simply a great many *other activities*. Truthfulness is necessary quite generally in cooperative activities that require communication among participants. Scientific inquiry is simply one such practice. That people can generally be trusted to be truthful is a condition of communication; that people should tell the truth is a norm of communication. That this standard applies widely in our lives reflects the fact that the phrase, "cooperative activity involving communica-

tion among participants," describes most, if not all, important human practices and activities. It applies to a very prominent and pervasive feature of human life.[43]

From this it seems to follow that, for virtually any practice or activity we might select, the story will be similar. Each will have a special norm of truthfulness whose meaning and authority derives from the nature and purposes of that practice or activity. If the importance of truthfulness for each practice or activity is understood in this way, it seems that what we have is simply a set of special norms, each of which happens to stress the importance of truthfulness for a particular practice or activity.

But this does not seem to capture Wallace's view. For him there is a strength in numbers (at least across practices and activities) that yields a moral, not merely a special, or "technical," norm of truthfulness. That is, truthfulness as a moral norm is to be understood distributively as one norm for all those particular practices or activities. From this perspective, truthfulness in science is an application of the moral norm rather than merely a special norm of a particular practice.

Still, we might, with Wallace, consider a scientist for whom truthfulness is only a "technical" norm rather than a moral norm, too; he is someone apparently committed to the norm of truthfulness specifically in science, but not in other activities generally.[44] Wallace says we should prefer a scientist who is more broadly committed to truthfulness than this. This is surely right. But it also seems questionable whether the more narrowly committed scientist understands the significance of the norm to which he is committed. After all, the "technical" is explained earlier as "getting its authority from the character of the practice of scientific inquiry and the concerns peculiar to this activity."[45] Well, what *is* the character of the practice of scientific inquiry, and what *are* the concerns peculiar to this activity?

If the scientist draws the lines around science too tightly, this begs the question against those many scientists who see science more broadly, say, in relation to values that science can serve and that may constrain both how science should proceed (for example, in experimenting on humans and animals) and what it should undertake (for example, whether developing bacterial weapons is acceptable). If Wallace says that the more narrow conception of science is defensible, another problem arises. If this more narrow view is accepted by scientists, then they may not view the norms governing their activities more broadly either; they will see them as applying only within science, narrowly understood as a "technical" practice whose norm of truthfulness is "technical," too.

In a broader view of science, scientists can see how the moral norm of truthfulness should work its way through scientific practice. Thus, it will incorporate the "technical" norm of truthfulness, insofar as it is acceptable. This seems to be precisely what has happened recently in national efforts to define "research misconduct" as an aspect of research ethics.[46] Two of the three provisions that are now standard are prohibitions of fabrication and falsification of data. Both pivot around the fundamental value of truthfulness in science. So, it seems that there is no need to posit two norms of truthfulness for science, one moral and the other "technical." The so-called technical norm, taken alone, would simply be an inadequately understood norm for those scientists who do not appreciate the moral importance of truthfulness for science. It is inadequately understood both because of an inadequate understanding of truthfulness as a moral norm and because of an inadequate understanding of the nature and purposes of science insofar as it embraces not only the norm of truthfulness but other moral norms that are relevant to science fulfilling its appropriate role in society.

In this respect, the failure to understand science in these broader terms is comparable to Wallace's depiction of Albert Z. Carr's understanding of business practice as analogous to playing poker.[47] Neither science nor business can be compared to playing a game of cards, with its special rules that apply to an activity largely isolated from the practices and activities of those not playing the game. The stakes for those who are not in science or business are much higher than that. Poker is a game in which it is explicitly understood that bluffing is acceptable. Thus, deception is explicitly authorized, even for those who have the virtue of truthfulness.

TRUTHFULNESS AS A VIRTUE

Wallace holds that, because truthfulness is fundamental in a wide range of human practices and activities, we regard it as a virtue of moral character.[48] But, as a virtue of moral character, we hope that it begins to take hold in childhood. Even though the importance of truthfulness for a given activity or practice may vary somewhat for different activities or practices, we hope that the child will at some point grasp the general idea that being able to trust one another to be truthful is, as Wallace himself puts it, "a condition of communication."[49] What we expect from those who have the virtue of truthfulness is that they accept telling the truth as a norm of communication.

If this is right, then we should expect that by the time children begin to acquire an understanding of what science is, and what scientists do, they will already be well on their way to having the virtue of truthfulness. As they learn about biology, chemistry, and physics, we would expect them to assume that the scientists responsible for the content of what they learn were being truthful in reporting their findings. When they themselves are expected to do work in the laboratory and report their results, those with the virtue of truthfulness can be expected to manifest that virtue in their work. What they may not have thought about are all the various ways in which truthfulness in science is crucial to its success or about all the various ways in which departures from truthfulness can harm not only science but society in general. Still, they should have no difficulty understanding that falsifying or fabricating data is lying. Furthermore, they should be able to see that, as a departure from what standardly counts as scientific activity, it is a rather serious sort of lying, as it threatens to undermine the very practice that allegedly is being undertaken.

It seems reasonable to suppose that children can have a decent grasp of the basic idea that truthfulness is a norm of communication and the corresponding virtue of truthfulness. As they continue to be introduced to different kinds of activities and practices (including science), we can expect them to make discoveries about the special importance this norm has in those activities and practices. Since, as Wallace points out, truthfulness is not the only moral norm, they will also learn about important exceptions and come to recognize that truthfulness is only one among many moral values. They will also recognize that these values sometimes come into conflict with one another, giving rise to challenges both in making up their minds about where they stand and in dealing with the fact that others may make up their minds differently. However, none of this need upset their basic commitment to truthfulness.

REASONABLENESS IN FOLLOWING NORMS

Wallace says that reasonableness in following any one norm requires assessing its relationship to other norms that are also relevant to a given set of circumstances.[50] A surgeon performs many different tasks — talking with patients, working with other members of the medical staff, filling out prescriptions, making examinations, attending meetings, reading medical books and magazines, deciding whether to recommend surgery, performing different sorts of surgery (using various instruments at different times), deciding how many patients to accept, and so on. These are not all the same activities even though they might be said to serve the same set of purposes. A crucial factor that provides unity to this picture is the surgeon's sense of being a surgeon. These activities are all important to being a surgeon, but they must be done well, not only as individual activities but together as the work of a good surgeon; and this calls for intelligence, sensitivity, skill, and judgment. This lends unity to the diverse set of activities that constitute the surgeon's practice as a surgeon.

Reasonably following a moral norm is similar; it, too, must be done in conjunction with other norms, with a careful concern for what is appropriate in this or that particular circumstance. This requires not merely applying norms in particular circumstances, but also noticing those factors that make bringing various norms to bear on the situation important.[51] Evident failure in handling this well in any particular case may evoke guilt, shame, remorse, or the sense that one must try to make amends, improve, or change one's ways. In some instances, one may feel that one's integrity is on the line. These forms of self-appraisal (and there are positive ones, too) are features of one's sense of oneself as a moral agent. There are related attitudes that we have about others that are central to our conception of them as moral agents.

Wallace makes no attempt to assemble the moral norms with which we are familiar into a comprehensive, mutually consistent, set of rules of conduct. These norms do help us understand and appreciate the moral dimensions of our practices, but they do not provide us with algorithms for making moral decisions, and they do not offer the promise of resolving all moral conflicts in ways that all reasonable people must accept. Reasonable disagreement is still possible, and moral judgment is still necessary.

Given the possibility of reasonable disagreement, a skeptic might ask, how can we tell whether departures from moral norms are based on morally serious considerations or carefully disguised considerations of personal advantage? Temptations to act contrary to moral norms for reasons of self-interest begin in childhood and continue throughout one's lifetime. Here the question is more a matter of "Why be moral?" than "What does morality require?" One of the tests of the virtue of truthfulness is how one handles such challenges. This, we can say, is a test of integrity, the topic to be taken up directly in chapter 5. First, however, we will take a closer look at another important ingredient of professional reliability, good judgment.

CHAPTER FOUR

Good Judgment

Professionals have expertise that distinguishes them from the rest of us, including other professionals. This means that it would be difficult for those not sharing a professional's particular expertise to understand and assess the processes he or she uses in making judgments. If things obviously go badly (for example, the bridge collapses), we may suspect that bad judgment was employed somewhere along the line. But it still may not be evident just where, why, or even to what extent bad judgment was involved. Unlike problems that can be completely resolved through some sort of algorithmic process, the problems professionals address typically call for a kind of judgment that is anything but routine. It is expected that professional judgment is based on supporting reasons, but the reasons are seldom so compelling that no discretion is needed. Furthermore, even good judgment sometimes is not enough. The unexpected occurs, particular circumstances have unique features, nothing lasts forever, and so on. Finally, the work of professionals typically is not monitored closely, even by peers. We have neither the time, interest, nor expertise to do so. In short, to a large extent, we are not in a good position to evaluate directly the work of professionals, especially *before* something bad happens.

What counts as good professional judgment depends very much, of course, on the particular area of expertise in question. We should not expect to be able to say much of a general nature about this. However, some general things can be said about conditions that threaten to undermine good professional judgment. Perhaps the most obvious requirement for good judgment is competence. However, the competence of any given professional is limited. An ophthalmologist is unlikely to have expertise in cardiology. Nevertheless, she might notice irregularities from a patient's EKG that indicate a possible heart problem. Here we might expect the ophthalmologist to recommend seeing a heart specialist but not to present herself as if she had expertise in that area. Knowing when and how to refer patients and clients to other professionals itself requires good judgment.

Unfortunately, sometimes professionals take on tasks for which they lack competence. This is a real enough concern in engineering, for example, that nearly all engineering societies' codes of ethics specify, as a fundamental canon, that engineers are to provide services "only in areas of their competence."[1] Many engineering projects require the formal approval of a qualified, licensed engineer. A striking violation of this requirement is the case of Charles Landers, former Anchorage, Alaska, assemblyman and unlicensed engineer.[2] He was found guilty of using his partner's professional seal and forging his signature on at least forty documents. This was done without his partner's knowledge. The documents certified to the city health department that local septic systems met city wastewater-disposal regulations. Landers said he did this because his clients needed approval right away, and his partner was unavailable at the time. It was also confirmed in subsequent review that there were no violations of health standards, only the misuse of the professional seal and the forgery of signatures.

Circuit Judge Michael Wolverton, presiding in this case, said that Landers's actions betrayed the trust of the public, which relies on the word of those, like professional engineers, who are entrusted with special responsibilities. The judge also cited a letter from Richard Armstrong, then chair of the Architects, Engineers, and Land Surveyors Board of Registration for Alaska's Department of Commerce and Economic Development:

> Some of the reasons for requiring professional engineers to seal their work are to protect the public from unqualified practitioners; to assure some minimum level of competency in the profession; to make practicing architects, engineers, and land surveyors responsible for their work; and to promote a level of ethics in the profession. The discovery of this case will cast a shadow of doubt on other engineering designed by properly licensed individuals.

Deadlines and the desire to succeed can also pose problems in scientific research. A widely discussed case in point is John Darsee's fabrication of data in his research on the effects of heart drugs on dogs.[3] Regarded as a brilliant student and medical researcher at Notre Dame, Indiana, Emory, and Harvard, he had an impressive record of publications. Faculty at all four institutions saw him as a potential "all-star" researcher. However, colleagues finally observed Darsee labeling data recordings "24 seconds," "72 hours," "one week," and "two weeks," when actually only a few minutes had passed. Confronted, he admitted fabricating the data but claimed that he had never done this before and that there was heavy pressure to complete the study quickly. He added: "I had too much to do, too little time to do it in, and was greatly fatigued mentally and almost childlike emotionally. I had not taken a vacation, sick day, or even a day off from work for six years. I had put myself on a track that I hoped would allow me to have a wonderful academic job and I knew I had to work very hard for it."[4] However, further investigation revealed a long history of fabricating data. As a consequence, not only was Darsee's own research discredited, but much of the collaborative research he had engaged in was also thrown into doubt, thus seriously affecting the work of many others as well.

A positive outcome of the Darsee case is that it signaled to scientists that closer supervision of trainees should be taken more seriously, and it contributed to the development of guidelines and standards concerning research misconduct by federal agencies, medical associations and institutes, and universities and medical schools.[5] However, Darsee's former mentor, Eugene Braunwald, observes that there is no foolproof system of protection from research misconduct and that an atmosphere of "policing" of one another's work can interfere with good science: "The most creative minds will not thrive in such an environment and the most promising young people might actually be deterred from embarking on a scientific career in an atmosphere of suspicion. Second only to absolute truth, science requires an atmosphere of openness, trust, and collegiality."

Outright fabrication of data is a clear instance of research misconduct in research, however difficult it might be to detect. There are other ways of preparing data that are less clear cut. Trimming data by smoothing out irregularities or cooking data by keeping only data that supports one's theory are also regarded to be research misconduct. However, it is sometimes acceptable not to include certain data in one's reports, particularly when some irregularity has occurred in the gathering of that data. Here judgment is unavoidable, on the part of both the researcher and those evaluating his or her work. A much-discussed controversy in this regard is the case of the celebrated physicist Robert A. Millikan, accused by some of misrepresenting data from his oil drop experiment to determine the uniformity of electron charge.

Scientists who have analyzed Millikan's presentation of his data point out that it is not always easy to distinguish between responsible interpretation of laboratory data, inappropriate but unintentional distortion of data, and the intentional cooking of data. There is consensus that there can be circumstances in which it is appropriate to disregard certain data. In many situations it must be left to the judgment of the scientist to decide if a problem with the equipment or some other consideration justifies not including data in one's analysis.

Millikan's procedure in trying to determine the charge of electrons involved watching the behavior of oil droplets in an electrically charged field. A droplet is allowed to fall between two plates, and then an electric field is created that pulls the droplet upwards. Millikan published tables of his measured drops and their rise times. These tables indicated that the charges on the droplets were multiples of the same number, the charge of the electron. Eventually he won the Nobel Prize for his work.

However, Millikan's notebooks indicate that he exercised judgment in deciding which drops he would include and which to exclude in his published accounts. Sometimes he mentioned that he was doing this, but not always. The locus of controversy revolves around an assertion made in his 1913 paper, which presents the most complete account of his measurements of the charge on the electron. Millikan says: "It is to be remarked that this is not a selected group of drops but represents all of the drops experimented upon during 60 consecutive days." But his notebook appears to conflict with this, indicating that of the 189 observations he made, only 140 are presented in the paper.

Ultimately, Millikan's conclusions seem to have been confirmed. However, the ethical issue pivots around his reporting procedure; and on this matter there is still divided opinion. One view is that Millikan should at least have mentioned in his published statement that only 140 of 189 were being used, along with a brief explanation of why the other 49 were not. Others defend Millikan as meaning that all data taken when the apparatus was working properly were included.

If it is neither possible nor desirable to closely monitor the work of professionals, this places a responsibility for self-monitoring on individual professionals. It should have been obvious to Charles Landers and John Darsee that what they were doing was unacceptable. In Robert Millikan's case, perhaps much of the controversy could have been avoided by explicitly mentioning in the published account that 49 observations were not included because the apparatus was not working properly. Presumably, despite this acknowledgment, other scientists could still be as convinced as Millikan himself that he had drawn the right conclusions from his data. However, much must still be taken on trust, as no one but Millikan was present when the observations were made.

Unfortunately, there are subtle ways in which one's judgment can become skewed or corrupted, even sometimes without self-awareness. Two such ways will now be discussed: bribery and conflicts of interest. Both are commonly addressed, but not explained, in codes of ethics. As we shall see, explaining these concepts poses challenges of its own.

BRIBERY

Despite the thoroughgoing nature of its discussion of whether Socrates should escape, Plato's *Crito* ignores an issue that would require attention if Socrates were seriously tempted to accept Crito's offer.[6] This is the question of how the escape would be accomplished. Crito is ready with an answer: They would bribe those responsible for keeping Socrates imprisoned. Socrates had other reasons for not escaping. But what might be said about using bribery as a means of escape? Calling an act a bribe invites philosophical discussion, as this identifies the act as being of a certain kind, one that bears significant moral weight. What kind of act is it? Answering this question moves us to a more general level of inquiry.

Bribery, like lying, is not a value-neutral concept. It has a negative connotation and is regarded by most as generally, although not necessarily universally, wrong. At the very least, those who resort to bribery bear a burden of justification for what they do. This is no small point, as no such burden must be borne for the vast majority of human activities, such as engaging in conversation or taking a walk, which normally do not. As Sissela Bok says of lying, we might say that a negative moral weight attaches to every act of bribery; it may be possible to counter this negative weight in some instances, but not without an argument (the provision of good reasons).[7]

Why should a negative moral weight be attached to every act of bribery? It might be thought that, even if most instances of bribery are morally objectionable, the concept of bribery itself is morally neutral.[8] However, enticing people to violate what they take to be their duty does seem to call for some sort of moral justification. This seems to be so even in extreme cases, for example, when bribing a Nazi guard to allow concentration camp prisoners to escape. The ready availability of a moral justification in such circumstances does not eliminate the need for one.

Bribery continues to pose serious practical problems for many today; and getting clearer about just what it is about bribery that is morally problematic is an important task of practical ethics. Here are a few representative, fictional examples with which we might begin:

- Anderson Suppliers wants a sales contract with Barlow, Inc.; so its sales representative offers Barlow's purchasing agent a substantial sum of money in an effort to secure a contract.
- Compton Builders knows that the condos it has just built fail to meet some of the building code standards. It offers the building inspector a substantial sum of money to "look the other way."
- Tom wants a better grade in his philosophy class. He also manages a car wash facility. So he offers to give his professor free car washes for the next year if his grade is raised.
- Jane is coach of the women's soccer team at the local high school. Alex desperately wants his daughter, Cindy, to make the team. However, competition for spots on the team is stiff and Cindy has marginal talent. Alex offers Jane a free membership in his tennis club if she awards Cindy a place on the team.

- Brad is caught speeding in a residential area. He will lose his driver's license for six months if he receives another ticket. He offers the police officer $100 if no ticket is issued.

By any reasonable account, each of these is a clear instance of attempted bribery. Although their legal statuses may vary, as well as accompanying sanctions, each is morally questionable. What kind of account might explain this? Thomas Carson offers the following as a common denominator in discussions of bribery: "An individual (the briber) pays another individual (the bribee) something of value in exchange for the bribee's doing something that violates a special duty or special obligation that attaches to an office occupied, or a role or practice participated in, by the bribee."[9] The five examples share this common denominator. In each case, bribing explicitly includes the notion of an inducement to violate a duty or obligation as an essential element; the briber's intent is to get the bribee to violate a special duty or obligation. Carson suggests that, insofar as accepting a bribe is wrong, it is also wrong to attempt to induce someone into accepting a bribe. So, assuming that these examples do capture a common feature of bribery, there seems to be good reason to accept the notion that an act of bribery bears an initial negative moral weight.

BRIBERY, EXTORTION, AND TIPPING

Even if bribery is viewed as bearing an initial negative moral weight, there can be difficulties in determining just what counts as a bribe. It is important to distinguish bribery from both extortion and tipping. Extortion is the attempt to coerce someone into making payment by threatening harm. Both extortionists and bribers take the initiative; however, extortionists seek payment, whereas bribers make an offer. In contrast to extortion, successful bribery is best viewed as a mutual exchange, a voluntary relationship. Tipping is payment for performing routine tasks (such as passing goods through customs), and it does not provide the payee with special favors that conflict with fulfilling his or her duties.

Tipping is commonly done openly; bribery is not (a point that Carson does not emphasize). Richard DeGeorge argues that concealment is an essential feature of bribery:[10]

Bribery is a means of bypassing the normal way of doing business. If it were the accepted norm, it would simply become part of the price one paid to do business. It would be open, above-board, required, and legally sanctioned; it would cause no harm and require no deception. It would then not be bribery. Bribery is a way of getting preferential treatment. If the practice were ethically justifiable and acceptable to the public, the whole point of paying bribes would be lost.

DeGeorge notes that there simply are no countries that openly defend bribery as ethically permissible. Given the undesirable consequences that can come from widespread bribery, this should not be surprising. What are these undesirable consequences? DeGeorge cites three.[11] First, it would compromise open, fair competition. Second, it is symptomatic of a manipulated, inefficient market. Third, it is not clear that the recipients of payment deserve any compensation at all. To this list we can add a fourth possible consequence: Bribes may be made to take shortcuts or avoid meeting standards, thus compromising quality and, quite possibly, safety.

FAIRNESS, TRUST, AND INTEGRITY

What Scott Turow finds most objectionable about bribery is its inherent favoritism.[12] Each of us, he says, stands as equal before the law, and government has an obligation to treat like cases alike. The briber, he objects, "asks that that principle be violated, that some persons be allowed to stand ahead of others, that like cases not be treated alike, and that some persons be preferred." So, for Turow, bribery is fundamentally unfair — some will gain unfair advantage over others.

Turow extends this to the international sphere. It is, he says, just as wrong to try to induce foreign officials to violate fundamental moral principles. Furthermore, he doubts that other governments accept the idea that their officials are morally permitted to deal with their citizens in "a random and unequal fashion."[13] This does not mean that bribery is not a common occurrence. It means only, as DeGeorge insists, that bribery is not openly approved even in other countries. (Evidence of this is the ousting of Japanese prime minister Tanaka when he was implicated in bribery in the early 1970s.)

Turow also points out that bribery's secrecy raises serious doubts about the integrity and reliability of those party to the bribe once it is discovered; and these doubts extend beyond current decisions to all prior and future ones (not just ones directly associated with bribery). The worry is that, once a bribe is accepted, the bribee's judgment will be tainted. Thus, Turow holds, bribery is a crime against trust. Bribery is especially worrisome in settings that require trust in the discretionary judgments of decision makers (as is the case in many bureaucratic and governmental structures).[14]

WHEN IN ROME?

But what about the old saying, "When in Rome, do as the Romans do?" DeGeorge has some very useful things to say about this old saying in the context of bribery. First, he points out that one seldom hears the argument that, although something is permissible at home, it is wrong to do it in Rome. That is, more stringent standards elsewhere are seldom advocated.[15] So, we should be suspicious of rationalizations posing as justifications. Second, he points out that, as a general rule, we don't find the "When in Rome" line convincing. We would not, for example, accept slavery as all right for us when operating internationally simply because it is accepted in the host country. Third, we must carefully distinguish what may be a common practice and what is tolerated, but not necessarily approved; and both of these must be distinguished from what is morally required. If we do this, we may more readily see how unlikely it is that any country holds that bribery is morally required; at most it is tolerated, and even then it might be viewed with moral disapproval.

THE FOREIGN CORRUPT PRACTICES ACT

Complicating matters in the United States is the 1977 Foreign Corrupt Practices Act (FCPA), which prohibits the bribing of foreign government officials. The unlawfulness of bribery provides additional reasons for abstaining from bribery. On the one hand, bribery risks sanctions that can be quite costly to companies that resort to bribery. On the other hand, the fact that bribery is unlawful creates some expectation that other U.S. firms will not bribe; so, those that do may be regarded as acting unfairly in relation to those who refrain.

However, many complain that unilateral restraint on the part of U.S. companies places them at a competitive disadvantage internationally. DeGeorge replies that there is little evidence that this actually has resulted from FCPA. In fact, he adds, some U.S. companies have joined hands to fight extortion payments to Mexican border guards who demand special payment to expedite the passage of trucks. Moral imagination can suggest alternatives to capitulation. DeGeorge comments, "When a customs official assessed one firm a higher-than-normal fee, company officials sent 500 letters to various government offices asking for an explanation."[16] The official in question lowered the fee in order to avoid the hassle.

What if it could be shown that U.S. companies are at a disadvantage in some places because they do not resort to bribery? DeGeorge's answer is that, as a world economic leader, the United States should lead the way to less corrupt practices and work toward getting others to join in opposition to bribery. (If those who can most afford to take such an economic risk are unwilling to take it, who else can be expected to?)

A common objection to the Foreign Corrupt Practices Act is that it prohibits not only bribery but also extortion. Extortion, some argue, should not be prohibited, since harm is threatened and the initiative is made by the extorter, not the briber. However, Turow points out that the law does not regard extortion and bribery as mutually exclusive. Although extortion is connected with the apprehension of harm and bribery with the desire to influence, actual circumstances often obscure their differences. What has to be shown, Turow insists, is more than the convenience of profitableness of making payment, "but that the situation presented a choice of evils in which the [payment] somehow avoided a greater peril."[17]

One might still wish to argue that parts of the FCPA are unduly restrictive. Nevertheless, the point here is simply that we should be wary of permitting bribery (or giving in to extortion) for anything but very powerful reasons. Given all the harms that bribery (and extortion) can bring upon us, such reasons are harder to come by than many may think.

A FINAL EXAMPLE

The five examples of bribery with which we began fit Thomas Carson's analysis of *bribery* quite nicely. Here is a sixth example, one that is not such a good fit. Followers of the comic strip *Calvin and Hobbes* may recall how Calvin's mother replies to the question of how she gets her six-year-old son to pick up his toys: "I bribe him with cookies." Unlike the other five examples, this is an instance of a "briber" making an offer to induce someone to do what he *ought* to do, rather than to violate his duties or obligations. Admittedly, Calvin is offered an incentive to do something that he would otherwise be much less likely to do. This fits in with the notion that bribees need some sort of inducement to depart from duty, and it may be what inclines us to agree that Calvin's mother is resorting to bribery. Without an offer, Calvin will not pick up his toys; so Calvin's mother resorts to cookies to get him to do what she wants. However, this sort of inducement may actually, for a time at least, stand in the way of Calvin acting as he ought (namely, picking up his room simply because he has created the mess — i.e., because it is his responsibility). In this sense, what she is doing may seem to her to be slightly corrupting, even as she deems it expedient to get Calvin eventually to accept responsibility.

We could regard Calvin's case as bribery in only a very loose sense and retain Carson's account as central. Nevertheless, this example helps us see why bribery and extortion are not as clearly distinct as might otherwise be thought. Suppose Calvin realizes that if he holds back on picking up his toys, one of two things will happen: either his mother will offer him cookies or she will pick up his toys for him. However, clever as he is, Calvin makes no overt demands (such as "Give me cookies or pick up the room yourself"). He simply waits until she offers; and she knows that this is how he will operate. This may seem to Calvin's mother as much a matter of extortion on his part as bribery on hers. In the business world things may sometimes appear this way as well, thus blurring the line between extortion and bribery. The framers of the Foreign Corrupt Practices Act may have thought so, too. If a firm makes it clear that, because of the FCPA, it is not permitted to offer bribes, but that making payments for extortion is not forbidden, those who wish to receive payments can simply make the adjustment. (Rather than wait for his mother to offer cookies, Calvin will demand them. His mother has already indicated her willingness to part with some cookies. The only question is what will facilitate this.) So, before attempting to expunge making extortion payments from FCPA's list of prohibited activities, we should make sure that this would not enable adult Calvins to get what they want under a different label — leaving the problems caused by bribery untouched.

CONFLICTS OF INTEREST

Conflicts of interest rightly occupy the attention of every profession. Although the terminology might suggest otherwise, a conflict of interest is really a conflict between certain interests and *obligations,* not simply other interests. Thus, to say that a professional, *as a professional,* has a conflict of interest is to say that he or she has certain professional obligations. Furthermore, these obligations are to others, not to oneself. So, to explore the possible range of conflicts of interest for a professional is to explore his or her range of professional obligations. However, it is not necessary to have a completely theorized account of professional obligations in order to place the concept of a conflict of interest on solid ground. Nor is it necessary to have a completely worked out concept in order to have a decent grasp of what the basic elements of a conflict of interest are in standard cases.

Virtually all codes of ethics in business and the professions contain provisions about conflicts of interest. The details vary, ranging from opposition to even the appearance of a conflict of interest to requiring disclosure of an actual or potential conflict of interest. Unfortunately, codes typically assume that the concept of a conflict of interest is clearly enough understood that there is no need to explain it. However, it turns out that this concept is surprisingly elusive.

For some, it seems that virtually any situation in which two or more interests of any kind are in some sort of tension constitutes a conflict of interest. But, this broadens the scope of the concept of a conflict of interest at the expense of depriving it of any analytical power regarding the specific kinds of ethical concerns standard cases of conflicts of interest seem to raise. For others, it seems that only financial or familial interests should count. This takes us into the right arena, but too narrowly. It discourages us from recognizing that virtually identical kinds of ethical concerns can arise in situations involving neither financial nor familial interests. Admittedly, there are many cases that anyone with a minimal grasp of the concept will agree are conflicts of interest. However, generalizing from such cases to a satisfactory definition of conflict of interest is a challenging task.[18]

A good place to begin is with Michael Davis's very helpful essays on the topic.[19] In summary, he offers the following account of what he regards to be "the standard view": I have a conflict of interest if and only if

- I occupy a certain *role* in which (a) I have certain *obligations* that (b) require me to exercise good *judgment* in regard to certain matters.
- My being in this role justifies certain others relying on, or placing *trust* in, my exercise of judgment in regard to fulfilling those obligations.
- I am in a situation in which it would reasonable for others to wonder whether certain *interests* of mine might compromise my ability to exercise the good judgment that can be expected of me.

As a summary, this cannot do justice to Davis's more detailed and nuanced account. However, it can set a rough framework for a discussion in which the concepts of "interest," "role," "obligation," "judgment," and "trust" will be central elements.

Rather than offer a definition, I will discuss some of these central elements, with the aim of helping to explain why, and in what ways, conflicts of interest raise ethical concerns. This approach allows for the possibility, even likelihood, that there are some conflicts of interest that do not fit comfortably within Davis's standard view. Nevertheless, the advantage of having a standard view in mind is that it enables us to focus more clearly on what is ethically at stake.

Davis's 1982 article notes how surprisingly little analysis of the idea of conflict of interest appeared in the literature prior to that time. He suggests that we look to the legal profession for help. But even there the history of the expression "conflict of interest" is relatively short, making its entry into court decisions in the 1930s,[20] although a notion of "conflicting interests" was discussed in the American Bar Association's *Canon of Professional Ethics* in the very early 1900s.[21] This does not mean that the ethical issues posed by conflicts of interest were unfamiliar to people prior to the twentieth century. It means only that the first formal attempts to demarcate a special set of concerns in professional practice were made in the early 1900s. So what are the marks of this special set of concerns that the expression "conflict of interest" brings to mind?

This choice of words is suggestive but possibly misleading. Although it appropriately focuses our attention on conflicts, it may suggest to some the much looser notion that anytime one has conflicting interests one has a conflict of interest. But this would mean that I have a conflict of interest anytime I must choose between two things in which I have an interest, such as going out alone tonight to the basketball game or going to a play's final performance. No doubt this may present me with a difficult choice, but this sort of conflict lacks two elements standardly found in a conflict of interest. First, it is not evident that there is any duty or obligation involved. I could choose a third option, such as taking an evening walk rather than attending either the basketball game or the play, without failing to fulfill a duty, obligation, or responsibility. Second, there is only one party involved, myself. In short, this conflict does not seem to raise any ethical issues.

Actually, the expression "conflict of interest" is incomplete. It should be taken as shorthand for "conflict of interest *with*. . . ." A conflict of interest is a conflict of one or more interests with not another interest but with an obligation. Of course, I may have an interest in fulfilling my obligation, but it is the obligation rather than the interest that is the primary concern when it is said that I have a conflict of interest. An interest that conflicts with my obligation may itself involve another obligation; but the focus is on the fact that it is an interest.

In the context of a conflict of interest, what should count as an interest is not entirely clear. According to Davis, the standard view is that an interest includes any influence, loyalty, concern, or emotion that might interfere with fulfilling the relevant obligation.[22] However, without adding important qualifications, this list seems much too broad. For example, if I am very upset because I have just been issued a ticket and fined for going through a red light, this might well temporarily interfere with my ability to grade student papers fairly. Perhaps I should delay grading them for a while — until I am no longer consumed with anger at the officer for issuing such a heavy fine or making me late for an appointment, or distracted by my concern that my insurance rates may be raised or my driver's license suspended. But, thus described, I do not have a conflict of interest. My suggestion is that we think of an interest as something one might pursue, act in behalf of, or attempt to satisfy or fulfill. My anger at being heavily fined does not qualify as an interest in this sense.

Our emotions and concerns do reveal interests that we have. If I am angry because I have been heavily fined or concerned because my insurance rates may be raised, this reveals that I have an interest in the state of my finances. However, having an interest that, as it happens, may interfere with meeting an obligation is not in itself enough to create a conflict of interest with that obligation. I may have an obligation to meet a student during my office hours on the first sunny, warm day of spring and a strong interest in accepting the invitation of my friends to join them on the golf course at that very same time. I am faced with a conflict, one involving my interests and obligations, but this is not standardly viewed as a conflict of interest.

For the conflict to be a conflict of interest, there must be a more special relationship between the interest and the obligation. As a quite contingent matter, it turns out that I cannot fulfill the obligation to meet my student and play golf with my friends. However, there is nothing about the obligation in question or playing golf with my friends that creates the conflict other than the impossibility of being in both places at the same time. So, we might better call this a "conflict of place and time" than a "conflict of interest."

When a conflict of place and time involves a conflict between an obligation and interest alone, the ethical expectation is usually that the interest should give way to the obligation. If the interest is quite significant (for example, a "once in a lifetime" opportunity), the verdict might go otherwise, depending on what acting on the interest involves, the obligation in question, and the availability of alternative ways of handling the situation. However, there can also be conflicts of time and place that find obligations in tension with one another. One may have taken on too many obligations — several of which are "coming due" at roughly the same time. This is a "conflict of commitment," a problem busy professionals commonly face, whether through their own fault or not. Or one may have obligations to be in two places at the same time. This may be the result of poor planning or forgetfulness; but this can also happen through no fault of one's own (for example, one is scheduled to chair a meeting and one's child has become ill at school just before the meeting is convened). Such conflicts can be quite serious and difficult to resolve in a satisfactory manner. However, unless these commitments stand in some special relationship to each other that is more than simply a competition for time and place, we do not yet have a standard conflict of interest.

My suggestion is that we reserve "conflict of interest" for those conflicts between interests and obligations that involve an inherent conflict between them. Here is an illustration. Imagine I am serving on a National Science Foundation panel reviewing research proposals. As I examine the packet of proposals I am to review, I discover that I am listed in one of them as a paid consultant. My obligation is to exercise independent, impartial judgment in evaluating the proposals. But, seemingly, I have an interest in this particular proposal being funded. Precisely because of this, others may reasonably wonder whether this very special interest could bias my judgment.

It is noteworthy that this instance of a conflict of interest does not preclude my attempting to fulfill my obligation. I may even believe that my interest in a favorable outcome will not bias my judgment of the proposal. In contrast, I know I cannot both go to the game and go to the play. I know I cannot both keep my appointment with my student and join my friends on the golf course. What can be seductive about conflicts of interest is that I might well believe I can "have my cake and eat it too." This is so for at least two reasons.

First, I may not recognize that I have a conflict of interest. This is because, in general, it is quite acceptable to act in behalf of the interests involved in conflicts of interest. Of course, one might be so determined to obtain a grant or publish one's results that he or she is seriously tempted to fabricate or falsify data. Giving in to this temptation is not acceptable; it falls under the standard view of "scientific misconduct." There is no need to designate this further as a conflict of interest. The concern in the case of a conflict of interest is often not so much that one will engage in behavior that is otherwise objectionable; it is that, because of the relationship between certain otherwise perfectly legitimate interests and certain obligations, there is an ethical concern that must be addressed. So, in contrast to cases of deliberate misconduct, finding that I have a conflict of interest may come as a surprise to me — especially if no one is asking me to examine my circumstances to see if I have one.

Second, even if I realize that my circumstance bears all the marks of a conflict of interest, I might believe that my interests pose no serious threat to fulfilling my obligations. Although I am sitting in review of research proposals, I may think that I can fairly evaluate my own proposal along with the rest. Or, if this seems a bit much, I might think that I can fairly evaluate the other proposals provided that I leave the room when mine is being evaluated. However, even this second procedure is very problematic. Once the results are announced and it is learned that I am among the winners, others outside the review process may reasonably wonder whether my judgment was nevertheless affected by my interest in being funded; and the worry might well be shared by other committee members, who were perhaps all too aware of my presence in the review process.

Here, it might be said, we have the appearance of a conflict of interest. Once the doubts are raised, how are they answered? Decisions in such cases are not algorithmic. They call for judgment, which, as Davis points out, involves discretion, not simply doing sums. How can I convincingly show others that my judgment was not biased by having a proposal under consideration? How can I convincingly show myself?

The difficulty, if not impossibility, of satisfactorily answering these questions raises two concerns. Both are related to the reliability of judgment. First, there is the question about whether the judgments rendered were, in fact, influenced by my serving on the committee that reviewed my proposal. Conceivably, despite the "coziness" of the arrangement, good judgment may have been exercised. Second, absent any way of determining that good judgment was exercised, there remains a question of *trust*. If the appearance of a conflict of interest cannot be removed in such cases, we have reason not to place full confidence in judgments rendered, even if, in fact, good judgment was exercised. Given the importance of trust in so many ways, it is important to make serious efforts to minimize risks to that trust. In this case, not allowing one to serve on the committee and submit a proposal at the same time is a positive step. However, depending on other relationships and research interests of committee members, this may not be sufficient.

Bearing all of this in mind, it is important to realize that merely having a conflict of interest is not, in general, to have done anything ethically suspect or wrong. This is illustrated in the National Science Foundation example above. When I discover that I am listed as a paid consultant on the proposal I am asked to review, I discover that I have a conflict of interest in my role as reviewer. So far, I have done nothing wrong. What I do next is crucial. Normally, it would be expected that I would recuse myself from reviewing this proposal. Suppose, however, that I am not listed as a paid consultant, but I discover that this proposal is very familiar to me. In fact, I realize, I worked closely with the applicant as he prepared it, and it was clearly understood that I would be working closely with him on the project if it is funded. Lest there be any suspicion of complicity on my part, let us suppose that I was led to believe that the proposal was being prepared for a funding agency other than the National Science Foundation, but that the applicant changed his mind without telling me. I have a conflict of interest that only I know about (assuming the applicant did not know I was serving on the NSF panel). This does not constitute wrongdoing on my part. But, again, what I do next is crucial.

Of course, if I have colluded with the applicant and urged him to send the proposal to NSF because I am on the review panel, I can hardly plead moral innocence. The conflict of interest is of my own, deliberate making. However, there should be no presumption that this is typical of those who have conflicts of interest. This is an ethical point of some practical importance. If acknowledging that I have a conflict of interest is taken by others, or myself, as some sort of admission of "guilt," it is understandable that I might be reluctant to disclose that I have an actual or possible conflict of interest. For this reason it is important to remove the accusatory label from "conflict of interest" insofar as it is plausible to do so. This can be done while still signaling that there is something ethically significant to which careful attention should be given. Many acceptable, if not required, courses of action may be available at this point, ranging from disclosure to recusal.

Speaking metaphorically, we might think of actual, and even potential, conflicts of interest as yellow traffic lights. Caution must be taken. Depending on the available alternatives, the light may turn red or green — or it may remain yellow for the duration. One significant departure from the traffic signal metaphor is that what happens when the light turns yellow is to a large extent a function of what those addressing the actual or potential conflict of interest do. Thus, the conflict of interest signal is quite unlike traffic lights that are preset to turn green, yellow, and red in an invariable, timed sequence independently of driver behavior. Just as professional expertise in general calls for good judgment rather than algorithmic determination, so does the responsible handling of actual and potential conflicts of interest.

CHAPTER FIVE

Professional Integrity

INTEGRITY

The integrity of professionals is a function of how they handle themselves in the various professional roles they assume. As the previous chapter suggests, this is especially so in regard to their exercise of professional judgment, both in general and in the more particular cases of bribery and conflicts of interest. Stephen Carter traces the etymological origins of "integrity" to the Latin root it shares with "integer," which conveys a sense of "wholeness," suggesting that a person of integrity, "like a whole number, is a whole person, a person somehow undivided."[1] Although in this generic sense, "integrity" makes no explicit reference to one's sense of right and wrong, integrity in the moral sphere obviously does; and no account of professional integrity that lacks such a reference will be plausible. Carter continues:

> The word conveys not so much a single-mindedness as a completeness; not the frenzy of a fanatic who wants to remake all the world in a single mold but the serenity of a person who is confident in the knowledge that he or she is living rightly. The person of integrity need not be a Gandhi but also cannot be a person who blows up buildings to make a point. A person of integrity lurks somewhere inside each of us: a person we feel we can trust to do right, to play by the rules, to keep commitments.[2]

Furthermore, Carter notes that we can see and admire the integrity of others even as we find ourselves in sharp disagreement with them.

Carter also insists that integrity requires some level of reflection and discernment. If we decide we don't have time to stop and think about right and wrong, this means we think we don't "have time to live according to our model of right and wrong, which means, simply put, that we do not have time for lives of integrity."[3] Of course, there can be no guarantee that the person of integrity will always come up with the best decision. Integrity, says Carter, requires trying to get it right, not necessarily actually getting it right.[4] It also requires seriousness of commitment, which involves acting in ways consistent with our judgments about right and wrong.[5] Finally, willingness to make personal sacrifice in order to do what is right is expected of professionals.[6]

A CHALLENGE

Although not questioning the importance of professional integrity, Damien Cox, Marguerite La Caze, and Michael P. Levine complain that most philosophical work on the concept of integrity treats it as a generic concept, one that is not sensitive to the differences among agents and their circumstances. "Integrity is seen as the one virtue — essentially the same virtue expected of one's life partner, a friend, an employee, a priest, a teacher or a politician. Professional integrity then becomes a matter of the extent to which a person displays personal integrity in their professional lives."[7] It is likely that they would regard Carter's treatment of integrity as falling under their criticism.

They offer several reasons for resisting this way of characterizing integrity. First, our legitimate expectations from professionals should be sensitive to the particular roles they play as professionals, and our judgments of their professional integrity should reflect an understanding of those roles. Because different professions are marked by different competencies and responsibilities, we should not expect any necessary carryover of professional integrity from one profession to another.

Second, they claim that the concept of personal integrity is not well equipped to serve as a generic concept. Attempts to analyze it in this way focus too much on the individual as such rather than on what might be expected of him or her in particular contexts.[8] For example, "remaining true to oneself" will not do as an account because it is not clear what it amounts to in practice. The "self" is not sufficiently stable or fixed to enable us easily to determine what "remaining true to oneself" might come to. In contrast:

> Professional integrity is not a matter of remaining true to oneself; it is, very roughly, a matter of remaining true to the fundamental role and character of one's profession — to its principles, values, ideals, goals and standards. This requires that professionals not merely remain true to and publicly endorse personal values and principles but that they remain true to the role they are publicly entrusted with.[9]

Thus, they conclude that, although it is closely related to personal integrity, professional integrity in a particular profession is a virtue in its own right and calls for detailed specification in that context.[10] Because professional roles and values vary so much, professional integrity can have no uniform characterization.[11]

It is difficult to disagree entirely with Cox, La Caze, and Levine on this matter. However, their concerns seem overstated. Admittedly, what professional integrity requires of accountants, lawyers, doctors, nurses, educators, engineers, and so on cannot be determined independently of the specific features of those professions; and there are important differences, both in expertise required and services provided. However, as the authors say, professional integrity does require "being true to the profession" in question. This idea survives the differences that can be found in the specific roles professionals play in this or that profession. Being able to count on the professional's seriousness of commitment is the common thread for those said to have professional integrity.

Cox, La Caze, and Levine are right to question the notion that professional integrity in one profession automatically carries over to another. To understand what specifically counts as integrity for a professor of literature is not necessarily to understand much about what specifically counts as integrity for a physician. These are quite distinct professions, calling for different kinds of expertise and with different ends in mind. However, what if we think of an individual, Allison, who leaves academia for medicine? Shouldn't the integrity she exhibited as a professor give us some basis for predicting how she will conduct herself as a physician?

Of course, a particular individual may "have what it takes" to maintain professional integrity as a professor but not as a physician. Not everyone is well suited for the sorts of challenges that a particular profession may pose. However, regardless of the particular profession, what is crucial to professional integrity is the relationship the professional has to his or her acknowledged responsibilities.

The responsibilities a professional has are not simply a matter of individual determination; they are also determined by requirements of the profession itself and the particular setting within which a professional works. In that sense, they are not simply personal; and a generic notion of personal integrity cannot fill in the blanks in all their specificity. However, it is the individual who makes a commitment to become a professional; and what this commitment comes to is a matter of both personal and professional integrity. Those seriously lacking in personal integrity may, for that reason, also be seriously lacking in professional integrity.

A RING OF GYGES?

To ascribe integrity to a professional is to suggest that he or she should fare well when subjected to William F. May's test of character and virtue: What does a professional do when no one is watching? One way to try to find out how professionals fare in this regard is for some professionals to watch other professionals when they think no one is watching them. But this is impracticable at a very comprehensive level. It is also very expensive and time-consuming even as a random activity. Finally, as a secretive activity, such watching raises important ethical questions about professionals functioning as spies. So, largely, we infer what professionals do when they think they aren't being watched from the results of their largely unmonitored, ill-understood, activities.

Most of us are not very good at making such inferences. For example, we all know that wonderful as high technology's products can be, they are not perfect. Things can go wrong, no matter how dedicated, conscientious, and competent their professional designers and manufacturers may be. So, when something goes wrong, is it anyone's fault? And when nothing has gone wrong (yet), can we assume this is because of the work of dedicated, conscientious, and competent professional designers and manufacturers? In such a world, couldn't a clever professional try to calculate how good is just good enough — good enough to get by, get ahead, avoid being faulted, or get rewarded for "getting the job done"?

There is an ancient tale that should give us pause for worry. Plato's *Republic* recounts the story of the Ring of Gyges. A shepherd finds a fabulous ring and puts it on his finger:

> He arrived at the usual monthly meeting which reported to the king on the state of the flocks, wearing the ring. As he was sitting among the others he happened to twist the hoop of the ring towards himself, to the inside of his hand, and as he did they went on talking as if he had gone. He marveled at this and, fingering the ring, he turned the hoop outward again and became visible. Perceiving this he tested whether the ring had this power and so it happened: if he turned the hoop inwards he became invisible, but was visible when he turned it outwards. When he realized this, he at once arranged to become one of the messengers to the king. He went, committed adultery with the king's wife, attacked the king with her help, killed him, and took over the kingdom.[12]

It is tempting to say that this just shows how unprincipled that particular shepherd was. But the tale continues, challenging just such a reading:

> Now if there were two such rings, one worn by the just man, the other by the unjust, no one, as these people think, would be so incorruptible that he would stay on the path of justice or bring himself to keep away from other people's property and not touch it, when he could with impunity take whatever he

wanted from the market, go into houses and have sexual relations with anyone he wanted, kill anyone, free all those he wished from prison, and the other things which would make him like a god among men. His actions would be in no way different from those of the other and they would both follow the same path. This, some would say, is a great proof that no one is just willingly but under compulsion, so that justice is not one's private good, since wherever either thought he could do wrong with impunity he would do so.[13]

Insofar as we believe this thought experiment accurately depicts the human condition, we have reason to worry about whether we are adequately protected from professionals (not to speak of our neighbors). Are they rewarded enough for their services to be counted on to serve our interests as well as their own? Are the laws and threats of social censure sufficient to protect us from their willingness to exploit us at the first opportunity? For most professionals, we hope, the answer to both questions is, yes. But we may nevertheless worry a bit about the possibility, if not likelihood, of there being at least a few who cannot be trusted not to exploit the trust we invest in them; and we worry all the more because we are unsure who they are.

The story of the Ring of Gyges seems to exaggerate in two directions. First, the ring may not bring its bearer as much success as the story suggests. If the shepherd uses the ring to steal by making himself invisible, will the goods themselves be invisible as he transports them elsewhere?[14] It would seem that finding him in possession of the goods can serve as evidence that he is a thief. If he has to hide or disguise them, will it be worth the effort? And will he be successful? So, it seems that merely possessing the ring is not sufficient; one also needs prudence.

Second, we might object that even if we can imagine circumstances in which virtually anyone might be corrupted by such a ring, it is plausible to suppose that, for most people, these circumstances would have to be quite extraordinary. Short of such extraordinary circumstances, however, one could actually have self-sustaining virtues — that is, virtues that do not require external threats or promises of reward in order to be operative. To say that "virtue is its own reward" is not to say that its reward cannot be overcome in some extraordinary circumstances. But, in more ordinary circumstances such virtues can be expected to be effective even when no one is watching.

Still, there may be a few who are willing to take their chances and try to take advantage of others through their specialized knowledge and expertise. There may be nothing we can do to eliminate this possibility. However, there may be some things we can do to minimize it.

PRUDENT STEWARDS

One way to guard ourselves against the trust we extend to professionals being exploited is to try to find professionals who have the sorts of qualities that make them trustworthy. What are those qualities? First, of course, we expect basic competence. Evidence of competence is the completion of an educational program designed to prepare professionals for the sorts of work expected of them. In some instances, there are examination and licensing procedures that the would-be professional must successfully pass through in order to be certified to practice.

Let us assume that basic competence is not at issue. In searching for trustworthy professionals, why isn't it sufficient that they have the basic knowledge and skills that indicate competence in our areas of professional need? Immanuel Kant suggests why:

> Suppose someone recommends you a man as steward, as a man to whom you can blindly trust all your affairs, and, in order to inspire you with confidence, extols him as a prudent man who thoroughly understands his own interest, and is so indefatigably active that he lets slip no opportunity of advancing it. . . . you would either believe that the recommender was mocking you, or that he had lost his senses.[15]

What should bother us about prudent stewards is not that they lack basic competence. They may possess a high level of expertise in just those areas where our needs lie. Is it that *blindly* entrusting our affairs to such persons opens us up to exploitation? What if we *cautiously* entrust our affairs to prudent stewards? Much depends on what effect we might expect our caution to have on their conduct. The problem is that we are unlikely to be in a good position to monitor their conduct in any effective way.

Prudent stewards, too, will be cautious, but not in the same way we are. Presumably they understand what they are doing; and they are out to take advantage of all opportunities to advance *their* interests. Whether this will also advance *our* interests is not something we are particularly well situated to determine, let alone control. We might say, the less able we are to assess how well prudent stewards are representing our interests, the more vulnerable we are to being exploited. They may be particularly adept at making matters look much better than they are. But even if things go badly in ways that are obvious, prudent stewards may be able to reply that, unfortunately, very little is certain in this world. They may then plead that, despite their best efforts, bad luck was afoot. If they are sufficiently prudent, they will minimize such bad turns of events —

not necessarily to the fewest possible instances for us, but to the fewest possible instances in which they will be faulted.

Still, in order to advance their own interests by handling our affairs, prudent stewards are going to have to appear to be trustworthy. Otherwise we will not seek them out in the first place, let alone retain their services. So, they have a stake in achieving and maintaining the appearance of actually being competent and reliable. This means that, although they may be "so indefatigably active" in advancing their own interests that they never miss an opportunity to do so, they work very hard to conceal this from those they serve. That is, they will not tell us that they are such opportunists, for they realize that this will sow the seeds of distrust.

Although we may not be in a good position to determine whether we are dealing with prudent stewards, this is the sort of professional in whom we would prefer not to have to place our trust — certainly not blind trust. And, insofar as we have neither ability nor time to monitor how they would handle our affairs, the trust we extend to them would, in effect, be blind. Add to this the fact that we are probably not very interested in spending our time monitoring their behavior even if we had the ability and time to do so, and clearly we want the professionals on whom we rely to be more trustworthy than this.

SENSIBLE KNAVES

One reason for worrying about Kant's prudent stewards is that, for all we know, they are what David Hume calls sensible knaves.[16] Although committed only to that which serves their self-interest, sensible knaves realize the advantages that come from general compliance with common rules of morality and that it is in their self-interest to live in a society that endorses and largely operates in accordance with them. Furthermore, it is to their advantage to appear to be as committed to these rules as anyone. In this respect, the public good is also their good. So, as Hume points out, there is a large coincidence between the demands of morality and self-interest; and there is no reason to suppose that sensible knaves are incapable of appreciating this. Quite the contrary — this is why they are regarded as *sensible* knaves. Nevertheless, we must not forget that they are sensible *knaves* — roguish, deceitful, mischievous. As Hume puts it:

> And though it is allowed that, without a regard to property, no society could subsist; yet according to the imperfect way in which human affairs are conducted, a sensible knave, in particular incidents, may think that an act of iniquity or infidelity will make a considerable addition to his fortune, without

causing any considerable breach in the social union and confederacy. That honesty is the best policy, may be a good general rule, but is liable to many exceptions; and he, it may perhaps be thought, conducts himself with most wisdom, who observes the general rule, and takes advantage of all the exceptions.[17]

Hume offers an answer to sensible knaves, albeit one that is unlikely to move them but which can move the rest of us. Basically, it is an appeal to personal integrity. Knaves, it seems, are prepared to trade their integrity, and even their happiness, for "worthless toys and gewgaws."[18] This should be particularly worrisome if a sensible knave is also a professional.

SENSIBLE KNAVES AS PROFESSIONALS

What might we expect from sensible knaves who become professionals? Like Kant's prudent stewards, they will have gone through rather elaborate and rigorous educational preparation to become members of some profession or other. Whatever professions we imagine sensible knaves as entering, at some point they will present themselves to others as qualified and willing to do the work in question. In essence, they will attempt to provide assurance that they meet the standards of competency of the profession and that, if engaged, they can be trusted to conduct themselves as responsible professionals.

Deliberate failure to do competent work is a failure to fulfill the responsibilities that one has assumed by becoming a professional. This is also a failure of integrity but, as we have noted, others (including one's colleagues) may not be in a good position to detect this. Even competent, dedicated professionals sometimes fail. Honest mistakes are made and unexpected complications can arise. It may not be easy to tell the difference between such failures and failures due to knavish tendencies. Sensible knaves will try to conceal their less than satisfactory work from others. If this is unsuccessful, they will try to make it appear that they are, nevertheless, competent, dedicated professionals.[19]

What if, in the end, some sensible knaves fail successfully to conceal their knavishness? They may now no longer be entrusted with such work, perhaps even losing their license to practice. Their attitude and behavior may also cast a shadow of doubt over others in their professions, regardless of their apparent competence and dedication. After all, *sensible* knaves are likely to go undetected for the most part. But once one is exposed, we may wonder if there are others nearby — and worry that we are not in a good position to tell. Which others, we may ask? For all we know, it could be anyone. So, other professionals may be less trusted — a kind of "guilt by association."[20]

However, Hume's sensible knaves will be aware of such risks, too. Insofar as they wish to continue as professionals, it will be in their self-interest to take special care that they are not found out. So, sensible knaves will be quite cautious. They have already shown themselves to be quite intelligent (or at least clever) — they have made it through school and successfully entered a profession. But they are cautious in that, recognizing that they, too, can be harmed if it is discovered that they have shortchanged their employers, clients, or the public, they will normally perform at an acceptable level; and they will be on the front line with those in their profession who *publicly* insist on professional integrity.

What if we suspected some particular professionals to be sensible knaves? Would we place our trust in them as professionals? Perhaps we would if they are skilled and we have some external assurance that they will do the work well — for example, if they are being watched closely or they will be paid only if their work passes careful review. Would we regard them as trustworthy? To say that, in certain circumstances, they can be trusted is not to say that they are trustworthy. Trust is needed; but is it warranted, or deserved? Martin Hollis makes a crucial distinction: "Trusting people to act in their self-interest is one thing and trusting them to live up to their obligations another. The former does not capture the bond of society, since the bond relies on trusting people not to exploit trust."[21]

Without professionals having a sense of obligation to provide competent service, Hollis's problem of trust remains unresolved. It is, as Hume suggests, a matter of integrity that, assuming they present themselves as agreeing to provide competent service, professionals will make a good faith effort to do so. Furthermore, our understanding is not that they will do this, unless they think no one is looking. Even if this were agreeable to sensible knaves, it would not be to those they have persuaded to rely on them. The readiness of sensible knaves to commit acts of iniquity and infidelity for personal gain is, we object, a willingness to wrong the unsuspecting.

BAD CONSCIENCE

Sensible knaves probably handle their wrongdoing with equanimity, unless they fear getting caught. We can hope that, in fact, there are few sensible knaves — especially in the professions. For the rest of us, as Hume suggests, conscience can take a toll. For example, while taking the final exam in his doctoral program in history at the University of Washington, Norm Lewis excused himself to go to the bathroom, where he secretly consulted his notes.[22] He received his Ph.D. and eventually authored a number of books in his field. Over the next thirty-two years he told no one of his misdeed, not even members of his family. However, in the year 2000, at age eighty-three, he wrote to the president of the University of Washington, admitting that he had cheated on his final exam in 1968 and that he had regretted it ever since.

Lewis's late confession seemed to be an effort, finally, to "set the record straight." As might be expected, university officials were unsure about what, if anything, should be done. Others had mixed reactions, too. Jeane Wilson, president of the Center for Academic Integrity, commented: "I think there is an important lesson here for students about the costs of cheating. He has felt guilty all these years, and has felt burdened by this secret, believing that he never really earned the degree he was awarded." However, Wilson recommended that, in light of Lewis's confession, his age, and the fact that he completed his coursework and dissertation, the university should not take any action.

Had the facts been different, Wilson reflected, a different recommendation might have been in order: "On the other hand, I think an institution might feel compelled to revoke the degree if we were talking about a medical or law degree or license, or some other professional field such as engineering or education, and the individual were younger and still employed on the basis of that degree or license." Underlying Wilson's comment is the presumption that the professions, particularly those entrusted with providing vital services to others, cannot afford to allow their practitioners to get away with such cheating.[23] Not only is there the basic question of whether the cheater has basic competence in the field, there is also the question of whether he or she can be trusted as a professional. In Lewis's case, Wilson seems to have thought that his age mitigates against such worries; at this late date, what would revoking his degree accomplish?

Lewis's years of regret might be thought to be a sufficient price to pay for his misdeed. The important lesson for today's students would still hold: feelings of guilt can have considerable staying power and can take a tremendous toll on one's conscience. Of course, the prospect of possibly being stripped of one's degree, however long ago it was awarded, might discourage a few would-be cheaters, too. But the issue of how to deal with one's own conscience is the larger one for Lewis. Even if his degree were taken away, this in itself would not resolve his feelings of guilt.

So, there is an issue of integrity. That Lewis suffered regret for more than three decades could be regarded as evidence that, despite his aberration, his concern for integrity survived. When taking the final exam, the moment might have seemed right to Lewis to make himself the exception to the rule and engage in an act of dishonesty. Had he been Hume's sensible knave, his action would not have haunted him for thirty-two years. Instead, he would simply have taken it in stride, perhaps forgetting he had done it even by the time he strode across the stage to receive his diploma. However, Lewis clearly was not a sensible knave; and to his moral credit, he finally publicly acknowledged his wrongdoing and the deep regret it engendered.

Lewis's confession could be regarded as an effort, however belated, to engage in "rightdoing." Somewhat surprisingly, "rightdoing" is not a word found in standard dictionaries. However, it serves as a useful complement to "wrong-doing" in providing us with a more comprehensive picture of what professional responsibility can involve. Here, Lewis's acknowledgment of what he did could be viewed as primarily an attempt to somehow atone for his wrongdoing so that he can finally "live with himself." However, it could also be seen as an attempt to impart an important lesson to others — to alert young, aspiring profession-als that, although they might not think so at the moment, such cheating does matter — both now and later.

MIXED CONSCIENCE

Norm Lewis's bad conscience was triggered by one event, cheating on an exam; and this occurred before he launched his professional career. Many conscience-raising scenarios relate to a larger range of activities, are intimately involved in one's day-to-day work as a professional, and prompt a more mixed personal assessment. Mark Feith came to Hillenbrand Industries with an impressive record as an accountant and a former special agent for the FBI. Soon he received a general assignment "to gather information on the competition" — other com-panies in the business of making caskets and hospital beds. Before long he adopted cat-burglar tactics, engaging in searches of competitors' trash for secret information about such things as proposed mergers:

> Emboldened by his employer's approval, he says, he combed through dumps in the dark and paid a trash hauler for access to his truck, where he risked being crushed in a compactor. His endeavors became so well-known within Hillenbrand that one manager called him "director of covert activities."[24]

Initially assigned to analyze public information about acquisition targets, Feith gradually became a full-time cat-burglar. However, he then learned that Hillenbrand was reducing its acquisition plans. Discouraged by the belief that he was not in line for any further advancement in Hillenbrand, Feith began to see things differently: "It was clear that I wasn't getting ahead. Until then, I spied thinking I was on the way up. I stopped believing that."[25]

Eventually Feith turned on his employer, stealing confidential files from Hil-lenbrand and offering them for sale to its competitors. Feith admitted that "no one held a gun to my head" to spy on competitors, but he added: "I'll guarantee you that if I hadn't been spying for Hillenbrand, I never would have considered going against them. Some things I did to competitors weren't ethical. Once you start to sacrifice what you believe, where do you stop?"[26] So, in a striking turn of conscience, Feith turned to Superman TV re-runs for inspiration: "Superman was for justice, and somehow, doing to Hillenbrand what they had me do to others seemed so right."[27]

Identifying himself as Clark Kent to Service Corp., Hillenbrand's major competitor, Feith offered to sell inside information. However, Service Corp. was not interested. Instead, it blew the whistle on Feith, ultimately resulting in a two-month jail term. As for Feith's colleagues at Hillenbrand, all denied having sanctioned his activities.

So where did things go wrong? Perhaps it was the company's attitude, which Feith described in this way: "The only good competitor is a dead competitor. Hillenbrand's only concern seemed to be getting caught and embarrassed."[28] Initially this seemed to be Feith's attitude, too — as he undertook his ventures before dawn, wearing a ski mask, rubber gloves, and combat boots. Of course, this was risky business. He might get caught. Or he might get crushed. Given these risks, Feith's disappointment at not being promoted is understandable. Rather than elevating himself to the conscience of Superman, perhaps he was just out for revenge. If Hillenbrand was not sufficiently grateful, he owed them nothing — in fact, they owed him something, and he decided to take it.

Would Feith have felt differently if he had had access to something closer to Plato's Ring of Gyges? Suppose, for example, that everyone's files were computerized and that Feith was a computer technologist turned supersleuth. His spying task certainly could have been easier — and less risky. Perhaps he would have been able to raid competitor's files in just the way he raided his own employer's. No predawn dumpster searches. No fear of being crushed. Who could resist such an opportunity? No one, as the myth of the Ring of Gyges would have it — certainly not Hume's sensible knave.

But what about the conscience of "Superman"? The lure of his "Ring of Gyges" may have been more powerful. In the actual circumstances, it seems that Feith simply miscalculated. He thought Hillenbrand's competitors would buy his goods. Why didn't they? Like Hillenbrand, they may have drawn the line at what is undeniably illegal — buying stolen goods.

Of course, as computer-technologist-turned-supersleuth, Feith might have been less welcome at Hillenbrand than as a dumpster raider. If Feith were caught raiding dumpsters, Hillenbrand could first claim, "Competitors' trash is fair game once it leaves their offices. That's why there are shredders."[29] Or, if this didn't work, they could deny having authorized Feith to raid dumpsters. But it is doubtful that Hillenbrand could plausibly claim that competitors' files are fair game once someone figures out how to tap into them. Still, given their apparent support of Feith's initial activities as dumpster raider, they might well have thought an invisible raider who left no fingerprints was worth a somewhat greater legal risk.

Given this sort of corporate environment and the presence of skillful professionals with attitudes like Mark Feith's, the closer we are to having a Ring of Gyges, the more reason we have to be fearful, if not distrustful. The arrival of computer technology gives us reason to take the Ring of Gyges myth seriously. Theft from the unsuspecting can be very much like a Ring of Gyges operation. Insufficiently protected, confidential files can be raided from a distance. Sufficient protection requires even more sophisticated technology. But even more sophisticated technology cannot guarantee protection — clever thieves may break through. Stiff laws might help discourage some from making the attempt. But the thought, even if mistaken, that one might have the Ring can be alluring. "There are no guarantees," the thief might say, "but this is a pretty good risk."

To Mark Feith's credit, he seems to have sensed from the outset that what he was being asked to do was ethically questionable. As he said, "Some things I did to competitors weren't ethical. Once you start to sacrifice what you believe, where do you stop?" So, legal or not, the covert activities Feith undertook for his employer seemed unethical to him. Why, then, did he raid the dumpsters? He thought this would help him advance in the organization, and apparently he did not receive any signals from his supervisors that they thought his activities were ethically questionable. He may even have believed that his covert activities were quietly celebrated at Hillenbrand.

Mike Martin identifies two kinds of explanations of wrongdoing.[30] First, there are character explanations, which are cast in terms of features of persons, flaws of character, that play a significant role in wrongdoing. Second, there are social explanations, which are cast in terms of "outside structures and pressures that contribute to misconduct, including influences within professions, corporations, and the wider society."[31] Mark Feith's downward spiral seems to involve both character and social explanations. He was ambitious, and Hillenbrand offered a working environment that encouraged, or at least did not discourage, the use of questionable means in advancing its interests. Although willing to use such means himself, Feith retained some sense of his own wrongdoing. When Hillenbrand failed to show the appreciation for his work Feith thought he deserved, he stole from his employer — in the name of justice. Although no sensible knave, Feith's moral concerns seem too selective and self-serving to count in favor of his professional integrity; but Hillenbrand seems to deserve some responsibility for his moral slide.

CHARACTER EXPLANATIONS AND SOCIAL EXPLANATIONS

Martin seems right in arguing that it is a mistake to think that character and social explanations must be opposed to one another. As he says, "Professionals are not merely hapless victims of external forces (although occasionally they are). They are responsible moral agents who make choices in response to outside influences."[32] Thus, it seems that some space should be allowed for character in explaining wrongdoing and in explaining responsible practice. At the same time, the influence of external social forces, institutional structures, and specific working environments is undeniable.

For example, the workplace portrayed in the fictional video *Gilbane Gold* does not encourage proactive approaches to controlling environmental pollution, cooperative problem-solving, or full honesty in communicating with city environmental officials.[33] Z-Corp is emitting potentially harmful levels of lead and arsenic into the local waterway. This could result in the contamination of the waterway's sludge, known as Gilbane Gold, a profit-producing fertilizer used in the surrounding community. Z-Corp's young environmental engineer, David Jackson, is deeply troubled by his company's apparent indifference to it's environmental responsibilities, and he ends up talking with the local media. Unfortunately, even though the video portrays what has been happening at Z-Corp for more than a year after Jackson first raised his concerns, it never shows him working on alternative, technical solutions to the problem.[34] Phil Port, manager of environmental affairs, is not ethically troubled by how the company is operating—nor does he seem much concerned about the environmental damage his company may be causing. Other company officials, although eager to increase Z-Corp's profit line, are equally unconcerned about potential environmental problems. So, the social explanation model seems to be a good fit.

However, consider a nonfictional case, that of Minnesota, Mining, and Manufacturing (3M), which has adopted a strong pollution prevention program, with a corresponding reward system for success.[35] 3M claims that its 3P program has saved the company $810 million since 1975. Prior to adopting its aggressive pollution control program, 3M was regarded as a major polluter. Did the new program stir up the imagination of the Phil Ports and David Jacksons in their employ? Or did 3M have to go out and hire new engineers because too few at 3M cared enough, or were imaginative enough, about pollution prevention to meet the challenge? These questions are as much about individual character as the social environment of the workplace. A hopeful thought is that there already were engineers at 3M who were ready and willing to work on its 3P program — that 3M's history of polluting had not quashed their sensitivity to environmental concerns. If this is not simply a vain hope, then Martin's view that character explanations and social explanations can live side-by-side has credibility even in settings that might otherwise seem responsive only to strong external sanctions.

GOOD CONSCIENCE

Martin's examples of character and social explanations focus on wrongdoing. But what if, taking a cue from the 3M example, we shift our attention to "right-doing"? Character explanations of wrongdoing focus on flawed or failed character traits. On what might character explanations of "rightdoing" focus in professional ethics? At the very least, it seems, such explanations will need to discuss ways in which generic moral virtues such as honesty, trustworthiness, fair-mindedness, and caring for others blend with more specific character traits expressed in one's professional skills and expertise.

A case in point is computer scientist David Parnas.[36] In 1985 he was asked by the Strategic Defense Initiative Organization (SDIO) to serve on a $1,000-per-day advisory panel. He resigned from the panel two months later, convinced that SDI was both dangerous and a waste of money. Noting that "software is the glue that holds such systems together," he complained that there is no way that any software could adequately meet the requirements of a good SDI system. He based his resignation on three ethical premises:

1. I am responsible for my own actions and cannot rely on any external authority to make my decisions for me.
2. I cannot ignore ethical and moral issues. I must devote some of my energy to deciding whether the task that I have been given is of benefit to society.
3. I must make sure that I am solving the real problem, not simply providing short-term satisfaction to my supervisor.[37]

While these premises may explain Parnas's resignation, they do not explain his subsequent active, public opposition to SDI. What apparently pushed him from passive resignation to active opposition were the responses of SDIO and his fellow panelists. None of them, he says, responded with serious, scientific discussion of the technical problems he cited. Had they done so, he might have been satisfied to resign quietly, respecting their right to differ from him in technical judgment. Instead of challenging his technical arguments, Parnas claims, he received responses like this: "The government has decided; we cannot change it." "The money will be spent; all you can do is make good use of it." "The system will be built; you cannot change that." "Your resignation will not stop the program."[38]

In Martin's terms, these responses seem to offer a social explanation as justifying, or at least excusing, continued participation in the SDI program. This did not satisfy Parnas:

It is true, my decision not to toss trash on the ground will not eliminate litter. However, if we are to eliminate litter, I must decide not to toss trash on the ground. We all make a difference.

Similarly, my decision not to participate in SDI will not stop this misguided program. However, if everyone who knows that the program will not lead to a trustworthy shield against nuclear weapons refuses to participate, there will be no program. Every individual's decision is important.[39]

Parnas says that his protest was not a call for computer scientists to take political positions on government projects. Rather, it was an appeal to their professional integrity: "They need only be true to their professional responsibilities."[40] Given reliable information, he was confident that the public would decide against the project.

It is interesting that in making a public statement about his resignation Parnas went well beyond his initial three ethical premises for leaving the SDI project. He accepted the responsibility of challenging his fellow professionals to follow his example. If other computer experts acted as he did, he reasoned, there would be no one to design the software. But he went even further. He accepted the responsibility to try to help the public (nonexperts) understand why the project was not technically feasible; only experts like himself could do this.

It is also noteworthy that Parnas extends his comments about professional conduct to other areas:

> My years as a consultant in the defense field have shown me that unprofessional behavior is common. When consulting, I often find people doing something foolish. Knowing that the person involved is quite competent, I may say something like, "You know that's not the right way to do that." "Of course," is the response, "but this is what the customer asked for." "Is your customer a computer scientist? Does he know what he is asking?" ask I. "No" is the simple reply. "Why don't you tell him?" elicits the response: "At XYZ Corporation, we don't tell our customers that what they want is wrong. We get contracts." This may be a businesslike attitude, but it is not a professional one. It misleads the government into wasting [the] taxpayer's money.[41]

MEANINGFUL WORK

Despite the positive side of the David Parnas story, much of it dwells on the negative: the problem of preventing the waste of public funds and creating a false sense of public security. Mike Martin's *Meaningful Work* raises another issue. Shouldn't, he asks, professional ethics also be concerned with the idea of *meaningful* work? Parnas expresses a personal commitment to working on projects that pose real problems and that offer some promise of benefiting society. He complains that, because the SDI project lacks these features, it is unprofessional for computer scientists to accept public funds to continue working on it. Although he finds it meaningful and important to oppose such work, he might also find projects like SDI themselves to be essentially meaningless.

Martin discusses Akira Kurosawa's fictional character, Kanji Watanabe.[42] As Watanabe looks back at his thirty-year career as a city manager, he says he has forgotten all the particulars; he remembers only that he was always busy — and always bored. There is no hint of wrongdoing, only meaninglessness. However, in the end, he finds meaning in responding positively to a citizens' petition to drain a dangerous, polluted swamp and build in its place a community playground. Might Watanabe have overlooked other opportunities in his capacity as city manager to do things he regarded to be meaningful? If so, this is to be regretted. If not, it can be regretted that his work was so inherently unsatisfying.

Professionals typically require a great deal of higher education in preparation for their work. That this work can, nevertheless, seem dull, repetitive, and meaningless to some is ironic. The exercise of trained judgment and expertise in the service of others might seem in itself to add zest and meaning to one's life. But the story of Kanji Watanabe is sobering. The hope is that it will not take thirty years for most professionals to find their way to work that amounts to more than the avoidance of wrongdoing and that they can regard as meaningful and worthwhile.

Martin's view is that professional ethics should make room for personal commitments as well as the sorts of basic duties typically found in codes of ethics. Given this, a qualification of Sidgwick's view of practical ethics may be in order. In areas where agreement is needed and sought, Sidgwick urges that we not insist on getting to "the bottom of things." However, for professionals whose personal commitments inform their sense of professional responsibility, those commitments might well reflect what for them is "the bottom of things." Integrating personal commitments with professional responsibilities can pose difficult challenges. There are some situations in which the cost of compromise is harm to one's integrity. Those who can see that accepting a certain sort of employment is likely to pose such a challenge may decide against accepting the job. However, not everyone may be fortunate enough to have such foresight. In such cases, preserving personal and professional integrity may require one to choose between conscientiously objecting to doing certain sorts of work (thereby risking losing one's job), or resigning.

Sensible knaves seem, as David Hume says, willing to trade their integrity, and even their happiness, for "worthless toys and gewgaws."[43] Such trades are rejected both by common morality and by professional ethics. But integrity typically requires more from us than resisting the lure of the sensible knave, or simply refraining from wrongdoing. Within professional life, what else one will see as required is determined by the particular tasks at hand — and, equally importantly, one's personal sense of responsibility.

It has been the burden of this chapter to make the case that we count on something from professionals that neither Kant's prudent steward nor Hume's sensible knave can be expected to provide. This will not necessarily show up in the quality of the services they render; circumstances may, in fact, commend reliable work to them in most instances. But at least occasionally the lure of self-interest may lead them astray; and it is self-interest, not professional service, that is their primary commitment. This means that they are not fully trustworthy, indicating a serious shortcoming in professional integrity. In any case, professional integrity is not simply a spin-off of calculated self-interest; and, as we shall see in subsequent chapters, its requirements reflect joint as well as individual commitment and understanding.

CHAPTER SIX

Basic Duties and Codes of Ethics

BASIC DUTIES

Codes of professional ethics emphasize duties or obligations deemed so basic that failure to fulfill them warrants reproach or even formal sanctions. Many basic duties of professionals are simply extensions of what J. O. Urmson more generally refers to as "rock-bottom duties which are duties for all and from every point of view, and to which anyone may draw attention."[1] However, other basic duties derive from professional roles or take on special significance because of those roles. This is Bernard Gert's understanding of common morality's requirement that we fulfill our duties as nurses, physicians, police officers, teachers, or other professionals.[2] These duties may be to do specific things, such as making rounds; but they may also be requirements to do things in specified ways, such as a judge making decisions impartially.

Gert is not using "duty" in the broad sense in which some philosophers do — namely, as equivalent to "moral requirement" (so that there would be a duty to keep one's promises, a duty not to kill, and so on). Instead, says Gert: "In ordinary usage, 'duty' is not used in this very wide sense but is restricted to moral requirements that stem from a social role or job or from being in some special circumstances."[3] The scope of "duty" is further restricted, he adds, because "duty" has a moral connotation that limits our duties to what is morally allowable; thus it retains strong ties to common morality.

CODES OF ETHICS: THE VERY IDEA

The codes of ethics of professions represent the efforts of their members to organize in a systematic way basic ethical standards, rules, and principles of professional conduct. Although these codes articulate standards, rules, and principles for practitioners in particular professions, if they are well grounded morally, they should make good sense from the standpoint of common morality. Professionals provide services that profoundly affect the well-being of others and therefore should be held accountable to them, as well. However, as expressions of shared commitments by a broad spectrum of practitioners, codes must navigate a course that is compatible with a wide range of moral and religious differences.

How well framed and suitable the provisions of any particular code are is a very contingent matter. Differences among practitioners may be buried in somewhat vaguely stated moral requirements or in broad statements of ideals that are regarded as aspirational rather than mandatory. Some codes capture the basic responsibilities of professional practice better than others. Codes sometimes contain provisions that seem designed more to protect the economic interests of its members than to promote responsible practice. Codes also vary in regard to enforcement provisions. Nevertheless, they are a good starting point for obtaining an overview of major areas of ethical concern regarding particular professions.[4]

However, at the outset it is necessary to respond to a radical objection. Since codes of ethics are sometimes used to sanction the conduct of those to whom they apply, some object to their being referred to as codes of ethics.[5] The coercive use of a code renders it a code of conduct, they argue, but not a code of ethics. Ethics is supposed to respect our autonomy. This does not exempt us from criticism, or even strong persuasion; but it should be free from coercion through the enforcement of sanctions.

In response, it should be pointed out that codes of ethics typically do not, by themselves, have the force of law. Although commitment to a code's provisions may be understood as a condition of membership in a professional society, membership itself may be voluntary and in no way required in order to engage in professional practice. Courts occasionally use a society's code as a basis for imposing sanctions, but this is not a provision of the code itself. Whether or not this is an appropriate use of a code of ethics, such external sanctions do not seem to vitiate its status as a code of ethics.

There are several functions a code can serve that do seem to warrant calling it a code of ethics.[6] First, it can express a shared commitment on the part of a professional society's members to strive to satisfy certain ethical standards and principles. Second, it can be used by members to resist pressure from others to engage in unethical behavior ("I cannot do that — it is prohibited by my profession's code of ethics"). Third, it can help foster an environment in which ethical behavior is the norm. Fourth, it can serve as a guide or reminder in specific situations. Fifth, developing and revising a code of ethics can be a valuable exercise in ethical reflection for a profession. Sixth, a code can be a valuable educational tool for seminars, workshops, courses, and professional meetings. Finally, as a publicly declared statement, a code of ethics can indicate to others that members are seriously committed to responsible conduct. In the case of engineering, for example, such assurances are especially important because of the impact that engineering practice has on public health, safety, and welfare, and in light of the fact that the public, largely ignorant of, but very dependent on, the expertise of engineers, must trust that this expertise will be exercised responsibly.

At their best, codes of ethics are the result of the careful deliberation of experienced professionals whose recommendations have received the approval of members of their respective professional societies. Codes of ethics are hardly the last word in professional ethics; but unless there is reason to believe that professional societies are incapable of identifying the major ethical dimensions of their profession, it is wise to begin with their consensus views on these matters.

AGREEMENT DESPITE DIFFERENCES

Typically, a code of ethics will endorse commonly agreed upon major services provided by the profession and proceed from this to an articulation of principles, rules, and guidelines that should govern the provision of those services. It is important to realize that the main principles, rules, and guidelines specified in the code will already have gained broad acceptance among practitioners. That is, they will not come from "thin air," so to speak. They might appear in more refined form, but they will not depart widely (or wildly) from ongoing norms that are broadly accepted. This means that a well-crafted code will endorse rather than create basic professional responsibilities. Furthermore, by and large, practitioners would be regarded as having these responsibilities even if they were not specified in a code, or even if there were no explicit code at all.

So, although an adopted code of ethics might imply a kind of "social contract" among members of a profession, this explicit agreement should be understood as a statement of commitment to principles, rules, and guidelines that are already acknowledged as binding by responsible practitioners. An explicit statement of commitment can provide reassurances to one's fellow professionals, employers, and others for whom they provide services and whose lives might be affected by their work. However, this does not mean that, without a formal statement of commitment, professionals do not have those responsibilities.

An implication of the above is that, although philosophers and others who specialize in teaching ethics might be of some help in framing a code, practitioners themselves should be quite capable of doing this themselves.[7] A good code is not a philosopher's invention. This is implied by the moral agency of the practitioners and the understanding they have of their own professional field. Ethicists might be of assistance in articulating and organizing basic principles, rules, and guidelines. Also, as outsiders, they may have an advantage of disinterestedness that can assist members of a profession from unduly favoring themselves as well as help them see themselves from the perspective of recipients rather than dispensers of services. Of course, members of a profession can benefit from the observations of ordinary citizens in all of these regards as well.

All of the above presumes that, at some level, there is attainable ethical agreement among members of a given profession. Nevertheless, a well-crafted code will fall short of the mark for many practitioners, in particular, those whose sense of professional responsibility goes beyond the common denominator that cuts across all moderately responsible practitioners. This additional dimension of responsibility will be addressed later in this chapter. For now, the focus will be on agreement.

Some might think that, given the diverse background, beliefs, and ambitions of practitioners, it is naïve to believe that there is enough agreement to form the basis of a code of ethics, however minimal. However, there need not be agreement about everything, and at every level, in order for there to be substantial agreement at the level of professional practice. Cass Sunstein's notion of "incompletely theorized agreement" can help us to understand and appreciate this.[8] Sunstein points out that it is possible to achieve agreement on particular judgments in a group context (for example, a court of law) without achieving agreement on underlying theoretical commitments.[9] He endorses Amy Gutmann and Dennis Thompson's idea of economizing on moral disagreement: In political life, do not challenge one another's deepest moral convictions when it is not necessary to do so.[10] Applying this to the professions, the advice is to try to solve problems of disagreement through incompletely theorized agreements. Although there can be disagreement about certain underlying beliefs and commitments, there might nevertheless be attainable agreement at a very concrete level, or even at a relatively abstract level. The favored strategy "enlists silence, on certain basic questions, as a device for producing convergence despite disagreement, uncertainty, limits of time and capacity, and heterogeneity."[11]

Sunstein notes two advantages provided by this strategy. First, proceeding in this manner can be a source of social stability. Agreement promotes mutual understanding and mutual expectation among members of a profession, both of which are important in practice. Second, proceeding in this manner is a way of demonstrating mutual respect despite differences. In the case of professional practice, this mutual respect would also seem to allow for significant differences regarding one's religious commitments, personal ideals, and basic attitudes toward one's work, as long as this is compatible with whatever agreements are otherwise present. So, through silence, or perhaps through somewhat open-ended provisions, a code of ethics can provide space for important differences while nevertheless expressing agreement on basic responsibilities shared by all.

Sunstein illustrates what he has in mind by focusing on politics and the courts. However, research ethics is another area that shows the advantage of settling for shared ground rather than insisting on starting from first principles. In the mid-1970s the National Commission for the Protection of Human Subjects of Biomedical and Behavioral Research was given the task of formulating ethical guidelines for research involving human subjects (or participants). As described by Albert Jonsen, a member of the commission, and Stephen Toulmin, a consultant, commission members tried initially to come to agreement on first principles.[12] Given the makeup of the commission, it is not surprising that this posed difficulties: "The eleven commissioners had varied backgrounds and interests. They included men and women; blacks and whites; Catholics and Protestants, Jews, and atheists; medical scientists and behaviorist psychologists; philosophers; lawyers; theologians; and public representatives. In all, five commissioners had scientific interests and six did not."[13] Given this range of differences, it should not be surprising that their efforts to articulate shared first principles ended in failure.

However, when they turned to particular cases, especially ones showing disrespect for, harms to, or injustices to humans, they found themselves in substantial agreement. Generalizing from particular examples, the commission finally formulated *The Belmont Report,* which endorses three principles governing appropriate research involving humans (respect for persons, beneficence, and justice).[14] These principles provide an agreed-upon framework around which decisions about the acceptability of research involving human subjects are now made by institutional review boards at colleges and universities across the country. Avoiding overstating the usefulness of the principles on which they agreed, the commission modestly and wisely stated at the outset of its report:

> Three principles, or general prescriptive judgments, that are relevant to research involving human subjects are identified in this statement. Other principles may also be relevant. These three are comprehensive, however, and are stated at a level of generalization that should assist scientists, subjects, reviewers and interested citizens to understand the ethical issues inherent in research involving human subjects. These principles cannot always be applied so as to resolve beyond dispute particular ethical problems. The objective is to provide an analytical framework that will guide the resolution of ethical problems arising from research involving human subjects.[15]

Despite not "getting to the bottom of things" from a theoretical perspective, the commission found shared confidence in particular cases and even at the level of general principles. Sunstein's account of "agreement without theory" seems as apt here as in the judicial realm: "The agreement on particulars is incompletely theorized in the sense that the relevant participants are clear on the result without agreeing on the most general theory that accounts for it."[16] The commissioners succeeded when they tried to reach agreement at a more particular level than the level at which they disagreed.

CONSTRUCTING A CODE

We might expect similar success if those attempting to formulate a professional code of ethics adopt a similar procedure. In fact, this seems to be very much like the way the code of ethics of the American Association of Engineers (AAE) was established in the early twentieth century.[17] AAE was founded in 1915. Intended as an umbrella organization for all engineers, one of its major tasks was to formulate a code of ethics. In 1922, H. W. Clausen, treasurer of AAE, wrote:

> Effective bodies have long been in existence to deal with the technical side of engineering service and in the course of their work much has also been done to advance the standard of practice from an ethical standpoint as well. It was thought, however, that the establishment of the American Association of Engineers would be helpful in providing a means for determining a general code of ethics and in interpreting that code in specific problems of everyday practice.[18]

Dr. Isham Randolph, an engineer noted for his integrity and high standards, was asked to draft a code for the association's consideration. The code, consisting of a small set of general principles and a small set of more specific articles, was adopted by the association members.

But AAE also established a "Practice Committee," which had the job of helping members interpret the code in specific instances. This committee's task was to analyze nearly fifty cases and recommend the adoption of its decisions as setting precedent for appropriate behavior in similar circumstances. The intention was that these might serve as something similar to court decisions in common law. Clausen reported that the committee was to "continue to study and work out the itemized list of specific principles of good professional conduct in such completeness that infractions of ethical practice may be specified by clause and sentence." Prior to adoption of their views, the committee's analyses of cases were published for AAE members, who were invited to discuss the cases and make suggestions.

The Practice Committee's 1921 annual report provides some measure of its success. The committee identified two general classes of cases. The first, it said, consists of cases in which no facts are in dispute. The only question is whether the conduct in question conforms to the adopted code of ethics. The second consists of cases in which the facts are in dispute. This second kind of case, the committee said, requires very careful analysis and should be decided only after "a thorough examination of all facts and circumstances surrounding the controversy."[19] These cases can be resolved only with great difficulty.

It might be thought that the committee's view was that cases of the first kind, those in which no facts are in dispute, are amenable to easy and definitive resolution. But this is not what the committee said. Although it thought that approved decisions should function like common law, the committee insisted that "these decisions are subject to change from time to time as engineering opinion becomes more and more crystallized resulting from experience and investigation. They are of prime importance because they are written and can be referred to from time to time."[20]

So, although the committee helped establish a reliable set of ethical guidelines for engineers, it did not regard its work as settling matters once and for all. Carl Taeusch described the committee's work in this way:

> After some forty practice cases had accumulated, the AAE made a compilation of specific principles from the recorded decisions in these cases and then proceeded to accumulate a further set of practice cases authoritatively interpreted by a representative and responsible committee. The Code of Specific Principles is amended as new rulings or decisions are formulated.[21]

So, AAE regarded the Practice Committee's work as ongoing rather than as something to be finally completed.

In keeping with its focus on analyzing and categorizing cases, the committee seems to have employed an essentially *casuistic* method.[22] One begins with particular cases rather than first principles, looking for relevant paradigm cases of appropriate or inappropriate conduct that can serve as a reference point for more complicated cases. Current cases under consideration are compared with analogous cases, with relevant similarities and differences carefully noted. In striving for consistency, cases are linked to relevant principles that can be used to provide guidelines for future cases; but principles, in turn, are regarded as provisional, liable to exceptions, and subject to revision in light of new cases and circumstances.

AAE was relatively short-lived, fading away before the end of the 1920s, perhaps too short a time to expect many dramatic revisions in its developing code. However, particularly noteworthy is the first Specific Principle listed in the code once the Practice Committee completed its first forty cases: "The engineer should regard his duty to the public welfare as paramount to all other obligations." This reflects the committee's observation that public welfare is often at stake in engineering practice. This principle is very much like those appearing in nearly every engineering society's code today — but only after an absence of nearly forty years. This does not mean that engineers had no responsibility to uphold this principle during that forty-year hiatus — nor even that this was not acknowledged by practicing engineers. Why it took forty years for any engineering codes to reintroduce this principle is an interesting question, but the validity of the principle itself does not hang on the answer.

REVISING A CODE

It is clear from the history of engineering practice that even general framing principles of engineering ethics do not necessarily remain fixed. As just noted, AAE originally had as a framing principle the paramount duty of engineers to hold public health and safety paramount. This principle vanished along with AAE in the 1920s. The code of the National Society for Professional Engineers (NSPE), like most other engineering codes, for years emphasized fidelity to employer or client as the engineer's first duty. It was only in the mid-1960s that NSPE adopted a section specifically devoted to the engineer's paramount duty to protect public safety, health, and welfare in the performance of one's professional duties.

From its inception, NSPE, like AAE, aspired to be an umbrella organization for all professional engineers. Founded in 1934, there is some evidence that NSPE may have adopted a code of ethics as early as 1935. But by the mid-1950s it had already undergone many changes. In June 1954, NSPE established a Board of Ethical Review (BER). Its task was to analyze real and hypothetical ethical cases in engineering practice and to publish its decisions in *Professional Engineer*. Thus, the BER procedure, like that of the AAE committee, is essentially casuistic. In 1965, NSPE published its first volume of BER decisions and commentaries. Seven other volumes have subsequently been published, thus making more than 300 case analyses available to NSPE members.[23] Since the code has changed several times over that period, BER commentaries have undergone changes. However, many of the code's revisions have resulted from BER recommendations based on its efforts to apply sections of the code to particular circumstances.

Each volume numbers its cases and lists them according to the kinds of ethical issues they raise in relation to the code current at that time (for example, conflict of interest, public safety, expert witnessing). Subsequent cases refer to previous cases as paradigms of appropriate or inappropriate behavior, as establishing precedent for the current case, or as being relevantly different from the current case.

Prefacing a departure it makes from a specific code provision in a previous conflict of interest case, the BER commentary in Case 85-6 observes: "While that provision of the Code has been interpreted many times over the years, it is, as are all Code provisions, subject to constant examination and reinterpretation. For any code of ethics to have meaning, it must be a living, breathing document which responds to situations that evolve and develop." The earlier provision said that an "engineer will endeavor to avoid a conflict of interest with his employer or client," which requires either divesting oneself of the interests in question or declining to perform services. Noting that this requirement was replaced with a less restrictive one (one requiring only initial disclosure), the BER goes on to explain why. It does not reject the notion that there are clear cases in which engineers ought to avoid conflicts of interest. The concern, rather, is with those cases in which this is not a reasonable option:

> These difficult, multifaceted situations require discussion and consideration as they are complex and sometimes irresolvable. A code should address and provide guidance for these kinds of conflicts of interest. We believe the new code provisions sought to establish the ethical obligation to engage in dialogue with a client or employer on the difficult questions relating to conflicts of interest. We think that it was for this reason that the Code provisions were altered.

Given this alteration, the BER concludes:

> We are not willing to state as we did in BER Case 69-13 that the engineer can only avoid such a conflict either by "disposing of his land and holdings prior to undertaking the commission or by declining to perform the services if it is not feasible or desirable for him to dispose of his land at the particular time."

So, the more settled, determinative language of the earlier provision is now seen to be inadequate to deal reasonably with certain cases. Good judgment must replace straightforward application of an overly restrictive rule.

Refinements in the NSPE code seem to have resulted from reflection on the nuances of particular cases brought before the BER, rather than simply from reflection on abstract principles. Principles do enter into BER analyses, but always with an eye on practice. Broader principles of engineering ethics are viewed by the BER as providing a framework within which ethical analysis is to be understood. But these principles must be interpreted within the context of engineering practice, thereby being constrained by that practice even as they frame it; thus, principles are driven by practice rather than the reverse.

SOME LIMITATIONS

It might well be argued that engineering practice has always had a "direct and vital impact on the quality of life for all people." NSPE and other engineering societies have just been late in acknowledging the full ethical implications of this. Nevertheless, there is a distinction to be made between the ethical implications of a practice and a professional society's ability and willingness to make a collective, public commitment on these matters. NSPE's ultimate success in this regard is a significant accomplishment, however late in the day. At the same time, this reveals some of the limitations of casuistry in engineering ethics.

As Jonsen and Toulmin point out, casuistry operates within certain kinds of social contexts.[24] Historically, they say, conscience for casuists is a kind of "knowing together" (*con-scientia*). This presupposes shared institutions within which ethical reflection can take place with others. Traditionally, Jonsen and Toulmin say, such institutions have a body of public interest, expert scholarship, and professional support. They argue that medicine and health care are major areas that have at least begun to provide a suitable setting for casuistry. Engineering seems also to have made a beginning, but it is only that.

Most practicing engineers do not belong to any professional engineering society, let alone NSPE. So, there is a problem determining the proper reach of engineering societies and their codes. Even if their reach could be said in some way to include all practicing engineers, a code such as NSPE's is limited in another way. It represents, at best, the highest common ethical denominator among those to whom it applies. At worst, it may include provisions that themselves are ethically questionable (for example, former restrictions on advertising and competitive bidding, or provisions that seem designed to benefit engineers, even at the expense of the public). Furthermore, there are matters of ethical importance that go virtually unmentioned. The most conspicuously underplayed area of concern in engineering is the environment. NSPE's code, like most others, has no special sections directly addressing environmental responsibilities. Thus far, only a handful of the major U.S. engineering societies make explicit reference to protecting the environment. Perhaps someday, as has happened with public safety, health, and welfare, NSPE will introduce special provisions of this sort.

However, until it does, NSPE's Board of Ethical Review (BER) is limited in what it can provide by way of casuistic reasoning about environmental concerns. BER's function is primarily to provide guidance to NSPE members by interpreting the code in regard to particular kinds of cases that fall under the purview of the code. On matters about which the code is silent, either the BER is itself silent or it gives the verdict of "it would not be unethical" as far as the code is concerned. Yet, it is ethically important for engineers to reflect further about such matters, even if they cannot expect consensus with their professional peers.

Another limitation is that many of the provisions of the NSPE code of ethics do not easily lend themselves to casuistic interpretation. Cases that require interpretation of the engineer's paramount duty to protect public safety, health, and welfare are discussed relatively infrequently in BER commentaries, and typically the discussion is restricted to whether there is a duty to report violations to appropriate authorities. This is in line with the code's own further specification of the paramount duty. Its only direct elaboration concerns what to do when an engineer believes the provision is being violated.

However, if it is an engineer's duty to hold paramount public safety, health, and welfare in the performance of his or her professional duties, there should be a more proactive side as well. What does it mean for an engineer to strive to meet this duty? The answer is perhaps best understood in terms of an engineer's overall dispositions rather than in terms of particular cases to be analyzed.[25] For example, if an engineer is disposed to spot trouble, take preventive measures, alert others to problems, work on imaginative ways of improving the quality and safety of products, or become involved in projects that promise improvements in safety or health, he or she is, to that extent, meeting this duty. It is difficult, if not impossible, to encapsulate any of this in a "case" that invites casuistic reasoning. By and large, there is no specific ethical issue to be resolved. The BER commentaries address cases in which the question is whether certain conduct is ethical or unethical (according to the code).

In fact, the NSPE code does call for attitudes and conduct that do not fit well into an ethical/unethical dichotomy in a case-by-case context. The code stresses the importance of integrity, honor, and other commendable qualities that, it is expected, will have a positive impact on engineering practice and, at least indirectly, society. However, these appeals are expressed in aspirational terms rather than as duties or obligations, and they leave unspecified the sorts of conduct that would exemplify them. These limitations do not imply that the casuistic reasoning that can and does take place in regard to engineering practice is somehow inappropriate or unimportant. All that should be concluded is that casuistic reasoning is not everything when it comes to ethics in engineering — or anywhere else, for that matter.

There are other serious limitations of codes of ethics, particularly insofar as professionals work in large corporate settings. For example, although the vast majority of engineers are corporate employees, this is not adequately reflected in existing engineering codes of ethics, which seem written mainly with relatively independent, consulting engineers in mind. Engineering ethics is also about the ethics of large organizations, which raises challenging questions about collective responsibility, relationships between engineers and managers, and authority in hierarchical organizations. Thus, professional ethics cannot be separated from the problems of business ethics.

Furthermore, as a consensus document, a code of ethics must leave much to individual discretion, both within the code itself and outside the code. The engineer's paramount duty to protect public health, safety, and welfare is broadly stated and is consistent with a wide range of conduct. Although blatant disregard for public safety is ruled out, varying levels of commitment to improving safety seem permissible. This is reflected in the language used in BER opinions: "It would be unethical to. . . ." "It would not be unethical to. . . ." "It would be ethical to. . . ."

However, an individual engineer facing an ethical question may not be satisfied to learn simply that the code does not prohibit a certain course of conduct. Of those options the code does not prohibit (and there may be many), the engineer might want to determine which is ethically best. This, one might contend, is more a matter of personal rather than professional ethics. Even so, it is a matter of personal ethics about what, in one's professional role, one should do. For the individual engineer, it is still a question about what, as an engineer, he or she should do. It is also possible that, although a professional engineering society has been unable to come to a consensus on the point in question, there is a defensible ethical perspective that speaks to the issue from more than a personal perspective. In fact, this is a plausible way of viewing the duty to protect public health, safety, and welfare prior to its inclusion in engineering codes of ethics. It may also be a plausible way of viewing the virtual silence on environmental concerns in the current codes.

Nevertheless, just as consensus is difficult to obtain at a sufficiently specific level in professional engineering societies, it is also difficult to obtain among philosophers, theologians, and other reflective persons. Meanwhile, professionals still have to decide what to do, despite the fact that well-informed, reasonable persons may differ. This, however personal it may be, is an important part of professional ethics.

There is a related aspect of professional ethics, largely unexplored but to be taken up in chapter 8, "Working Together," that merits some discussion. Typically professionals not only work in large organizations, they also work in teams. This means that the problems they try to solve are not simply the problems of this or that individual professional. They are the problems of a group, or team. That is, a particular problem may be "ours," not simply "mine"; and this holds for problems that have ethical dimensions as well as those that do not. Furthermore, the group, or team, may need to decide *together* what should be done.

This means they will have to negotiate their differences, and this may call for compromise. How, ethically, should such negotiations proceed? What are the responsibilities of individual professionals in this process? Given the likelihood that one's own views will not be found completely acceptable by others, to what extent can one compromise without compromising one's integrity?[26]

Finally, professionals face questions about career choices and about whether to abstain from undertaking certain projects they find ethically problematic. Some engineers, for example, regard it as ethically important to avoid engineering careers or projects that directly involve the military. For others, certain engineering projects in third world countries are problematic. Still others are concerned about the appropriate development and use of technology. Professional engineering societies cannot be expected to settle these issues for engineers. Yet, reflective discussion is called for, whether within the meetings and publications of engineering societies themselves, or in higher education and other forums that provide space for vigorous examination of ethical issues related to engineering. The same should be possible for other professions.

THEORETICAL AMBITIONS

Some might wonder if Sunstein's notion of "incompletely theorized agreement" reaches high enough. If theoretical questions remain unanswered, how can we be confident that our agreements are well grounded? Before addressing this question, however, we might ask a related question, one that Sunstein does not ask, at least not directly: What would it mean to attain "*completely* theorized agreement"?[27] Or, more modestly, what would it mean for an individual to hold a *completely* theorized moral belief, whether or not others agreed with this view?

Sunstein does say that "it is quite rare for a person or group completely to theorize any subject, that is, to accept both a general theory and a series of steps connecting that theory to concrete conclusions."[28] It may be more than rare; Sunstein offers no examples of completely theorized views, at either the individual or group level. When might I justifiably conclude that one of my own moral beliefs is completely theorized? I might be confident that some particular course of action is right for me, but I may be uncertain about any more general appeal to ground it than the initial reasons I am able to provide.

Of course I would say that relevantly similar circumstances, for myself or others, justify the same conclusion. But this hardly requires me to embrace a completely theorized position. Furthermore, having learned the Euthyphro lesson, I might be very hesitant to proclaim that I have anything like a satisfactory general theory. Instead, like Socrates and Crito, I might be content to rely on "mid-level" principles in resolving moral issues. Socrates and Crito do come to agreement, but neither offers a "completely theorized" view. Nor need those who take issue with their agreement.

Two or more parties may find themselves in agreement at the particular level about some course of action being right but realize that they may diverge somewhat at a "higher" level — not because each has completely theorized in a different direction, but because they seem to have different leanings. None may believe he or she has, or is even capable of formulating, a completely theorized position. As Sunstein says, people may agree on a rationale in terms of low- or mid-level principles, even though "what accounts for the outcome in terms of a full-scale theory of the right or the good, is left unexplained."[29]

As the high-level theoretical excursions in *Euthyphro* illustrate, there may be good reason to explore the "lower" regions more thoroughly first. Furthermore, going to a more general level isn't necessarily searching for a more foundational level. One might simply be extending the same sort of thinking to other cases, working out the implications of taking a certain perspective on this or that particular issue. Or one might be trying to work out more fully a concept like "equal treatment," "equal opportunity," "disloyalty," "friendship," and so on. Dividing a cake into equal pieces for a group of hungry eight-year-olds would be equal treatment at a birthday party. So would giving each a turn at bat. Would lending one of one's children $5,000 to buy a car and the other $5,000 for college expenses be equal treatment? We may not know precisely how to extend the concept of equal treatment, or even how far we should try to extend it. But this need not make us hesitate in dividing the cake into equal pieces, nor in seeking more nuanced ways of understanding equal treatment in more complex circumstances.

Sunstein observes that ordinary people tend to proceed from firm judgments to more difficult ones by employing analogical reasoning.[30] This sort of reasoning has four main features:[31] (1) It strives for principled consistency; (2) it focuses on particulars; (3) it employs incompletely theorized judgments; and (4) it employs principles operating at a low or intermediate level of abstraction. Furthermore, ordinary people typically begin their reasonings from their understanding of familiar social roles:

> In social life, people reason in ways that grow out of the particular role in which they find themselves. They know what actions are permissible, and what actions are off-limits, only because of their role. As practical reasoners people take their roles for granted and live accordingly. Consider the close relation-

ship between reasoning and the role for such diverse figures as parents, students, waiters, doctors, employees, consumers, and automobile drivers.[32]

This may seem to have an overly conservative ring to it. However, unless social roles and practices are rather thoroughly corrupt or confused, it would seem that they contain much that is normatively reliable and worth preserving. At the same time, Sunstein cautions: "when defining commitments are based on demonstrable errors of fact or logic, it is appropriate to contest them. So, too, when those commitments are rooted in a rejection of the basic dignity of all human beings, or when it is necessary to undertake to resolve a genuine problem."[33] Furthermore, the notion of "incompletely theorized agreement" itself suggests an openness to change. As Sunstein notes, "Incompletely theorized agreements are valuable when we seek moral evolution over time. Consider the area of equality, where considerable change has occurred in the past and will inevitably occur in the future."[34] Completely theorized agreement in such areas suggests a kind of inflexibility that would resist change.

Still, Sunstein concedes, there is the risk that everyone who participates in an incompletely theorized agreement is actually mistaken.[35] It is also possible that there are reasonable people who have not been parties to the agreement and who, if they were included, would undermine the consensus. Thus, he concludes that from time to time incompletely theorized agreements should be subject to critical examination. Actually, the same might be said of completely theorized agreements, should any be achieved, unless we have a guarantee that premises of those arguments are *both* true and comprehensive. But what would guarantee that? In any case, since completely theorized agreements are, as Sunstein points out, rare at best, this is not likely to become a practical issue.

As an incompletely theorized agreement, a professional code of ethics can serve as a reliable, but corrigible, guide to responsible conduct. As suggested earlier, a professional society's code is a reasonable place to look for an articulation of standards of responsible conduct. However, for reasons already given, one should not expect a code to cover all areas that engage the sense of responsibility of professionals; nor should one expect the provisions of a code to provide algorithms for appropriate conduct.

CHAPTER SEVEN

Good Works

Reflecting on his earlier essay, "Saints and Heroes," J. O. Urmson reminds us that there is a "vast array of actions, having moral significance, which frequently are performed by persons who are far from being moral saints or heroes but which are neither duties nor obligations, nor involve conformity to principle as I use that term."[1] Related to this is another array of actions, not mentioned by Urmson, but also morally important and not widely discussed. These are actions that, while connected with one's duties or obligations, are not fairly describable as "just doing one's duty." How one goes about fulfilling one's duties can vary in morally significant ways. How perceptively, competently, or conscientiously one proceeds can make a critical difference to what does or does not happen. So, in addition to actions that clearly go "above and beyond the call of duty" (supererogatory actions), there are ways of pursuing one's professional duties that can be commendable, if not exemplary. For want of a more suitable expression, and without making any claim to precision, I will call all of these actions, supererogatory or otherwise, "good works."[2]

What would be an illustration of what Urmson has in mind? Here is an example outside of professional life. Several years ago I lived in a rural setting nearly twenty-five miles from the university where I teach. My unpaved driveway was several hundred feet long. I had a snow shovel, but no snowblower or snowplow. One morning in the dead of winter I awoke to eight inches of freshly fallen snow in my driveway. I had not planned my departure to the university around a major shoveling job, and I worried that I would be late for my class. As I trudged out to my driveway, shovel in hand, one of my neighbors drove up in his pickup truck with a snowplow attached to the front end. "Looks like you might be late for work today. Can I help you with your driveway?" he asked

The first several sections of this chapter are adapted from my article "Good Works," in *Professional Ethics* 1, nos. 1–2 (Spring/Summer 1992): 155–177. The discussion of service-learning is based on my "Service-Learning and Engineering Ethics," in *Science and Engineering Ethics* 6, no. 3 (July, 2000): 413–422.

cheerily. Refusing my offer of compensation, he replied, "It'll only take a couple of minutes; besides, I enjoy using my plow."

This example has several important features. First, my neighbor noticed that my driveway was drifted; like the vast majority of my neighbors, he might not have noticed it at all. Second, he might have noticed it, but not in such a way that it prompted him to action. He might not have connected it with my need to get to work. Third, he might have noticed it and connected it with my need to get to work, but thought to himself: "He's going to have a tough time getting to work today. This isn't the city. I don't know why that guy doesn't get some kind of plow."

That he noticed my need in the way he did inclines me to regard him as a good neighbor — a very good neighbor, at least under these circumstances. Noticing my need in just the way he did was, I am inclined to think, a manifestation of thoughtfulness and goodwill. However, if he had not noticed my need at all, or even if he had noticed it but had done nothing, this alone would not incline me to think of him as thoughtless, or as a bad neighbor. Prior to his thoughtful action, my neighbor and I had had only a nodding acquaintance with each other. Despite living near each other for more than two years, our social contact had consisted of occasional greetings from across the street when retrieving our mail. His deed was special, unexpected, and more than I had a right to expect from a neighbor. What he did was not a basic duty. My neighbor's thoughtful act did not require a great deal of time or sacrifice on his part. Yet, in admittedly less than "life-or-death" circumstances, it was helpful, much appreciated, and morally commendable.

Not everyone in my rural setting regarded my neighbor's actions in this way. When I mentioned this example to another neighbor, he replied, "I don't want him plowing my drive. He's not very careful, and he's plowed up some of my flower beds along the edge of the drive." His point is well taken: Trying to be helpful is no guarantee of success. A corollary is that, even if one has no basic duty to help others in circumstances like this, taking up the task incurs certain responsibilities (not damaging property). What is required is some assurance that the effort is welcome, that the helper is capable of carrying out the task well, and that the helper will carry it out well (rather than, say, piling the snow at the bottom of the drive and leaving to "help" another neighbor). In my case, the effort was welcome (my neighbor did ask before beginning his work); I simply assumed (correctly in this instance) that my neighbor was capable of carrying out the task well and that he would finish the job.

In cases where the need for help seemingly is more urgent, we may think that those nearby who are capable of helping have a duty to do so. Herbert Fingarette offers psychological evidence that we at least believe we have a duty to help someone in distress. This is the fact that we often carry on an inner debate when confronted with a stranger who apparently is in serious need of help: "It's none of my business — I don't know what's behind this; I might even aggravate the injury; there might be trouble later for me or for my family; besides I'm late for my appointment; anyway, why should *I* be the one to stop? Maybe someone else has already gone for help."[3] Fingarette holds that such debates would be pointless if we were not tacitly acknowledging that we do have a duty to help, at least if we are in a good position to do so without undue risk or sacrifice.

However, for some, personal risk and sacrifice do not stand in the way of offering assistance. During World War II, the residents of the little French Protestant village Le Chambon understood very well what was happening during the Vichy regime in France. Led by Andre and Magda Trocme, they saved the lives of hundreds of fleeing Jews by hiding them in their homes. Philip Hallie's *Lest Innocent Blood Be Shed* describes in great detail the efforts of the Le Chambon villagers.[4]

Hallie notes that Le Chambon stood virtually alone among French villages in the area in providing refuge for Jews. However, rather than suggest that other villages failed to recognize or act on a basic duty to offer assistance, he concentrates on depicting the goodness of the residents of Le Chambon. In so doing he draws a striking contrast between Magda and Andre Trocme:

> Magda Trocme believes that something is evil *because* it hurts people. Hers is an ethic of benevolence: She need only to look into the eyes of a refugee in order to find her duty.
>
> But her husband had a more complex ethic. He believed that something is evil both because it hurts somebody *and* because it violates an imperative, a commandment given us by God in the Bible and in our particular hearts. He had to look up to some authority beyond the eyes of the refugee to find that commandment, but having found it, his duty, like hers, lay in diminishing the hurt in those eyes.[5]

Despite their apparent differences at this "foundational" level, the Trocmes stood as one in protecting the Jews by secretly hiding them in their home.

It is interesting that in this passage Hallie uses the language of duty. Elsewhere he makes clear that neither Trocme was concerned to judge those who saw things differently as falling short of their duty. Surely the Trocmes would urge others to join them, but "duty" here seems highly personalized, even in the case of Andre Trocme, who found the commandment, not only in the Bible, but "in our particular hearts." Magda Trocme, like most of the others in Le Chambon, seemed uncomfortable with judging and being judged in ethical terms. Hallie comments:

Often moral praise is an interpretation, a grid laid upon the facts by an outsider's hand. An outsider may see goodness or decency in an action, as an integral part of, say, Magda's invitation to the police to join them at the big dining table, but the doer of the deed, who often acts on the spur of the moment, sees nothing "moral" or "ethical" in that deed. For Magda Trocme and most of the other people of Le Chambon, words of moral praise are like a slightly uncomfortable wreath laid upon a head by a kind but alien hand.[6]

This passage brings out important differences between first- and third-person perspectives.[7] Those who have the most admirable moral traits may not see themselves as we see them. They may severely reproach themselves for not doing something, whereas we would not reproach them at all. Contrasted with this is a third-person notion of "duty" that focuses on Urmson's "rock-bottom duties" and their minimal satisfaction. This is not what Hallie has in mind when he refers to the Trocmes' sense of responsibility. Urmson's complaint is that we overemphasize "rock-bottom duties" at the expense of recognizing other important features of moral life. Whether it is my neighbor plowing my driveway or Le Chambon villagers providing refuge for Jews, Urmson's notion of "rock-bottom duties" seems to fall short of what needs to be acknowledged by third parties.

However they regard themselves, the Trocmes are regarded by their admirers in more exemplary terms than simply meeting one's basic duties. Through their words and actions they inspired an entire village. Had the Trocmes not stepped forward, would anyone (other than the Trocmes themselves) have said they were guilty of wrongdoing or that this was a failure of duty? If so, the same would have to be said of residents of the many other French villages that could have been Le Chambon, but were not.

Apparently the Trocmes were not inclined to say this of those villages. What would they have said of the residents of Le Chambon if they had not responded to their call? No doubt the Trocmes would have been quite disappointed, but there is little reason to think they would have regarded this lack of responsiveness as a failure to fulfill basic duties. This may be obscured by the fact that, once the villagers did respond to the Trocmes' call, matters changed considerably. Shared commitments do give rise to basic duties — to those who have joined together and to those they serve. There are duties to do one's share, work cooperatively, not betray others, and so on.

However, even within the realm of shared commitment we can distinguish between basic duties and something more. Hallie describes Le Chambon as being remarkably unified in its efforts. Yet, it is clear that some villagers played a more instrumental role than others, some devoted more of themselves to the tasks at hand than others, and so on. In short, among those providing assistance, some stand out as exemplary, whereas perhaps the actions of the vast majority fall somewhere within Urmson's "vast array of actions, having moral significance, which frequently are performed by persons who are far from being moral saints or heroes."[8]

GOOD WORKS IN PROFESSIONAL LIFE

Professions typically are marked by their expertise, the services they provide others, and self-regulation.[9] Self-regulation may include not only articulating and enforcing a code of ethics, but also exercising control over qualifications for entering professional practice. These elements combine to place knowledge and power in the hands of professionals and create dependency in those whom they serve. However, there is a further complicating factor. A growing number of professionals work in large organizations. While these organizations themselves depend on professionals, they may have aims quite distinct from those of the professionals. At times those aims come into conflict with what professionals might otherwise want. Professionals may find their autonomy restricted by goals established by management, working with others, limited resources, deadlines, and so on. All of this defines the context within which issues of professional ethics arise.

Obviously this context differs significantly from the examples presented so far. My neighbor did not act in a professional capacity. His was the solitary act of someone coming to the aid of a neighbor. Neither were the Le Chambon villagers acting in a professional capacity. However, the collective assumption of responsibility of the villagers bears some similarity to professional responsibility. Once assumed, responsibility carries with it certain basic duties. Morally, we might say, the villagers did not have to assume responsibility for providing refuge for Jews; but once they did, they acquired basic duties to those they served, and to one another.

Those who join a profession are like the Le Chambon villagers in that, by virtue of joining, they take on new duties, albeit duties that go beyond what is ordinarily required. For most professionals this does not involve risks comparable to those of the villagers. Nor are most faced daily with the life or death of those they serve hanging on their every move. Yet, even the more everyday side of professional life is replete with significant, if less dramatic, moral concerns. Given the special roles they play in society, professionals do have basic duties that others do not have. Nevertheless, it seems that within professional life, too, a distinction can be made between basic duties and something more.

Consider some candidates:

1. A university professor in statistics agrees to help analyze data to determine whether it is safe for residents in Love Canal to return to their homes. Although modestly compensated for his services, he realizes there are many much more lucrative consulting opportunities. Asked why he accepted this task instead, he says: "Analyzing data just for the money doesn't mean anything to me. I want it to do some good."[10]
2. A faculty member agrees to serve on yet another important university committee, knowing full well that this will require taking even more work home in the evening.[11]
3. After spending nearly an hour on the phone trying to get an elderly patient admitted into the hospital, a physician finally succeeds. Tempted to give up and recommend to the patient's daughter that she call the city ambulance and hope that it takes her mother to an emergency room with a sympathetic physician, he decides instead to fight his way through the bureaucratic layers to make certain that the patient receives proper attention.[12]
4. A dentist finally prevails in his thirty-year struggle to overcome strong resistance to allowing the water to be fluoridated in his small community.[13]

Although basic duties come into play once responsibilities are assumed, in none of these cases is it plausible for us to say that the professionals involved are simply fulfilling their basic duties.[14] Yet, what they are portrayed as doing has, as Urmson puts it, moral significance.

Good works in professional life are easy to miss. Those who perform them may see themselves as simply doing what needs to be done. Not privy to what goes on behind the scenes, we may simply take for granted the benefits we receive from such efforts.

There is another factor that may account for our failure to recognize the good works of others for what they are. As the Le Chambon villagers illustrate, once one accepts responsibilities, certain duties do arise. But it is not clear that they had a basic duty to undertake that task in the first place. Similarly, if professors agree to serve on committees, then they have a duty to follow through by attending meetings, doing the work of the committee, and so on. So, as they fulfill these responsibilities, we may see them as fulfilling basic duties, while failing to notice that they may have had no basic duty to serve on the committee in the first place.

Although it is easy to overlook the good works of others for the reasons just given, there are occasions when the case is too obvious to miss. Several years ago I served as an outside evaluator on a committee reviewing nominations for another university's annual merit awards in the areas of scholarly work, teaching, and service. Each category had several nominees, and our task was to recommend a top candidate in each area. As we began looking at the file of the service nominees, another outside evaluator commented, "This one looks like a career academy award."

Indeed, it did. Near retirement age, this candidate had served with distinction on committee after committee and project after project for more than thirty years, serving not only his department and university, but the community as well. In reviewing his record and letters of support, we could not help but conclude that he presented an exceptional model of service. The same is true of the candidates for the teaching award.

What is noteworthy about service and teaching is that, of the three areas of professional activity, they are far and away the least likely to bring one fame or fortune. Scholarly work is the clear winner — both in regard to the number of those who attain fame or fortune and in the amount of fame or fortune attainable. Scholarly work is also the area faculty can least afford to neglect if they desire tenure or promotion. So, while we may have doubts about whether someone's scholarly productivity is best understood in terms of good works (as distinct from good work), the cumulative case is sometimes obvious in the other two areas.

It is especially implausible to look at the cumulative record of a teaching or service nominee and conclude that simply fulfilling one's basic duties adequately captures the moral significance of his or her professional life. This is also true, if to a lesser degree, of any number of faculty who are never nominated for such awards. However, it seems fair to say of many that their professional lives are not noteworthy at all for their good works, even though they may not be guilty of any significant lapses of duty. Still others, unfortunately, are noted for falling short in meeting their basic duties — some rather spectacularly so.

We might ask how important it is to emphasize good works in addition to basic duties in professional life. It might be thought that if only professionals would meet their basic duties, this would be sufficient to meet the needs of those whom the professions acknowledge they should serve. But a simple thought experiment shows that this is not so.

Suppose that, contrary to fact, every member of a given profession were to meet his or her basic duties, but only minimally. Further suppose that, as is often the case, certain areas of social need are underrepresented by the profession (for example, not enough physicians are available in an impoverished urban area). Since no specific physicians can be identified as having a basic duty to serve in those areas, the collective result is that the profession itself fails adequately to provide the services to society that it is (or ought to be) committed to provide (for example, minimally adequate health care for the poor). So, there is evident societal need for at least some professionals doing good works beyond any basic duties they might have. Something more than the ethics of basic duty is necessary if such broader needs are to be addressed.

This is even more evident if we consider the implications of the *absence* of good works. Disasters are averted not only by professionals fulfilling their duties, but also by doing more than this requires. So are less severe, but nevertheless unwelcome, consequences. For example, how would the university have fared were it not for the efforts of its "career academy award" candidate — as well as others like him in the university?

So far, good works by professionals have been portrayed as actions which are, if noticed, welcome. But they are not always welcome. In fact, sometimes they are discouraged, intentionally or not. We need to ask to what extent the organizations within which professionals work present obstacles to doing good works by, for example, defining professional tasks and responsibilities too narrowly, actively discouraging "do-gooders," or rewarding only those who do not "rock the boat." Good works may also be discouraged by the need to meet tight time schedules, limited budgets, and other priorities. Some of these obstacles are simply realistic and justifiable limitations. Others seem, in principle, alterable. When this is so, it is important to examine the extent to which changes might be desirable and feasible.

In this regard, it is interesting to note that university professors may have as much professional autonomy as any professionals who work in large organizations. Teaching schedules and office hours typically are flexible. Areas of research are rather wide open (although external funding is sometimes needed). Yet, hovering over the heads of younger faculty especially is a tremendous disincentive for taking teaching and service as seriously as they might otherwise prefer — namely, a reward system that is concentrated in published research and scholarship. Given that teaching and service are equally important functions of higher education, it is unfortunate that so little serious effort is spent trying to establish a more balanced system of rewards.

SHIFTING TO THE POSITIVE

Whether the focus is on individual professionals or the institutional settings within which they typically work, the major emphasis in current literature in professional ethics is on basic duties. There is likely to be the greatest consensus about ethics at this level, and failure to meet basic duties can have very serious consequences. Still, as just noted, the absence of good works can have very serious consequences, too.

How might that which goes beyond basic duties be fruitfully explored in the context of professional ethics? John Ladd's analysis of responsibility is very helpful in this regard.[15] His specific target of criticism is what he calls the "standard view of responsibility," a view that restricts itself to basic duties. Responsibility is linked with a liability to blame, very much like the liability to punishment in law. In contrast, Ladd advocates a more positive view of responsibility, one that sees moral responsibility as "something positively good, that is, as something to be sought after."[16]

This more positive view does not hold that the failure to meet responsibilities necessarily warrants blame. Instead, Ladd says, we should think of such failures as moral deficiencies, implying "the lack of an appropriate attitude of concern or caring."[17] This broadens the scope of moral responsibility to emphasize caring relationships with others rather than restricting it to the avoidance or prevention of evil. To move from fault or blame to deficiency, Ladd says, is to move "from the presence of an evil to the absence of a good, and, in general, to an orientation towards humanity or lack thereof."[18]

Ladd points out several advantages of this more positive view. Moral responsibility is more open-ended, admitting of varying degrees and stringency. Unlike the standard view, responsibility cannot be divided neatly into separate spheres warranting statements such as "It's my job, not his," or "It's his job, not mine." So, in the case of the Bhopal, India, disaster in 1986, the explosion of a chemical plant resulting in the death and injury of thousands, the positive view allows us to say that safety was a low priority for nearly everyone and that "oughts" apply to "the conduct of all the various individuals whose acts or omissions made the accident at Bhopal possible."[19]

What is true of moral responsibility at Bhopal applies as well to the more everyday, less dramatic workplace of engineers and technicians. Rather than accept industry's "normal accidents" as beyond human control, Ladd insists, "Good engineering, and consequently good technological practice, requires constant testing."[20] No doubt the standard view, too, requires vigilance and testing on the part of some as a basic duty. But responsibility as care goes beyond this, both for those with basic duties and those who might otherwise be in a position to help.

Although Ladd's notion of positive responsibility includes much of what I have been calling good works, it is not clear that it includes all of what I have in mind. Ladd concentrates on examples in which one's responsibility is, in some sense, based on his or her responsibility for those situations being as they are. Thus, if one is partially responsible for bringing about the conditions that could ultimately result in a mishap or disaster, then one has some responsibility for attempting to avoid or prevent such bad consequences. However, good works also include cases in which one responds to circumstances that are, in no obvious sense, of one's own making. For example, my neighbor had nothing to do with the drifting of snow in my driveway (or my not being equipped to remove the snow efficiently). The statistician had nothing to do with the conditions causing Love Canal residents to leave their homes or with the circumstances calling for the statistical analysis. The many, many people from around the country who volunteered their services in New York City after the September 11, 2001, destruction of the World Trade Center were not responsible for the attack, and so on.

Nevertheless, these illustrations all seem to be in the spirit of Ladd's fundamental view of responsibility as actively caring about the welfare of others. What is unclear is whether Ladd would say that not undertaking good works is necessarily a sign of moral deficiency. I am myself reluctant to go this far. In any case, Ladd is not claiming that positive responsibility requires us to undertake supererogatory or heroic tasks. Decrying our society's tendency to regard concern for others as supererogatory, Ladd says that positive responsibility, "like other virtues, is other-regarding, it is intrinsically motivational and it binds persons to each other." And it is not just for saints and heroes — it is for everyone.[21]

SERVICE-LEARNING

Ladd's emphasis on the positive in engineering ethics is a shift from the more standard focus on avoiding and preventing wrongdoing. It is encouraging that current Accreditation Board for Engineering and Technology (ABET) requirements for accredited programs in the United States open the door for a more positive emphasis in engineering education. These requirements include helping students acquire "an understanding of the ethical characteristics of the engineering profession and practice."[22] ABET 2000 more specifically requires engineering programs to demonstrate that their graduates also understand the impact of engineering in a global and social context, along with a knowledge of current ethical issues related to engineering. It also requires students to have a "major design experience" that includes ethical factors in addition to economic, environmental, social, and political factors.[23]

At the same time, in many academic areas there is a growing recognition of the educational potential of service-learning.[24] This involves combining community service and academic study in ways that invite reflection on what one learns in the process. Given ABET 2000's "major design experience" requirement, the idea of service-learning in engineering may be especially promising. But this idea is important for another reason.

When we consider the common association of engineering ethics with wrongdoing and its prevention, it might be asked whether community service should be regarded as a part of engineering ethics at all. However, it is not at all uncommon for other professions to include pro bono service as an important feature of their professional ethics. This is based in large part on the recognition that professions provide services that may be needed by anyone, but which not everyone can afford or easily access. Medical and legal services readily come to mind. But this is no less true of engineering.

Is this acknowledged in engineering codes of ethics? It is in at least two: The National Society of Professional Engineers' (NSPE) and the American Society of Civil Engineers' (ASCE). I will discuss each code's provision briefly. Emphasizing the crucial impact that engineering has on the public, the Preamble of NSPE's *Code of Ethics for Engineers* states that engineering "requires adherence to the highest principles of ethical conduct on behalf of the public, clients, employers and the profession." Following this, the code lists as its first Fundamental Canon that engineers are to hold paramount the safety, health, and welfare of the public in the performance of their professional duties. This provision is repeated as the first entry under Rules of Practice.

Unfortunately, the Rules of Practice section says very little about what specifically this provision requires of engineers. The only further specifications concern: (1) reporting to proper authorities when one's judgment is overruled and public safety, health, or welfare is endangered; (2) reporting alleged violations of the Code; and (3) approving only those engineering documents that show proper regard for public safety, health, and welfare. That is, there is a rather striking shift from the positive to the negative.

This shift is in line with engineering ethics' predominant emphasis on wrongdoing and its prevention. However, later the Code returns to the positive. Under Section III, Professional Obligations, the second entry says: "Engineers shall at all times strive to serve the public interest." Subsection a under this obligation reads: "Engineers shall seek opportunities to be of constructive service in civic affairs and work for the advancement of the safety, health and well-being of their community." Noteworthy here is the assertion that engineers are to seek opportunities to be of service to the community. Furthermore, there is no qualifier, "in the performance of their professional duties." This suggests that engineers' responsibilities in regard to public well-being are not restricted to their duties within their place of employment.

Again, there is no specification of what taking this responsibility seriously might entail. Perhaps the best way to illustrate what this might involve is through examples. However, the engineering ethics literature thus far has not devoted much attention to this aspect of engineering responsibility.[25]

ASCE's *Code of Ethics* differs from NSPE's mainly in regard to its explicit emphasis on enhancing the environment and complying with principles of sustainable development.[26] Its first Fundamental Canon reads: "Engineers shall hold paramount the safety, health and welfare of the public and shall strive to comply with the principles of sustainable development in the performance of their professional duties." Subsection e, directly under this, reads: "Engineers should seek opportunities to be of constructive service in civic affairs and work for the advancement of the safety, health and well-being of their communities, and the protection of the environment through the practice of sustainable development." Subsection f reads: "Engineers should be committed to improving the environment by adherence to the principles of sustainable development so as to enhance the quality of life of the general public."

Although the NSPE and ASCE provisions are rather broadly stated, they do provide a rationale for concluding that, at least from the perspective of two major professional engineering societies, community service is an important feature of engineering ethics. Service-learning provides an opportunity for students to understand and appreciate this. At the same time that many have complained that our students are part of a "me-generation," there has been a marked increase in student interest in volunteer work. Until fairly recently, however, there has not been a strong correlation between students' academic pursuits and the sorts of volunteer work they undertake. Noting this lack of correlation, organizations such as Campus Compact have made concerted efforts to encourage the development of academic programs that explicitly encourage students to seek volunteer work related to their course of academic study and to reflect quite self-consciously on the connections.[27]

Service-learning projects must do more than provide service to others. They must also contain a learning component for those who provide the service, one that focuses on the notion of service itself. That is, service-learning projects require some sort of self-conscious reflection on the nature and significance of providing service to others. They also introduce the ethical factor of service itself, which, as noted, is an aspirational goal in most engineering codes of ethics. This goes well beyond the aspirations of six-year-old Calvin in the comic strip *Calvin and Hobbes*. Calvin wants Santa Claus to reward him for being good: "How good do you have to be to qualify as good?" he asks. "I haven't *killed* anybody. See, that's good, right? I haven't committed any felonies. I didn't start any wars. I don't practice cannibalism. Wouldn't you say I should get lots of presents?" Pausing for a moment of reflection, Calvin's stuffed tiger pal, Hobbes, wisely replies: "But maybe good is more than the absence of bad."[28]

However, students may need guidance in determining what counts as doing good when engaged in a service-learning project. Acting on good intentions is not enough. As engineer and disaster relief specialist Frederick Cuny has repeatedly insisted, assistance must carefully take into account the context in which help is offered.[29] This may require sensitivity to not only individual differences among those with similar backgrounds, but also vast differences in cultural, environmental, social, and political circumstances. Exposing students to some of Cuny's reflections would be quite useful.[30]

Although a fundamental ethical dimension of service-learning is the notion of service itself, there are other dimensions that are likely to be encountered in virtually any workplace environment. For example, there may be challenges working in teams, satisfying a supervisor or others with whom one is working, deciding what to do when observing wrongdoing, and deciding what to do when one has made a mistake that has not been noticed by others. So, in addition to reflecting on the significance of community service itself, students may find themselves addressing ethical problems very much like those they will have to deal with in their eventual place of employment as well. What this means is that, assuming that service-learning projects encourage a full discussion of the ethical dimensions of the students' experiences, a much broader spectrum of ethical questions will be considered than community service.

Finally, precisely because they are closely related to students' preparation for their careers, service-learning experiences can stimulate reflection on directions they want their careers to take and on the values and ethical ideals they hope to sustain in whatever pursuits they do eventually undertake. All of this should seem especially appealing to those educators who want their students to become responsible professionals both in the workplace and in their lives in the community.

CHAPTER EIGHT

Working Together

WORKING WITH OTHERS

Professionals work and consult with others, and they have available to them a vast array of technical literature to assist them. Aside from needing the support of others to be effective in pursuing particular courses of action, professionals often need the assistance of others in seeing what the problems are and what constructive alternatives might be available. Shifting attention to what responsible practice requires of those working together does not really diminish the importance of the individual. However, it does require thinking of responsible practice more in terms of collaborative work than of individuals working alone.

A striking example of the importance of group approaches to ethical problems is that of human subject institutional review boards (HSIRBs) at medical and university research centers. Particularly in the arena of medical research, for example, there are complicated problems in determining risks and benefits of the proposed research, in determining how best to seek the informed consent of participants, and in ensuring that there are no serious conflicts of interest. It is not unusual for an HSIRB to discover complications unnoticed by even the most well-intentioned researchers.

Furthermore, partly because HSIRBs are designed to represent many diverse perspectives, the dynamic of group interaction often results in perceptions that individual members did not bring with them into board meetings. By complementing one another, members are able collectively to come up with important considerations that it is unlikely that any one or two individuals would have. Thus, there can be strength in numbers in addressing ethical problems.

WHOSE PROBLEMS?

When an HSIRB addresses its task of evaluating a complicated protocol, many problems arise. Whose problems are they? Let us imagine the problems facing individual board members as they deliberate together. Andrew Bartkowski has student papers to grade before he meets his class at 2:00 P.M. He is worried that if the HSIRB meeting goes on too long, he will have to break a noon tennis engagement in order to complete his grading. He has already taken more than a week to grade the papers, and he doesn't want to disappoint his students, especially since he promised he would return them today. Carol Sherman isn't sure she is quite prepared to give her lecture today, and she is finding it difficult to focus her thinking on the protocol under discussion. David Russell is upset that his paper has been rejected by a leading journal. He, too, is finding it challenging to concentrate on the protocol under consideration. These are all problems for individual members of the group.

However, pressing as these individual problems may be, they do not define the task before the committee, namely, to evaluate the complicated protocol. That task is *their* problem, *together*. Andrew Bartkowski's grading problem is *his*, not *theirs*. His problem may make it difficult for him to concentrate on the problem facing the committee, but it is basically his responsibility to resolve his grading problem, not the committee's. It may be the committee chair's responsibility to try to keep the members focused on the task at hand. So, in this respect, their individual problems directly pose a problem for her in her role as chair. But each member of the committee has a role to play that can be understood only in terms of their *joint* responsibility to complete certain tasks.

Each of us has problems that are best seen as *mine* rather than *ours*. At the same time, each of us has problems that are best seen as *ours* rather than simply as *mine*. This is because we do not always act alone. We may be tempted to think that, in the end, problems best seen as *ours* are simply an assemblage of problems that for each of us individually are *mine*, but which add up to *ours* because they have the same content. However, this does not capture the distinctiveness of *our* problems. Explaining why not is the next task.

EUTHYPHRO AND *CRITO* AGAIN

Chapter 2 drew some important contrasts between Plato's *Euthyphro* and *Crito* in regard to their treatment of issues of practical ethics. There is another contrast to be drawn, one that can help us understand the importance of the difference between problems that are *mine* and those that are *ours*. In *Euthyphro*, the initial focus is on what Euthyphro, acting *by himself*, should do; and the dialogue ends, however disappointingly, with Euthyphro going off by himself to do what he thinks is right, despite his failure to articulate sound supporting reasons. However, in *Crito,* Socrates frequently talks about what "we" should do, and about what "our" action would mean. Crito comes to Socrates with an offer. He and his friends want to help Socrates escape; and this requires more than persuading Socrates that he should escape. There is little likelihood of Socrates escaping unaided by his friends. Although they discuss what each might do individually (put up money, bribe guards, make arrangements for safe refuge, or walk out of the prison), the escape is a *collaborative* action. And it is in these terms that Socrates couches much of the discussion.

Dialogue in *Euthyphro* is cast largely in terms of "I" or "you." Socrates and Euthyphro present themselves to each other as having quite separate paths to follow. Euthyphro talks about his own take on the problem before him. Socrates generally avoids talking about his own views, concentrating instead on Euthyphro's views and their implications ("*You* say . . ."). The emphasis is on what Euthyphro should do, where Euthyphro's arguments lead, whether Euthyphro has anything to offer Socrates in his own defense, and the like.

In *Crito,* the emphasis shifts to what "we" should do, to whom "we" should listen, and how "we" should proceed in assessing different views. The objective is very different — it is Socrates and Crito acting together, from shared premises and shared goals. Each step of the way, Socrates asks whether Crito agrees with him. This is quite different from Socrates asking Euthyphro if he has understood Euthyphro's words correctly. In *Crito,* Socrates does not shy away from saying what he believes is right or wrong. He invites Crito to examine these beliefs to see if they are sound and if Crito, too, holds them.

We could try to explain this difference by saying that, after all, in *Crito,* Socrates states his own beliefs because the focus is on what he should do, whereas in *Euthyphro* the focus is on what Euthyphro should do. In either case, then, the beliefs of the one who has to decide are crucial because it is he who must decide. Socrates cannot decide for Euthyphro. Crito cannot decide for Socrates. This is true. However, in *Crito,* whatever Socrates decides has direct implications for Crito; and what Crito does has direct implications for Socrates. If Socrates refuses to escape, then either Crito and his friends will abstain from engineering an escape or they will attempt to remove Socrates from prison against his will. If Socrates accepts the offer to escape, then Crito and his friends will be implicated as co-actors in the escape. Thus, their fates are tied together in a way that makes good sense of Socrates and Crito examining the issues as theirs to resolve together, rather than each looking at the issues from individual, albeit related, perspectives. If they are considering acting together, then they must reason together; and "my problems" must become "our problems" in deciding what to do.

TAKING A WALK TOGETHER

Margaret Gilbert introduces the idea of a "plural subject," which consists of at least two individuals joined for certain purposes in one activity.[1] She begins with a seemingly simple illustration, taking a walk together.[2] However, the complexity of this idea becomes evident when we contrast it with walking alone.

As I am walking alone, I realize that someone has come up beside me. We greet each other and exchange comments on the surrounding sights. She turns left and says, "Have a nice walk." Have we taken a walk together? Gilbert rightly says no. Our paths crossed, we talked briefly as we walked, then we continued on our separate journeys. Both of us were taking walks — mine and hers, not ours. It could have gone otherwise. As we talked, one of us might have suggested that, assuming we have similar destinations, we could continue together. Then what began as her walk and my walk would become our walk together.

Gilbert does not say exactly what has to transpire for something to be one walk that is ours, rather than two, mine and yours. Instead, she talks about entitlements that go with being on a walk with someone. If Sue and Jack were on a walk together and he, without comment, were simply to turn left and walk away, she would be entitled to object. Taking a walk together is, as Gilbert puts it, a joint commitment. With this joint commitment comes the recognition of certain rights and responsibilities that fall on each. What each expresses is a willingness to join with the other in constituting a plural subject, whose goal is that "they walk along in one another's company."[3]

For a plural subject of this sort to be established, Gilbert says, it is necessary for individuals to commit to it "simultaneously and interdependently." An exchange of individual promises in which each unilaterally commits to the goal will not do.[4] Instead, each person expresses a special form of conditional commitment such that only when all have done similarly are any committed. From this it follows, says Gilbert, that one cannot unilaterally release oneself from the commitment. Each member of the plural subject "is obligated to all *qua* member of the whole; each is entitled to certain actions *qua* member of the whole."[5] Insofar as Sue sees herself as bound up in a plural subject, she understands herself to be bound to do what will best serve its goal.[6] This, in turn, means that Sue does not need her own separable goal ("my goal") in order to have a reason for action; "our goal" serves as a reason in its own right.

For Gilbert, taking a walk together is to be understood in terms of "our goal" rather than as two or more "my goals." This does not mean that I cannot have my own goals in addition to sharing in "our goal"; but, as the goals of a single individual, they are neither necessary nor sufficient for something being "our goal." Gilbert believes that taking a walk together is simply one of a great variety of activities that are like this. She suggests others: traveling together, eating together, dancing together, and investigating a murder together. Each of these activities involves a plural subject and a joint, or shared, goal. A mark of all social groups, Gilbert says, is that they have plural subjects. However, she cautions, a social group need not have a joint, or shared, goal. It can also be marked by shared or collective beliefs or principles.[7] Teams of professionals, or professionals in organizational settings, can be expected to have joint, or shared, goals. Members of a profession, whether or not they work on the same projects or in the same workplace, can be expected to have shared or collective beliefs or principles, as expressed, for example, in their profession's code of ethics.

Gilbert concentrates on a social group consisting of two people taking a walk together. Social groups that constitute plural subjects can be, and typically are, larger. In many kinds of joint activities of larger groups there can be complications that call for some modifications in her account. For Sue and Jack to be taking a walk together, a simultaneous and interdependent commitment is necessary. But, once a social group is initiated, others may later join. If a third person were to join in the walk, we might say that the plural subject is reconstituted by another simultaneous and interdependent commitment. Here we imagine all three parties consenting and committing in the presence of one another. However, an individual can be added to a plural subject without this being known immediately to the original members, as when someone is newly appointed to a committee or working group. So, we need an explanation of how a plural subject can change its constituency. Simultaneity of commitment may be impossible; but, in any case, it is not necessary. Interdependence of commitment must be sustainable even as the constituency of the plural subject changes.

This does not seem to pose a serious problem. Individuals, whether in on the ground floor or not, commit to an "us." This "us" need not be conceived as static and unchanging. New members of the social group are assumed to commit themselves to this "us" as others have before them. Gilbert's general account of mutual obligations and responsibilities remains unaffected. They are of "our" making, not "mine," regardless of when one's participation in a plural subject begins.

These ideas can be usefully applied to professional life. New professionals join ongoing professions, take on employment in well-established companies, and join others in projects already well under way. To a significant extent, this is true for all professionals, wherever they are in their careers. Thus, it is standard for experienced professionals either to join in establishing new plural subjects (for example, taking on new clients) or to become participants in ongoing plural subjects (for example, changing employment). In contrast to taking a walk together, the specific obligations and responsibilities of an individual professional can be expected to vary widely, depending on the overall objectives of the plural subject and the particular expertise the professional brings into the mix. One test of the professional's acceptance of his or her role as part of a plural subject is the extent to which problems are acknowledged as "ours" rather than simply "mine" and seen as entailing responsibilities that flow from that perspective.

Focusing too narrowly on the idea of taking a walk together may mislead us into thinking that the activities of a plural subject must involve joint activity that itself is simultaneous. If Jack walks too far ahead of Sue, this can give her cause for complaint; "I thought we were walking *together*," she might say. However, in a relay race members of the relay team take turns. In a walking race Jack could take the first leg and walk briskly to the station where Sue is waiting to receive the baton from him. Sue, in turn, walks briskly to Calvin's station. Calvin sets out with the baton but gets distracted by an intriguing path to the left, away from where Diane is anxiously waiting to start the final leg. Later Calvin explains that, although he knew the path to the left was off course, it looked more interesting to him. His departure from "the beaten path" has cost the team its chance to win the race, which, Sue, Jack, and Diane forcefully remind Calvin, was the main objective of their "walk together." Calvin allowed his personal interests to interfere with the team's objective.

However, it is important to realize that being a part of a plural subject need not rule out having personal goals that are not shared by the group. The shared goal ("our" goal) of a relay team in track is to win the race. Nevertheless, the individual runners may hope that, by being a part of the winning team, they will get a track scholarship to attend the college of their choice, with each having a different college in mind. In this instance, being part of a plural subject may actually enhance reaching the different personal goals of the teammates.

ENDURING LOVE

Establishing a plural subject does not ensure success for the resulting social group. In Ian McEwan's novel *Enduring Love*, five men rush to a large helium balloon that is being buffeted by heavy gusts of wind.[8] A child is crying in the basket as his grandfather futilely tries to bring the balloon under control. Only two of the men know each other. However, now they are joined in common cause. In their effort to keep the balloon aground, each takes hold of a rope attached to the balloon's basket. The balloon is brought under control long enough for the men to exchange shouts about what should be done next. Suddenly, a powerful gust of wind lifts the basket into the air, carrying all five men off with it, with the child still in the basket. All but one of the men drop to the ground just before the balloon has risen to a level from which letting go would be dangerous. One, however, continues to hang on, only to fall to his death a few moments later.

The story is narrated by a survivor of the failed rescue. He describes the lack of consensus among the five men about what they should do to get the balloon firmly under control, concluding that "any leader, any firm plan would have been preferable to none. No human society, from the hunter-gatherer to the postindustrial, has come to the attention of anthropologists that did not have its leaders and the led; and no emergency was ever dealt with effectively by democratic process."[9]

The narrator describes the chaotic scene. Despite their shared purpose, he says, the rescuers were never an effective team. There wasn't time for the necessary leadership to form. Had he emerged as leader, he says, there would have been no tragedy. But he notes that each of the others seems to have felt the same about himself. In the press of the moment no one was in charge; instead there was only a shouting match. Nevertheless, asked to explain what they were doing, we could imagine them saying, "We are trying to get this balloon under control." This was their joint aim — undertaken together, however much they failed in their efforts.

As the balloon ascended, it became apparent that the men were soon going to be at serious risk themselves. One let go and dropped to the ground. The narrator reflects:

> I didn't know, nor have I ever discovered, who let go first. I'm not prepared to accept that it was me. But everyone claims not to have been first. What is certain is that if we had not broken ranks, our collective weight would have brought the balloon to earth a quarter of the way down the slope as the gust subsided a few seconds later. But, as I've said, there was no team, there was no plan, no agreement to be broken. No failure. So can we accept that it was right, every man for himself?[10]

However, they could not rest easy with this conclusion, says the narrator, for in our nature is a deep covenant: "Cooperation — the basis of our earliest hunting successes, the force behind our evolving capacity for language, the glue of our social adhesion."[11] He adds:

> But letting go was in our nature too. Selfishness is also written on our hearts. This is our mammalian conflict: what to give to the others and what to keep for yourself. Treading that line, keeping the others in check and being kept in check by them, is what we call morality. Hanging a few feet above the Chilterns escarpment, our crew enacted morality's ancient, irresolvable dilemma: us, or me.[12]

In this case, the narrator concludes, "someone said *me*, and then there was nothing to be gained by saying *us*."[13] It might be thought that the narrator's view is that, in the end, it is always "me" over "us." However, he does not say this. Instead, he contrasts this extraordinary circumstance with how things are, for the most part:

> Mostly we are good when it makes sense. A good society is one that makes sense of being good. Suddenly, hanging there below the basket, we were a bad society, we were disintegrating. Suddenly the sensible choice was to look out for yourself. The child was not my child, and I was not going to die for it. The moment I glimpsed a body falling away — but whose? — and I felt the balloon lurch upward, the matter was settled; altruism had no place. Being good made no sense.[14]

But what about John Logan, a family man, a doctor, a mountain rescue worker? For him, says the narrator, "the flame of altruism must have burned a little stronger. . . . A delay of one second would have been enough to close his options."[15]

In more ordinary circumstances calling for cooperative action, the failure of one to come up to the mark does not necessarily render it senseless for others to stay the course. It may make it more difficult to succeed, or the results may be less satisfying than they would have been if everyone had cooperated fully. But all need not be lost. The defection of one need neither cause nor excuse a domino effect of nearly everyone else doing likewise.

Philosopher Martin Benjamin comments on the dramatic scene in McEwan's novel: "Each instinct — aiding and cooperating with others to benefit the group ('us') and looking out for oneself ('me') — is, as the narrator puts it, 'written on our hearts.' But how did these instincts come to be written there? And on what basis do we, in less pressing circumstances, reflectively decide between them?"[16] Benjamin attempts to answer both questions. However, I will pursue only the second here, ultimately with the aim of seeing what we might learn about cooperation in professional practice. No doubt professional life involves working cooperatively with others, but ordinarily in less pressing circumstances. Sometimes there is little time to reflect; even then, however, professionals and those with whom they work might prepare in advance for moments that call for quick action.

This is not something that McEwan's five would-be-rescuers could be expected to have had the opportunity to do. Basically, they were strangers to one another who, until that moment, had no occasion for acting together. Could we expect an effective emergency team to assemble on the spot and function well in the midst of a crisis unlike any they had faced before? Imagine a different scenario. Five members of a local firefighting team and their families are having a picnic in the vicinity of the runaway balloon. They rush to the balloon and one of them, accustomed to taking leadership on the job, quickly issues instructions for securing the balloon. Although they are off-duty, they retain team unity and operate much as they always do. The child is rescued; and because of their full cooperation with one another, everything is secured without serious risk to anyone.

In this second scenario, there is no need to suppose that anyone is struggling with a conflict between "me" and "us." It is all "us." Of course, this could have gone otherwise, too. Suppose one of the firefighters lacked enthusiasm for the rescue. After all, they were at a picnic, not on the job. While the others sprint to the balloon, he slowly saunters in that direction. By the time he arrives on the scene, a strong gust of wind has pushed the balloon into its fatal ascent. Four men are not enough to bring it under control. The question of "me" versus "us" rears its head again.

However, at this point we should ask another question: Just what is it that they are being asked to decide between? What is this "us," and how does it differ from "me"? If I am one of the firefighters, I regard myself as part of an "us." But what is this "us" — simply some sort of collection of individual "me's"? Gilbert's notion of a plural subject works against this sort of reductive analysis. Still, the example of taking a walk together lacks the sort of complexity that a cooperative and effective team requires. Regarding myself as part of "us" in such cases, I see myself as related to others in a way that cannot, morally at least, be reduced simply to a collection of individual "me's". This is what needs to be understood in order to grasp the nature of the conflict McEwan and Benjamin are suggesting.

McEwan's narrator says that they had neither time nor opportunity to form a real team. Let us consider a less dramatic example. On their way home, a grandfather and his grandson spin off the icy road. The little boy is frightened and unable to help. The grandfather is not strong enough to push the car back onto the road by himself. Five men stop to help. All but two come from different cars and do not know each other (or the grandfather and grandson). They begin pushing the car back onto the road. Wishing not to get splashed with mud, ice, and snow, four of the five stop pushing, without saying anything, leaving everything in the hands of the remaining person. He is pushing from the back of the car, and he cannot see that the others have stopped helping. Not only does he get splashed with mud, ice, and snow; he also strains his back.

Quite apart from the question of whether any of the five had an obligation to stop to help, they quickly formed a team. By joining in the effort to move the car back on the road, matters have changed. How? Each now has a basis for complaint if the others simply stop unannounced. They have become an "us." Not only have they joined together in a cooperative venture, they have created mutual expectations of one another. Four have let down one, with resulting harm.

McEwan's original example illustrates a natural pull toward "us" when others are in obvious need of help. This is also exhibited in the present example. In McEwan's case, collective confusion explains (and may excuse) the disaster that followed. In this case, there is no apparent confusion. Everyone knows what is required to push the car back onto the road; leadership and planning seem unnecessary. Each seems to have given initial indication to the others that he would join in the effort. In McEwan's example, four opt out in order to save their lives. In this example, four opt out, not to save their lives, but for a much less compelling reason. Creating such expectations seems to create obligations, obligations one is not warranted in silently ignoring.

This seems so even in cases in which someone's failing to do his or her part does not result in the collective effort failing to achieve its objectives. Perhaps, with additional effort, three are able to push the car back onto the road, while the fourth simply "goes through the motions" and does not contribute as others expected each other to do. Here they would seem to be entitled to complain about the unfairness of the "free-rider."

Now imagine a case of full cooperation, with a successful outcome. John comes home with mud and water dripping from his clothes. His family asks what happened. He replies, "I helped push a car back onto the road." Notice that he says he " helped." This indicates that he sees the situation as one in which he joined with others to push the car; they, not simply he, pushed it. It was "us," not "me." In fact, assuming that all five did fully participate, it would be difficult for John to describe just what *his* specific contribution was. Although he could describe how he positioned himself, and how hard he pushed, it was their joint effort that moved the car.

COMPROMISE

Given willingness to cooperate, a workable plan, and effective leadership, success may be attainable. However, as Benjamin points out, sometimes even within an otherwise cohesive social group conflicts arise that seem intractable. When these conflicts pose a barrier to accomplishing the aims of a social group, compromise may be sought.[17] Benjamin is especially interested in determining the extent to which compromise may be possible without compromising anyone's integrity. Insofar as it is, group cohesiveness and shared purpose can be sustained despite differences.

For Benjamin, moral pluralism is a guiding premise. There are, he says, good and important ethical values and principles that are inherently incompatible. These values and principles conflict "even when selfishness, prejudice, ignorance, bad reasoning, and so on have been overcome."[18] Reasonable people can disagree about the scope and relative importance of these values and principles in relation to one another in particular circumstances. Thus, says Benjamin, we can have reasonable pluralism. John Rawls says that this is a permanent feature of democracy.[19] Whether or not it is a permanent feature, it certainly is a present and persistent one. We seem far from being able to justify the claim that the only reasonably held positions are those that agree with our own. So, for practical purposes at least, accepting moral pluralism seems to make good sense.

This, for Benjamin, counsels a democratic temperament that combines commitment to one's own values with respecting those whose values are different, though possibly equally reasonable. Important as our particular set of values is to giving our lives meaning and identity-conferring structure, says Benjamin, we are also capable of adopting a more detached, impersonal perspective:

> From this standpoint we understand the sources of reasonable disagreement and acknowledge the fact of moral pluralism; there are, we can see, a number of occasionally conflicting, but nonetheless reasonable, worldviews and ways of life of which ours is only one. There are, moreover, no neutral criteria for determining that one reasonable worldview and way of life is in all respects superior to the others.[20]

So, says Benjamin, we are both agents (operating from our personal perspective) and spectators (looking at matters from a more detached perspective). "The trick — and part of being human — is being able to retain both standpoints while judiciously tacking between them."[21]

Those who share this democratic temperament, says Benjamin, are more attracted to sharing the power to shape and make decisions with those who have a stake in the outcome than to simply imposing their will. In his earlier work on compromise, Benjamin comments on the attitudes most conducive to success:

> As a rule, parties to this process try to see matters from the other's point of view, engage in various forms of give-and-take discussion, and are prepared, at least in principle, to make concessions for the sake of coming to terms. In so doing they acknowledge each other's viewpoints as having some claim to equal respect and consideration. In contrast to certain other forms of bargaining and negotiation, the emphasis is on rational persuasion, mutual trust, and reciprocal concession rather than on force, threat, or intimidation.[22]

Benjamin offers the following fictional illustration of what he has in mind.[23] Ann Chapman is an experienced critical-care staff nurse who is highly regarded by other members of the intensive care unit in a large medical center. However, she is at odds with most other members of the unit regarding the treatment of a patient who has suffered severe brain damage and has a very poor prognosis. Chapman believes that, because of the patient's poor prognosis, aggressive treatment should be reduced. She expresses concern about what she thinks the patient herself would want, the high cost of continuing aggressive treatment, and the benefits that could be extended to other patients if less time and effort were devoted to this patient.

Meanwhile, the aggressive treatment continues. However, after several days of treatment with no apparent improvement, several nurses shift to Chapman's position. Physician Susan Lehman, head of the unit, agrees to have another staff meeting to discuss the issue. Benjamin's characterization of Lehman is crucial here. She is "a fairminded person who generally does not settle such matters by appeals to authority, rank, or legalisms."[24] The case is marked by factual uncertainty and moral complexity. Lehman's willingness to arrange for another meeting to discuss the issues further shows respect for each member of the staff.

Eventually attaining some sort of consensus is conceivable in such cases. Initially holding opposing positions, staff members might reach agreement by changing some of their original beliefs. Already some staff members have changed their views. Here no compromise is needed, for they have come to fully accept the same position as Ann Chapman. However, sometimes the original positions do not yield even though a joint decision is needed. Here compromise may be an alternative. Concessions are made without a change in original beliefs. For example, one of the staff members might propose as a compromise the continuation of aggressive treatment for a specified period of time, checking to see if improvements are noted and reducing aggressive treatment if the patient's condition worsens or stays the same. Benjamin sees an additional benefit from this process even if the disagreeing parties continue to believe that their original views are still best: a reinforcement of a sense of community and mutual respect within the group.

Benjamin outlines the kinds of circumstances in which compromise may be possible. The "circumstances of compromise," he says, "are those conditions that provide both the motivation and the grounds for compromise."[25] He lists five: uncertainty; complexity; a continuing cooperative relationship; the need for joint decision; and limited resources. He uses the British Warnock Committee to illustrate what he means. The Warnock Committee was established in 1984 to address issues regarding embryo research. Uncertainty surrounded the moral status of the human embryo, raising difficult factual and metaphysical questions. Moral complexity was afforded by the values of respect for individual human lives and the utilitarian concern to sustain and enhance the lives of others. The committee members saw themselves as being involved in a continuing, cooperative relationship, with the expectation that one voice would emerge from their deliberations. In particular, it was expected that the committee would issue a policy recommendation on the permissibility or impermissibility of embryo research, and this recommendation could not wait on a final resolution of the moral, factual, and metaphysical uncertainties surrounding the status of the human embryo. Limited resources include both money and time that might be invested profitably in embryo research.

Now, says Benjamin, imagine yourself on the Warnock Committee, firmly committed to one or the other of opposite positions on the appropriateness of research on human embryos. Could you, nevertheless, seriously consider a compromise position? Benjamin's answer is yes, if you have a democratic temperament. You remain convinced that your position is the best one. However, you realize you are a member of a committee that consists of others who also think they have a reasonable basis for their views. Furthermore, as a member of the committee, you are committed to the task of coming up with a workable policy.

Your democratic temperament commits you to doing this in a way that respects the conflicting, reasonable positions and has a good chance of winning public acceptance as well. This democratic temperament is as much a feature of who you are as your personal stand on embryo research is. So, the task of compromising without loss of integrity has to take this into account, too. In short, says Benjamin, "your identity is constituted in part by a complex constellation of occasionally conflicting values and principles";[26] that is, the external conflict you experience with other people's values is also an internal conflict of your own values. It is not that you agree with their personal values, too; it is that your personal values regarding embryo research are partially in conflict with your respect for others — unless you can find a way to compromise. Benjamin concludes, "Endorsing the compromise position under such conditions is not to betray your integrity; it is rather to preserve it."[27]

What might work as an integrity-preserving compromise for an individual can be difficult to determine, and it will not be the same for each person. Benjamin says that compromise involves "mutual concessions for mutual gain."[28] It is one thing to compromise over the final price of an automobile or home; it is quite another to compromise over moral values. However, the final concession, "I can live with that," need not signify giving up one's original convictions. It is giving up the idea that, when it comes to policy, it must be "my way or no way." In cases of reasonable moral compromise, coming to this position is itself a moral accomplishment rather than a sacrifice of integrity.

UNCERTAINTY FROM THE START

Whether the process ultimately ends up with consensus or compromise, most of Benjamin's examples present the participants as beginning with rather firm positions on the issues under consideration. The participants move from an initial position of relative certainty to uncertainty and finally to resolution. However, it is also possible for participants to begin in relative uncertainty. In fact, Benjamin's fictional example of Nurse Chapman and Dr. Lehman might be seen as having such a beginning. Only later, after the issues have been rather thoroughly discussed do we see lines being drawn in the sand.

But joint exploration of issues from a standpoint of initial uncertainty can contribute to a clearer understanding of those issues and consequent agreement about what should be done. As we have seen, rules and principles of common morality are not embraced as absolute, exceptionless norms. They require intelligent application in particular circumstances. This, in turn, requires a solid grasp of relevant facts, an assessment of their relative importance, and, finally, good judgment. All five of Benjamin's "circumstances of compromise" can be present even when there is no need for compromise. Starting from uncertainty, it remains to be seen whether a final decision will require the resolution of serious conflict among the participants. Often it does not.

An advantage of having participants with a democratic temperament is that, in view of their own uncertainties and knowing that the final decision is a shared responsibility, they can be expected to be open to the ideas of others. Awareness of their own limited knowledge of the relevant facts, combined with the realization that the issues are likely to be quite complex, can encourage an initial atmosphere of modesty and cooperation rather than conflict.

DECIDING WITH OTHERS

Everyday social engagements illustrate the significance of starting points in group deliberation. Tom, Erica, Shannon, and Roger know they want to spend the evening together. However, they may not know how they want to spend the evening. All four like movies, but their tastes are not identical. Suppose Tom says, "Let's decide by secret ballot. We'll write down our first choices and see which one wins." However, Shannon objects: "If I were going by myself I might know what my first choice is. But we're going together, and I'd like to go to a movie that we'll all enjoy together." Is there a difference between enjoying a movie by yourself and enjoying it with others? It seems that sometimes enjoyment is different in the company of others — especially if the decision is made in light of that fact. Assuming that our foursome begins with this premise, it will see its task as deciding *together;* this is a matter of deciding what "we" want rather than an aggregate of what each "I," considered alone, wants. Carrying out this task is very different from trying to settle the matter by, first, counting up independent, individual preferences, and then, if necessary, resolving conflicting results.

Even if professionals perform much of their work by themselves, their work is seldom understandable independently of the cooperation of others. This can easily give rise to complications. Decisions may need to be made together, much as in the example of movie-going. But, even when final responsibility for making a decision lies in the hands of one person, other professionals may have crucial roles to play in processes that lead up to the making of the decision. They may be expected to provide crucial information, make suggestions, or even recommend a decision. The information one provides may be misused or ignored, one's suggestions may be misunderstood or snubbed, or a decision may be made that is contrary to one's recommendations. Still, the work goes on, and involved professionals must ask whether they handled their responsibilities well and what responsibilities now lie ahead for them.

I imagine myself as part of a research team whose task is to develop and implement a plan for improving one of our company's products. I am convinced that, had it been solely up to me, we would have followed a certain plan of action. However, a different plan was adopted, and now I am expected to play a role in its implementation. Should I now support the plan that I still regard as second- (or even third-) best? Normally, yes. Assuming I go along with it, how do I do this — with resignation, with firm support, or even with enthusiasm? There is no answer in the abstract, but there can be many possibilities. Although the decision to implement the plan was not mine, it is ours to carry out. The point here is that, in joint endeavors, what I should do next may not be entirely my call either.

GROUPTHINK

Groups that deliberately make room for integrity-preserving compromise have the virtue of encouraging open discussion of issues that require critical attention. However, groups with a common task often develop a cohesiveness that presents obstacles to the kind of critical thinking that is needed. Social psychologist Irving Janis's detailed study of groups characterized by high cohesiveness, solidarity, and loyalty reveals a tendency of such groups to become victims of their own "groupthink," the achievement of agreement at the expense of objective, critical thinking.[29]

The primary focus of Janis's work is a number of historical fiascos. He discovered that groupthink contributed to bad decision making by those responsible for security at Pearl Harbor before U.S. involvement in World War II. According to Janis, repeated warning signs that the Japanese would attack were ignored, resulting in the loss of an entire U.S. fleet and thousands of lives. Other misfortunes cited by Janis include the government's failure to realize that Communist China would retaliate after U.S. troops crossed the 38th parallel during the Korean War, the Kennedy administration's miscalculations concerning the invasion of the Cuban Bay of Pigs, and the Nixon administration's underestimation of the public outcry the Watergate affair would provoke.

An important feature of Janis's work is its observation that groupthink occurs in groups of all kinds — committees, boards, teams, work units, and so on. In the film *Group Dynamics: Groupthink,* Janis applied his theory of groupthink to a fictional case of a corporate decision to market a weight-reducing drug, Byrotonin.[30] The film portrays a board meeting to determine whether the drug is ready to be marketed.

The board president sets the stage for groupthink by making it clear that he thinks the drug is ready and by stressing the importance of group camaraderie and loyalty. He then asks for an update on some outside test reports that are not completely positive. However, rather than inviting one of the researchers to make a presentation, a board member blocks him from attending and offers to present a summary of the report himself. This illustrates a symptom of groupthink that Janis calls "mindguarding." Just as a bodyguard protects us from being harmed physically, a mindguard protects us from being exposed to disturbing ideas. The mindguard's presentation of the possibly troubling research reports illustrates another symptom of groupthink, "stereotyping." He says of the researcher, "His sentiments, as always, are basically conservative. Just the usual stuff about wanting to test more, and so on." This, says Janis, reinforces a group's "we-feeling" that stereotypes outside groups as adversaries or enemies.

Janis identifies six other symptoms of groupthink. An "illusion of invulnerability" runs through the entire board meeting. It underlies the group's willingness to take excessive risks regarding the safety of Byrotonin. Several instances of "rationalization" are noted, including statements that attempt to shift responsibility: "It's a strict prescription-only product. Any doctor who doesn't feel sure about it doesn't have to prescribe it."

The moral tone of rationalization contributes to an "illusion of morality," reflected in statements proclaiming the inherent morality of the group. By saying, for example, "We have built one of the finest reputations in the field by dealing squarely with the public," the group avoids serious discussion of the safety issues at stake and remains comfortable with the thought that the company has always "done the right thing."

In the Byrotonin example, no one seems to feel free enough to object: "Wait a minute. We're kidding ourselves. We may be about to make a terrible mistake." An irony of group psychology, says Janis, is that the freer the climate in the group seems to be, the greater tendency there is toward "self-censorship." Because they can speak out if they want to, members censor their own statements. Contributing to self-censorship is the "illusion of unanimity." Members do not express their doubts, even if they have them, because they assume that everyone else's silence implies consensus; and there is a reluctance to disrupt group unity. Finally, if a member does begin to express doubts, "direct pressure" is often applied to encourage conformity. When Harriet, one of the corporate attorneys, suggests that further testing might be a good idea, several board members object. The president quickly intervenes. But rather than asking Harriet to elaborate, he tries to bring the group back together by saying, "Let's try to stay together on this. I'm sure Harriet wasn't trying to upset the apple cart."

The concurrence-seeking tendency illustrated in the Byrotonin case is at the heart of groupthink. Janis explains that the group failed to explore clear indications that the drug might have problems:

> They didn't consider the possibility that they might be letting themselves in for some real trouble. This has happened in a number of instances in which drugs were marketed before they were adequately tested and has led to very serious consequences. So this is an example of how the failure to engage in critical thinking, as a result of this striving for concurrence, can lead to potential trouble. This doesn't always occur, but that potentiality is certainly there.[31]

Janis suggests some ways to promote critical thinking in groups. Primary responsibility falls on the group leader to provide an atmosphere conducive to critical thinking. Allowing adequate time for reflection and discussion is essential. The Byrotonin meeting was rushed. Either earlier meetings could have been arranged to discuss the testing problems, or the decision could have been postponed until the group had an opportunity to more thoroughly consider the issues raised.

A group leader can also encourage group members to accept a basic responsibility to serve as a critic. This requires adequate preparation for discussion, careful thought, good listening skills, and a willingness to share one's reflections with others. Responsible members who are not willing to support the group's recommendations should make their dissent known while the group is deliberating, not simply later. This role need not detract from group cohesiveness, as long as it is understood that serving as a critic is essential to promoting the group's ends. After the Bay of Pigs fiasco, Janis notes, President Kennedy explicitly assigned the role of critic to each of his cabinet members. He also called on outside critics. Finally, recognizing that the presence of the group leader might subtly suppress free, critical discussion, Kennedy sometimes deliberately stayed away from meetings about matters that called for independent, critical advice.

The hindsight of astute researchers such as Janis might suggest that groupthink phenomena are easy to detect. But this is not so. The fictional Byrotonin example was in many respects exaggerated in order to identify and illustrate the eight symptoms of groupthink Janis has identified. In this example, it is relatively easy to find explicit statements made by board members that match groupthink symptoms. However, groupthink can operate more subtly. For example, everyone might know about the troubling research data; but, suspecting that the president does not want to hear anything further about these concerns, members might decide not to mention them at all unless explicitly asked. Furthermore, groupthink need not be confined to a single boardroom meeting. It can pervade a work environment over extended periods of time.

One more problem associated with groupthink bears mentioning. Individuals in groups have a tendency not to accept responsibility for the decisions that emerge even though they may have participated in the process leading up to those decisions. "After all," a group member might say, "it wasn't *my* decision; it was the president's (or the group's). Even if I had opposed the decision, it wouldn't have changed anything — I'm only one person." However, as Janis's research shows, this excuse will not always work. Silence does not necessarily indicate consensus, and having the courage to speak up may encourage others to step forward as well. Furthermore, if everyone uses this excuse, the chances of important alternative considerations being aired will be greatly diminished. So, even if each of us is only one person, we can still bear some responsibility for bringing important considerations to the attention of other group members.

DISSENT

The Byrotonin case effectively illustrates the symptoms of groupthink and the dangers they pose. However, in a revised version of the original video portraying this case, the 1986 Challenger space shuttle disaster has replaced the Byrotonin story. This revised version simulates the deliberations that took place the night before the fatal launch. Prominent in these deliberations is Roger Boisjoly, then Morton Thiokol's chief O-ring engineer, who more than a year earlier had issued an internal memo specifying safety risks posed by the O-rings. Although Boisjoly is noted for his critical testimony before the Rogers Commission,[32] he is portrayed in the video as being silent when his fellow engineers seemed finally to have dropped their opposition to the launch. He had vigorously articulated his concerns and felt that he had done all he could to convince others to oppose the launch. However, the Marshall Space Agency's pressure on Morton Thiokol engineers and managers to approve the launch apparently was too much to resist. Although those at the Marshall Space Agency might have construed Boisjoly's eventual silence as evidence of consensus among the engineers at Morton Thiokol, it seems clear from his later testimony before the Rogers Commission that he never changed his mind about the inadvisability of the launch. So, important as Janis's suggestion that group members serve as critics may be, internal protest is not necessarily sufficient to overcome the challenge of groupthink.

Despite receiving awards from science and engineering societies for his courage in testifying before the Rogers Commission, Roger Boisjoly has suffered the fate of so many who have "blown the whistle" on others. His career as an engineer has effectively ended, and he has been shunned by members of his community. However, in recounting the course of his professional life, he conveys a positive message for engineers beginning their own careers. He recalls a lesson he learned near the beginning of his career. Noticing a problem with a project, it nevertheless took him several days to muster up enough courage to tell his superior about it. Rather than thanking him for bringing the problem to his attention, his superior severely criticized Boisjoly for taking so long to do so, pointing out that such delays can cost the company considerable money and time. Boisjoly said that from that point on he spoke up without delay when he saw problems, and this worked very well for him — right up to the night before the fatal launch of the Challenger space shuttle. Although he did not anticipate that following his early lesson would lead to his undoing as an engineer, he has no regrets for having done what, after all, was the right thing to do.[33]

There is no denying that whistleblowers commonly endure great loss and suffering for stepping forward. They may become targets of discriminatory treatment in their workplaces, be pressured to leave, lose friends, become pariahs in their communities, and find it difficult, if not impossible, to find comparable employment elsewhere. As in the case of Roger Boisjoly, whistleblowing can effectively end one's career in a given profession. It is no wonder most would prefer to avoid finding themselves in situations that might call for blowing the whistle on others; and it certainly would be desirable to find alternatives to whistleblowing that avoid its often sad consequences but which are equally, if not more, effective in addressing the problems at hand.[34] Given the unavailability of such alternatives in particular cases and the heavy costs whistleblowers are likely to bear, we may be tempted to excuse them from stepping forward. However, frequently overlooked is the fact that many who find themselves in such situations apparently would not excuse themselves.

CHAPTER NINE

Dispositions, Perception, and Imagination

RESPONSIBILITY AND DISPOSITIONS

Using engineering as an illustration, this chapter will explore the role that character, perception, and imagination can play in responsible professional practice.[1] Engineering ethics literature quite appropriately emphasizes the importance of ethical principles, rules of action, justification, and decision making in particular circumstances that call for good judgment. Should a vendor's offer of a free round of golf at an exclusive country club be accepted? Should shortcuts be taken in order to meet a deadline? Given expected low temperatures and evidence of O-ring erosion in cold temperatures, should a delay in launching the Challenger space shuttle be recommended? Engineers are counted on to employ their professionalism and expertise in exercising responsible judgment in such circumstances.

Discussions of ethics in engineering practice commonly focus on specific events, typically events that are newsworthy because of their unfortunate, if not tragic, consequences. They also tend to focus on questions about alleged wrongdoing and its avoidance or its prevention. Important as such discussions are, responsible practice involves more than this. Given the importance of responsible professional practice, it is perhaps surprising how little attention has been directed to this more positive side of ethics in the literature.

In shifting to the positive, this chapter will concentrate on the responsibilities of engineers to protect public safety, health, and welfare. These are by no means the only sorts of responsibilities engineers have, but I will focus primarily on them. My basic thesis is that fulfilling an engineer's responsibilities to protect public safety, health, and welfare calls as much for settled dispositions, or virtues, as it does for performing this or that specific action.

My reflections take their cue from William F. May's previously noted observation that it is particularly important for professional ethics to pay attention to moral character and virtue, as these dispositions shape professionals' approach to their work.[2] He observes that professionals typically work in institutional settings, often making it difficult to determine just where things have gone wrong and who should bear the responsibility. Also, professional expertise, particularly in large organizations, is not widely shared, even by fellow professionals. So, May concludes, we need professionals to have virtues that warrant their being trusted: "Few may be in a position to discredit [them]. The knowledge explosion is also an ignorance explosion; if knowledge is power, then ignorance is powerlessness." He adds, "One test of character and virtue is what a person does when no one else is watching. A society that rests on expertise needs more people who can pass that test."[3]

What counts as "passing" this test of character? Especially when bad consequences become apparent only after the passage of considerable time, it can be very difficult to discredit specific professionals. This suggests that, when no one is watching (which is much of the time), professionals may be able to get away with shoddy, if not deliberately wrongful, behavior. So, "passing" the test seems to require avoiding such behavior even when no one will notice. But this is essentially negative — the avoidance of behavior that would be to one's discredit if noticed by others. Although this is the dominant emphasis in literature on professional responsibility, we should also want to know what contributions professionals make to desirable outcomes when no one is looking. This can be equally difficult to notice and to assess. We typically take for granted the reliability of the work of engineers. For example, we assume that the elevator will work, that the bridge will bear the weight of traffic, that the building will not fall, and so on, even though we have little understanding of the work that is required to make this so — let alone the special engineering efforts that may have prevented failures or improved reliability.

When we shift our attention in this more positive direction, it quickly becomes apparent that what might count as responsible (as distinct from irresponsible) professional practice can vary widely. Furthermore, professional skills may be well developed or poorly developed, conscientiously employed or lackadaisically employed, and so on. Of course, we would prefer the services of conscientious professionals who have well-developed skills, good judgment, and the like. However, we may end up with a professional who is content to stay out of trouble and to exert the least effort necessary for "success"; and if May is right, we may not be in a good position to know just how marginal the services are. By the same token, we may not be in a good position to know just how competent and conscientious other professionals are.

Whether or not we are in a good position to determine these things, our well-being, both as individuals and as a society, is at stake. As we reflect on the extent to which our well-being is dependent on the performance of professionals whose expertise and organizational workplace we do not understand, we can see why it is not only moral dispositions such as honesty, fair-mindedness, and benevolence that are important to professional ethics; equally important are those dispositions that relate to professional competence. Professional ethics calls for a level of performance, not just good moral purpose and intention. Competence needs to be linked with commitment to ethical values that are basic in a given profession — for example, public safety, health, and welfare in engineering. But commitment, like competence, can range from the minimal to the exemplary. Unfortunately, by emphasizing wrongdoing and its avoidance, most of the engineering ethics literature slights the more positive end of the responsibility spectrum. Even if falling short of the exemplary does not warrant discredit or blame, our needs exceed what merely avoiding discredit or blame provides. What follows will expand May's concern about what professionals do when no one is watching to include the exemplary as well.

Although May intends his remarks to apply to all the professions, they are especially apt for engineers. Clearly, the public depends heavily on, but is not privy to, the expertise of engineers. Furthermore, from the public's perspective, the work of engineers is largely anonymous; few members of the public ever meet the engineers whose work they depend on. But even engineers who work in the same organization, or even on the same projects, may not be in a good position to check on each other's work. Insofar as engineers do not share one another's expertise, or do not have time to check up on each other, there is an important sense in which engineers are not being watched by each other either. In short, largely unwatched by those who depend on them, engineers are expected to conduct themselves responsibly. Hence the special pertinence of May's question: "What do professionals do when no one is watching?"

DEDICATION TO SAFETY

As a glance at engineering codes of ethics reveals, many of their most important provisions are stated in such a way that what might count as satisfying them is open to considerable interpretation. The National Society for Professional Engineers (NSPE) code of ethics, like most other engineering codes, identifies protecting public safety, health, and welfare as the engineer's paramount obligation. It is interesting to notice how little assistance the NSPE code provides in interpreting what this responsibility entails. The Preamble says that, because engineering work has a direct and vital impact on everyone's quality of life, engineers must be *dedicated to* the protection of the public health, safety, and welfare. The first of the Fundamental Canons says that engineers shall *hold paramount* the safety, health, and welfare of the public. Under Rules of Practice this same language is used. But just what does this come to? And what is implied by being dedicated to protecting the public?

As noted in chapter 6, at its best, a code of engineering ethics prescribes the highest *common* denominator for members of its society. This means that individual professionals may have higher aspirations than the code requires. Much is left to individual interpretation. For example, under the Rules of Practice, the NSPE code offers guidance for only two kinds of circumstances that have to do specifically with protecting public safety, health, and welfare: (1) an engineer should inform appropriate persons if his or her engineering judgment is overruled when the public is endangered; and (2) an engineer should approve only those engineering documents that protect the public safety, health, and welfare. Can this be all that the framers of the code had in mind in saying that the engineer's paramount responsibility is to protect public safety, health, and welfare? Clearly the answer is no. However, this may be all that can be identified in terms of specific courses of action that are required (and even "appropriate persons" is left open to interpretation). In any case, being dedicated to protecting the public and holding paramount public safety, health, and welfare seem to be more enduring requirements; they refer to dispositions engineers are expected to have. They mark a readiness to take safety, health, and welfare into appropriate account. Sometimes we can see this exemplified in particular actions. But there does not seem to be any way to prescribe a certain set of required courses of action.

THE IMPORTANCE OF DISPOSITIONS

What I hope to show is that an engineer's dispositions can contribute to protecting the public in ways that no list of required courses of action can specify. Here there are no algorithms. Despite this, we should be able to list a number of dispositions that, by framing an engineer's approach to his or her work, can importantly contribute to protecting public safety, health, and welfare.

Several years ago, my colleague James Jaksa and I undertook a project to develop educational materials that illustrate responsible, if not exemplary, engineering practice.[4] We sought stories from engineers and their managers. To give them some idea of what we were interested in, we first asked them what characteristics they would look for if they were trying to hire a highly responsible engineer. Then we asked them if they could provide illustrations of engineers who exemplified these characteristics in their engineering practice. Although hardly a scientific survey, a list of commonly mentioned dispositions emerged. Many items on the list seem to have an inherent connection with ethics and would be expected to appear in one form or another on virtually anyone's list of virtues. For example:

- integrity
- honesty (even candor)
- civic-mindedness
- courage (to speak up, to "stick to one's guns")
- willingness to make self-sacrifice (including willingness to assume some personal risk)
- not being too personally ambitious

Virtues such as these are quite generic, not only in regard to the professions, but in regard to ordinary, nonprofessional life as well. How they might manifest themselves in engineering practice requires special attention to the working environment of engineers.

As attention shifts to the context of engineering practice, other items show up on the list. However, these items are less obviously connected with ethics, and several can readily be associated with undesirable behavior as well:

- competence
- ability to communicate clearly and informatively
- cooperativeness (being a good "team player")
- willingness to compromise
- perseverance
- habit of documenting work thoroughly and clearly
- commitment to objectivity
- openness to correction (admitting mistakes, acknowledging oversight)
- commitment to quality
- being imaginative
- seeing the "big picture" as well as the details of smaller domains

As with the first group of virtues, when listed abstractly they are not engineering-specific. To understand how they might manifest themselves in the lives of engineers, they must be seen in the context of engineering practice. However, it is conceivable that an engineer could have all of the dispositions in this second group and still be dedicated to any number of morally reprehensible engineering projects.

This may suggest to some that items in this second group of dispositions should not be included in an account of the virtues of responsible engineers. Admittedly, *having* these dispositions is not sufficient for responsible engineering practice. However, *lacking* them detracts from responsible engineering practice in general and exemplary practice in particular. Furthermore, having these dispositions is a fundamental part of what we admire in those engineers who are likely to be identified as morally commendable. It is fundamental because, without these dispositions, in addition to the more obvious virtues of honesty, justice, and benevolence (to take three traditional moral virtues), there is little reason to expect even competent engineering practice. In short, having the virtues of honesty, justice, and benevolence does not qualify one as a competent engineer. In fact, many who have these virtues might correctly conclude that they should not try to become engineers — they might be better suited for other kinds of work.

Given their fundamental role in responsible engineering practice, it is no accident that this second group of dispositions shows up on the list of characteristics engineers and their managers would look for if they were trying to hire a highly responsible engineer. What still needs to be explained, however, is the specific fit these dispositions might have in engineering practice. Simply listing a set of desirable dispositions, or virtues, does not tell us how they might play themselves out in responsible engineering practice. A good place to begin is with examples that show concretely that the presence or absence of some of these dispositions can have an important impact on ethical values in engineering.

AN ILLUSTRATION

Engineer William LeMessurier designed the structural frame of Manhattan's Citicorp Center, built in 1977.[5] In 1978 he discovered a structural problem that, because of the building's unusual features, rendered the building vulnerable to storms that could come along as frequently as every sixteen years (as distinct from the hundred-year storm vulnerability for which he thought he had designed the structure). He knew how to correct the problem, but only at the cost of millions of dollars and at the risk of his career if he were to tell others about the problem. Nevertheless, he promptly notified lawyers, insurers, the chief architect of the building, and Citicorp executives. Corrections were made, all parties were cooperative, and LeMessurier's career was not adversely affected.

In response to Joe Morgenstern's *New Yorker* article recounting the Citicorp story, LeMessurier received phone calls and letters of praise from engineers around the country acknowledging that they, too, had faced similar challenges. Some asked whether, faced with a similar situation, "Would I be this good?" This is an interesting question, since once he discovered the problem, it seems clear that LeMessurier had a duty to take some sort of action; this was not an instance of going "above and beyond the call of duty." In fact, this is explicitly acknowledged by LeMessurier himself. After mentioning LeMessurier's brief consideration of two unacceptable options (keeping silent or committing suicide), Morgenstern writes:

> What seized him an instant later was entirely convincing, because it was so unexpected — an almost giddy sense of power. "I had information that nobody else in the world had," LeMessurier recalls. "I had power in my hands to effect extraordinary events that only I could initiate. I mean, sixteen years to failure — that was very simple, very clearcut. I almost said, 'Thank you, dear Lord, for making this problem so sharply defined that there's no choice to make.'"[6]

That is, although it would still take courage to take constructive steps to protect public safety, there was no ambiguity or unclarity about having this duty in these circumstances. However, to focus primarily on this moment is to miss an important dimension of the story. This moment of truth for LeMessurier was of a piece with what led him to the discovery in the first place. But when we look at that trail of discovery, it is somewhat less clear what his responsibilities were.

When he first learned that Citicorp braces had bolted rather than welded joints, apparently LeMessurier had no special reason to be concerned. Morgenstern says:

> The choice of bolted joints was technically sound and professionally correct. Even the failure of his associates to flag him on the design change was justifiable; had every decision on the site in Manhattan waited for approval from Cambridge, the building would never have been finished. Most important, modern skyscrapers are so strong that catastrophic collapse is not considered a realistic prospect; when engineers seek to limit a building's sway [the purpose of having welded joints], they do so for the tenants' comfort.[7]

Instead, what initially aroused LeMessurier's interest was a phone call from an engineering student whose professor told him that the building was poorly designed (with supporting pillars being at the center of each side rather than at the four corners). He explained to the student that his design could handle quartering winds more effectively than more standard structures, and he referred him to a technical article on the matter written by one of his engineering partners. Next he decided to share technical aspects of his design with students in one of his own classes. It was determined, he told his class, that the building would be vulnerable only to one-hundred-year storms, well beyond the minimally acceptable requirements.

As already noted, even after learning that the joints were bolted rather than welded, LeMessurier remained confident that the building would still more than satisfy the New York building code, which required wind resistance tests only at a 90-degree angle. However, Morgenstern comments, "in the spirit of intellectual play, he wanted to see if they were just as strong in winds hitting from 45 degrees." It is this that ultimately led LeMessurier to his shocking conclusion that the building was much less safe than he had thought.

What I would like to suggest is that this "intellectual play," this exercise of engineering imagination, displays LeMessurier's abiding concern for public safety. However confident he may have been that his calculations would show that the building was as safe as he initially thought, without a firm commitment to safety it is not clear why he would have been interested in undertaking the calculations. Further evidence of this commitment is LeMessurier's persistence in working out the calculations to their disturbing conclusion.

We could imagine different scenarios. He could have simply dismissed the student's challenge. Confident that everything was according to code, LeMessurier might have decided he had other things to do with his time. Instead, he seemed to take particular pride in trying to show the student that the building was first-rate in every respect, but especially in regard to safety. Confident that the structure was in compliance with code, other engineers might well have simply turned their attention to other matters. Even in the remote chance that something bad would happen to the structure, how could they be faulted for this?

It seems plausible to say that what LeMessurier did from the moment he learned that bolted rather than welded joints were used expressed his character and imagination as an engineer. Despite his self-confidence (or perhaps even because of it), LeMessurier is the sort of engineer who is prepared to acknowledge mistakes and take necessary action, even at his own expense. Getting it right, we might say, is more important than preserving his reputation — particularly when public safety is at stake. Aiding him in this is his very active engineering imagination. As an illustration of LeMessurier's imagination at work, Morgenstern points out that the building's wind braces were "first sketched out, in a burst of almost ecstatic invention, on a napkin in a Greek restaurant in Cambridge: forty-eight braces, in six tiers of eight, arrayed like giant chevrons behind the building's curtain of aluminum and glass."[8] In some respects, we could say William LeMessurier was just doing his job. However, I think this understates matters a great deal. Engineers like LeMessurier exemplify what it means to *dedicate* oneself fully to the protection of public safety, health, and welfare.

However, in response to a talk I once gave on the Citicorp story, a member of the audience posed the following challenge. Why, he asked, should LeMessurier be lauded for his handling of the Citicorp problem? After all, once he discovered the problem, it was, as he himself acknowledges, his duty to report it to the appropriate authorities. In response, although acting on his duty may not be "going above and beyond the call of duty," a reason for lauding LeMessurier is that it did take a fair amount of courage to do this. Admittedly, failure to report the problem would have been blameworthy, but doing what is right under such challenging circumstances can nevertheless merit praise. In addition, how LeMessurier handled this duty also seems to warrant praise. He not only reported the existence of the problem, he also proposed a solution; and his ability to do so, especially in such circumstances, reflects his character and imagination as an engineer. There can be, we might say, better and worse ways of fulfilling one's duty; and LeMessurier's was exemplary.

Wasn't LeMessurier lucky that the student called him and that he learned about the bolted joints? Yes, but it is precisely his character and imagination that accounts for his making something of these crucial moments. Many engineers would not have capitalized on these events in the way he did. They could not fairly be faulted for this. But LeMessurier can be praised for his perceptiveness, persistence, and imagination — and his unqualified commitment to safety and quality. Engineers like LeMessurier seem to be somehow prepared to be lucky.[9] That is, because of their skills and commitment, they are prepared to pick up cues and run with them, to notice what others fail to notice, and so on.

In the end, ethical values appropriate to a profession must be joined with professional commitment, competence, and imagination in order to provide a complete picture of the virtues in professional life. It is important for professionals to be prepared to be lucky. This requires a blending of moral dispositions and professional expertise; and this is not primarily a matter of making this or that momentous, ethical decision. It is a way of (professional) life.

ON BEING PREPARED TO BE LUCKY

Although the importance of combining ethical principles and guidelines with engineering expertise is implicit in engineering codes of ethics, the codes give little attention to details. Instead, the fundamental principles and rules of practice largely consist of lists of "do not's" (for example, not divulging confidential information, not allowing one's judgment to be affected by conflicts of interest, not misrepresenting findings, and so on). However, in a more positive vein, it should be noted that, guided by ethical principles, the exercise of technical expertise is not simply technical; it is infused with positive values in ways that can significantly affect what is noticed (or perceived), how what is noticed is taken into account, and what alternatives are given serious consideration. At the same time, developing and maintaining expertise is essential for fulfilling responsibilities to one's employer, as well as to the public.

To illustrate this last point, consider W. Gale Cutler's fictional case study, "When 'Johnny' Won't Read," which recounts the failed effort of two young engineers to develop a more efficient heat transfer surface.[10] Their manager is angered at learning that neither engineer had consulted the company's filed report of a nearly identical failed effort by another team just five years earlier. In fact, neither had consulted any current technical literature for related publications. This seems to the manager to fall well below an acceptable threshold for responsible engineering research. Apparently the manager holds the view that engineers have a responsibility to try to avoid repeating mistakes, particularly when contraindications are so readily available.

Did the two engineers fail to meet their responsibilities as professionals and employees? This question addresses issues of competence and professional development. The code of ethics of the Institute for Electrical and Electronics Engineers (IEEE) addresses these concerns more explicitly than most engineering society codes. Two provisions (numbers 5 and 6) are particularly relevant here. Committing themselves to "the highest ethical and professional conduct," IEEE members also agree:

To improve the understanding of technology, its appropriate application, and potential consequences

To maintain and improve our technical competence and to undertake technological tasks for others only if qualified by training or experience, or after full disclosure of pertinent limitations[11]

Arguably, failing to consult current technical literature, or even the company's recent history in this area, falls below an acceptable threshold of responsibility. This could be regarded as a failure of professional duty or obligation.

However, in many cases it is not so clear whether one is simply fulfilling a duty in acquiring information that will prevent bad things from happening. Responsible practice can be exemplary ("above and beyond the call of duty") as well.[12] A celebrated example from the world of science is that of Dr. Fran Kelsey. In the early 1960s, despite severe criticism of her refusal and considerable pressure to change her mind, FDA official Dr. Kelsey refused to approve the marketing of Thalidomide as a sleeping pill in the United States.[13] She had read an article indicating that the pill failed to put many of the test animals to sleep, and she had read a letter in a British medical journal that reported that patients taking Thalidomide for a long time experienced tingling nerve inflammation in the fingers. And then in 1962 it was discovered that Thalidomide was responsible for thousands of physically deformed children in Europe.

Unlike the two engineers in "When 'Johnny' Won't Read," Fran Kelsey did consult literature relevant to the area of research under her purview. Should she have been faulted if she had not noticed the article about test animals failing to fall asleep or the letter in the British journal about tingling inflammation in the fingers? Or, if reading the article and letter had not raised her concerns, should she have been faulted? Given the extreme pressure she was under to approve the drug, this is unlikely. Nevertheless, her active search for reports on the drug's performance, even in other countries, and the salience of certain things she read resulted in preventing a major tragedy in the United States. It might be argued that the combination of running across the relevant literature, reading it, and worrying about its possible implications for Thalidomide was as much a matter of luck as evidence of her competence. But, even if Fran Kelsey was somewhat lucky, this is only because she was prepared to be lucky.[14] It was for her thoroughness, persistence, perceptiveness, and courage — not simply her (or the public's) good luck — that she was awarded a presidential medal of honor by President Kennedy.

The importance of noticing and following up on cues is equally evident in engineering. The 1978 collapse of the Hartford Civic Center roof is the story of a costly engineering disaster that, fortunately, did not result in injury or loss of life. Eugene Ferguson explains what happened, and what might have prevented the collapse:

> The roof failed under a moderate snow load because some of the long compression members buckled and brought the rest of the truss down in domino fashion. The programmer apparently had not expected those long members to be subjected to anything but pure compression. The possibility that a partial roof collapse might cause one or more members to buckle and thus nullify most of the assumptions made by the programmer either was not considered or was judged to be too remote to warrant inserting the several hundred stiffening braces necessary to arrest the domino action of an unbraced truss. Now this is a small decision in the scheme of things, although it will no doubt be a big consideration in the design of future space trusses. If somebody involved in the Hartford design had seen or had been able to visualize some of the buckling accidents that have occurred since the 1907 collapse of a railroad bridge under construction at Quebec City, stiffening stays or braces might have been added. In any case, assumptions and matters of judgment will always be present in engineering design, whatever the format of the design.[15]

It is noteworthy that Ferguson avoids the language of blame in this account. His fundamental point is that it is crucial for engineers to be prepared to examine assumptions, look for trouble, and imagine alternatives and to exercise good judgment — all the while realizing that crucial items may go unnoticed or underappreciated.

The Hartford design problem was not unique. In fact, in principle, a seventy-year history could have been written. Access to only a small part of that history might have been sufficient. However, it may not have been as readily available as the company's history of failure in W. Gale Cutler's fictional example. So, a much more interesting story of how someone involved in the Hartford design might have come to see the problem would have to be told.

Such a story might well have involved an engineer, or group of engineers, with professional qualities as commendable as Fran Kelsey's. However, it is unlikely that this story would have been widely circulated, for it would lack the drama of the Thalidomide story. In the case of Thalidomide, disaster was prevented in the United States but not in Europe; and the disaster in Europe is what initially attracted the media's attention. We have little idea of the number of accidents that have not occurred because of the timely dedication, perception, and imagination of engineers. Stories of accidents that never happen because of the efforts of engineers are seldom told.

As in the case of Fran Kelsey, one might ask to what extent LeMessurier's discovery of Citicorp's structural problems was a matter of luck. After all, the discovery was triggered by two fortuitous events: a phone call from a student who, at his professor's prodding, questioned the structural integrity of the building; and LeMessurier's discovery that, contrary to his specifications, Citicorp's structural joints were bolted together rather than welded. Can luck have a significant role to play in engineering ethics? One might think not. Ethics has to do with right and wrong, good and evil, praise and blame, virtues and vices, and the like. Certainly these notions have a place in engineering ethics. Luck, however, seems to be more a matter of chance than anything for which one can appropriately be credited or praised, discredited or blamed; it is, we might say, a matter of good or bad fortune. Nevertheless, it is important to explore ways in which luck can be intimately related to character and imagination, both of which are fundamental in ethics. In short, being lucky in engineering practice in the way LeMessurier was seems, like the case of Fran Kelsey, to depend on his being prepared to be lucky. In such cases, unlike winning a lottery, luck can be understood only against the background of the settled dispositions and imagination of engineers.

The particular twists and turns of LeMessurier's investigations indicate that his engineering imagination, or as he puts it, his "intellectual play," has special connections with his sense of professional responsibility. They reveal his abiding concern for public safety, his curiosity, his persistence, and his willingness to take the chance of discovering that his work was flawed. Had the student's call not prompted him to reexamine his structural design, perhaps LeMessurier would not have engaged in this particular "intellectual play." If so, then, indeed, the student's call was a piece of luck. And, had the question of the cost of welds not come up in Pittsburgh, there would not have been an occasion for recalculating. This, too, was a piece of luck. But had LeMessurier not responded in the ways he did, neither the phone call nor the question would have been matters of luck; they would simply have been unremarkable, and ignored, events.

So, the key point seems to be this: In order for such events to have counted as lucky, as distinct from simply uneventful, something had to be made of them. But this, it seems, was very much a function of special qualities of character and imagination possessed by William LeMessurier. He seems to be disposed to see things differently than most engineers. Like scientist Fran Kelsey, engineers like LeMessurier seem to be prepared to notice what others fail to notice, and to respond imaginatively and responsibly.

Such scientists and engineers occupy the high end of responsible practice. They are exemplars for others, and it is important that their stories be told and understood. Of course, insofar as these are stories of bad things that did not happen, there may be some difficulty in gaining access to them. LeMessurier's story itself could easily have gone untold. In fact, it was told only after seventeen years had passed since the drama was played out.

Even less likely to be told are stories of preventive actions taken by conscientious and imaginative engineers before a problem develops. LeMessurier discovered a problem after the structure was completed, and he faced a series of dramatic challenges. Had he been fortunate enough to learn during the construction phase that switching from welds to bolts was under consideration, he might have made his calculations earlier and spared everyone the excitement and expense that eventuated. But this story would not have attracted writer Joe Morgenstern's attention. In fact, it might have seemed rather routine for LeMessurier himself. "Luckily," he might have thought, "I found out about this before it was too late." That would have been the end of the matter.

MORAL PERCEPTION

Lawrence Blum has taken moral philosophy to task for focusing its attention on moral principles, justification, and decision making to the exclusion of what he calls "moral perception."[16] Although perception plays an essential role in decision making, it typically precedes the judgments we make when deciding what we should do.[17] Blum asks: "How do agents come to perceive situations in the way that they do? How does a situation come to have a particular character for a particular moral agent?"[18] To explain what he has in mind, it will be helpful first to look at a fictional everyday example he provides.

John and Joan are both seated on a subway with no empty seats and some people standing. One of the standing passengers is holding two relatively full shopping bags. Blum comments on John's and Joan's perspectives: "John is not particularly paying attention to the woman, but he is cognizant of her. Joan, by contrast, is distinctly aware that the woman is uncomfortable."[19] The main contrast, Blum goes on to say, is what is salient for John and Joan in this situation. What is salient for Joan is the woman's discomfort. Even if John is vaguely aware of her discomfort, this is not salient for him.

There are many possible explanations of the perceptual differences between John and Joan in this particular case. John may be preoccupied with worries about the workday ahead of him, the illness of his daughter, and so on. Joan may have noticed the woman struggling with the packages as she boarded the subway, whereas John noticed her only after she settled into her current position. However, Blum continues, if this is how John typically perceives others in such situations, this suggests that he often fails to see vital aspects of the moral world in which he resides. This does not necessarily mean that John is callous or uncaring. When someone's discomfort is brought to his attention, he may respond as sympathetically as we might imagine Joan does. The connection between perception and decision making here is this. For Joan, and perhaps for John, if the woman's discomfort is brought to his attention, the perception of her circumstance provides a reason for action, a reason that is grounded in her discomfort. Joan may be more readily disposed than John to fully notice and respond sympathetically to the visible discomfort of others.

In contrast to both Joan and John is Ted. Ted may be fully aware of the woman's discomfort but remain indifferent to her circumstance. If this is characteristic of Ted, his shortcoming is that he does not care enough about others to act in their behalf even when their discomfort is quite transparent to him. John's shortcoming is that he does not see with sufficient salience the discomfort of others; and it is this that accounts for his inaction.

Sometimes our failure to take sufficient note of the circumstances of others is because, bearing no special responsibility for creating or controlling those circumstances, we may be preoccupied with other matters. Perhaps the woman's discomfort was not salient for John because it was not of his making, even though he was in a position to offer some relief. However, it is clear that we often are responsible for putting others at risk of discomfort, or even harm. Recently, for example, we were visited by an elderly friend. When she arrived, I stepped out the front door to greet her, only to see her struggling to get past the tangled garden hose draped across our narrow walkway. Prior to her arrival, had I simply asked myself whether our walkway was clear, I would have known the hose was there even without looking. So, in one sense, I knew everything I needed to know in order to prevent a possible accident. Nevertheless, I failed to prepare properly for her arrival. Fortunately, no accident occurred. (I can only hope that this illustrates an occasional lapse rather than a character trait!)

At least with occasional prodding, it is relatively easy to avoid putting others at such risk in the first place. Better yet is developing habits that minimize risk and inconvenience to others. Putting tools, garden hoses, and the like out of harm's way rather than letting them lie about when not in use is one example. Slowing down in play areas for children and stopping at stop signs even when it looks like no one is around is another.

However, even good character and good habits cannot guarantee good consequences. Normally sensitive and compassionate, Joan's frustration at being late for work might interfere with fully appreciating the discomfort of fellow passengers. Preoccupied with finishing an exciting novel, I might neglect to clear the sidewalk for a visitor. Aside from occasional lapses, sometimes there are problems that could not have reasonably been anticipated. Driving down a two-lane road after dark, your headlights suddenly reveal a young skateboarder moving in the opposite direction; she is swerving back and forth, coming dangerously close to crossing the center line. Whether we become aware of such problems in time to handle them well may be, to some extent, a matter of luck. Nevertheless, given all the ways in which things can go badly, it is desirable that we prepare ourselves to notice and respond appropriately to both the expected and the unexpected.

PERCEPTION IN ENGINEERING

Keeping one's sidewalk clear and maintaining good driving habits are ways of caring about others even when they are not in view — something engineers need to bear in mind, for they typically do not directly encounter those most affected by the bridges, elevators, and microwaves they design, build, and maintain. Furthermore, engineers are employed in specialized work that creates risks that only they may be in a good position to perceive in advance — and only if they are adequately prepared and properly disposed to do so. Thus, what is salient in the perceptions of engineers is crucial to what they do; and this is a function of the basic dispositions and skills they bring to their work. But the perceptual dynamics are likely to be quite different than in the examples discussed so far. In Blum's example, the woman is in the presence of John, Joan, and Ted — quite literally "before their eyes." No special expertise is required in order to respond sympathetically to her discomfort. In engineering, expertise plays a special role both in detecting and in resolving the problems at hand.

Blum's questions about agents in general could be reformulated for engineers (or professionals in general): "How do engineers come to perceive situations in the way that they do? How does a situation come to have a particular character for a particular engineer?" The answer to both questions is the same. How engineers come to perceive situations in the way that they do and how those situations come to have a particular character for them is a function of their engineering experience and the dispositions they bring with them into those situations.

In engineering, as in everything else, even the most well-intentioned plans can go awry. For example, when shoulder safety belts were introduced in automobiles, they were automatically operative, whereas passengers had to manually engage the accompanying lap belts. Most consumers were unaware that failure to engage their lap belts placed them at higher risk of serious injury or death than having no seat belt at all. It seems that engineers did not take this sufficiently into account. Feeling the shoulder belt across their bodies frequently lulled drivers into thinking they had also engaged their lap belts. In fact, I frequently found this happening to me; and I was among those unaware of the increased risk. When I learned about the higher risk from an engineer, I asked how consumers standardly were informed about it. I was told that warnings are supposed to be placed on visors on the driver's side. Never having noticed this warning in the several years I had driven my car, I was surprised to find it on the backside of my seldom-used visor! No doubt, on those few occasions that I might previously have moved the visor, I was concentrating more on the glaring sun and the road in front of me than on the warning patch on the back of my visor. Of course, it could be argued that I bore responsibility for my own ignorance, as the warning was there; and it is likely that there was also a similar warning somewhere in my owner's manual. However, even had I known about the higher risk, I might still occasionally have been lulled into thinking my lap belt was engaged. The rather simple engineering solution was to attach the shoulder and lap belts in such a way that they engage together, manually. Sacrificing the automatic feature of the shoulder belt was rather insignificant compared to the resulting benefit.

This is a case of a safety innovation that, contrary to expectations, actually had the opposite effect for many. Here is another, a recent traffic light problem in the United States. Instead of having the light turn green as soon as the crossing light is red, traffic lights at many intersections now delay the onset of the green light until the crossing traffic has had a red light for a few moments. Some drivers have adjusted in the following way: When approaching an intersection, they estimate that they will still be able to pass through it even if the yellow light has been on for some time — or even a few moments after their light has turned red. This means that crossing traffic cannot be confident that it is safe to proceed when their light turns green. In fact, now it is much more likely that cars will go through red lights. (I've counted clusters of as many as six cars passing through a red light at an intersection I travel through each day.) This also causes problems for those waiting to turn left once the oncoming traffic has stopped. One needs to proceed cautiously even if there is a green left turn arrow. It is even worse at intersections that do not have left turn arrows. Typically the first car in line edges up so that at least it will be able to complete a left turn before crossing traffic can proceed. Uncertainty about whether oncoming traffic will stop when their light turns yellow, or at least once it is red, makes this a hazardous practice. Furthermore, if the car turning left has moved far enough into the turning area that it must complete the turn, crossing traffic may have to delay their start even longer.

Had traffic light programmers anticipated how drivers would respond to the changes, perhaps they would have left things as they were until other alternatives occurred to them. Unfortunately, better alternatives often come to mind only when one sees the shortcomings of decisions already made. However, examples like this are a reminder that professionals need to prepare themselves for unexpected and unfortunate consequences by readying themselves to make needed adjustments when necessary. A highly publicized instance is the response of Johnson & Johnson in 1982 when three people died from cyanide planted in their Extra-Strength Tylenol capsules.[20] Not only did Johnson & Johnson immediately recall its product, it promptly repackaged it in tamper-proof containers; in short, its packaging experts were well prepared to respond to the crisis quickly in a way that restored consumer confidence and enabled Johnson & Johnson to regain its standing in a highly competitive market.

CONCLUDING THOUGHTS

In the end, professional ethics must address questions about ethical principles, rules of practice, justification, good judgment, and decision making. However, as this chapter illustrates, it must also address questions about character, perception, and imagination. When it does, it becomes clear that what is required is the integration of ethical values and professional expertise, such that, in the midst of professional practice, the perceptions, imaginings and, finally, judgments of professionals reflect their blending in responsible practice. There are times when it is important for professionals to pause reflectively and ask whether what they are contemplating doing is ethically justifiable. As a subject of study, professional ethics needs to examine ways in which such questions might best be answered. However, equally important are the dispositions and values reflected in the very ways professionals come to perceive problems and possibilities in the first place. Professional ethics needs to pose for professionals the questions Lawrence Blum poses for all of us: "How do agents come to perceive situations in the way that they do? How does a situation come to have a particular character for a particular moral agent?"

CHAPTER TEN

Moral Development

ON BECOMING A RESPONSIBLE PROFESSIONAL

This book has concentrated mainly on factors that contribute to the responsible practice of those who are either already professionals or soon will be. However, the brief discussion in chapter 3 of how a child's understanding of the moral importance of truthfulness might come into play as he or she becomes a professional suggests that a more complete account of what is needed to become a responsible professional should begin in childhood. After all, professionals once were children; and today's children will become tomorrow's professionals. So, we can ask: What, if anything, can be done to help children eventually become responsible professionals? Of course, not all children will become professionals; and, in any case, all of them will certainly become more than professionals. Nevertheless, we live in a highly professionalized society, and we all have a vested interest in professionals being responsible. Even if we are not engineers, architects, scientists, doctors, nurses, lawyers, bankers, accountants, journalists, or professional educators (and no one of us can be all of these), whether we like it or not we all depend on a vast array of professionals for our well-being.

Standard educational preparation for entering a profession emphasizes the knowledge and skills that are necessary for competent performance. This preparation may or may not include an explicit focus on ethics, either for that particular profession or more generally. Clearly competence is a fundamental feature of responsible practice. However, responsible practice requires competence *and* good intentions. Without both we will have something less than a trustworthy, or fully reliable, professional. Furthermore, as pointed out by William F. May, a trustworthy professional must have both the ability and the commitment to exercise good judgment even when others are not in a good position to assess it.

The origins of trustworthiness (and its opposite) precede explicit training for a profession. Insofar as the trustworthiness of professionals depends on, say, basic skills in math, writing, and communication, these earlier origins are obvious enough. Engineers and accountants, for example, begin developing their math skills long before entering their professional programs. The same is true of writing and other communication skills for all the professions. The importance of these skills is, of course, not exhausted by their contribution to the professions; but they are essential for professional competence, and there is no point in denying that this is part of the rationale for including math, writing, and communication in the schools.

Why not stress moral education, too? Just as an introduction to the math, writing, and communication skills professionals will need has an early start in the schools, the moral education of those who will become professionals can also be supported in the schools.[1] Of course, the moral education of those who will become professionals will not end there, as there is much to be learned about the specific sorts of moral challenges posed by particular professions that will come only later. Likewise, math, writing, and communication skills will be shaped and refined in ways appropriate for particular professions. The point is that education for a specific profession must build on whatever earlier foundations have been laid, including moral foundations.

MORAL EDUCATION

We can think of the moral education of children as having two basic purposes. One is to help children develop their moral capacities *as children*. Rather than think of children simply as future adults, it is important to respect them during that part of their lives that we refer to as childhood. Children are, in their own right, moral agents. The other basic purpose is to help children develop those moral capacities they will need *as adults*. These two purposes parallel those we have for the education of children in general. History, mathematics, science, the languages, literature, art, and health education should aim to enrich the lives of children while they are children, as well as to prepare them for their future lives as adults. Both purposes are important and surely connected; however, here the focus will be on only the second: How might the moral education of children help prepare them to become morally responsible professionals?

Schools across the country are developing "character education" programs. This is the most recent version of the push for moral education in the schools, whose predecessors include "values clarification" programs and the "moral dilemmas" approach of Lawrence Kohlberg and his followers. Not in dispute is the fact that for years the vast majority of American adults have long favored some sort of moral education in the schools. In dispute is just what form this should take. At opposite ends of this dispute are models of firm indoctrination, on the one hand, and extreme pluralistic relativism and toleration of differences, on the other hand. Both extremes strike fear and apprehension into the hearts of large numbers of people.

Character education advocates respond to such worries by maintaining that there are some basic virtues that are essential for responsible citizenship in a democratic society and that it is the business of schools to help students appreciate their importance. Presumably, they would also agree that these same virtues are indispensable for responsible professionals. Their view is that, whatever deep moral and religious differences there may be among us, there is also widespread consensus that there is a set of virtues that cuts across these differences. The Character Counts movement, for example, promotes "the six pillars of character": trustworthiness, respect, responsibility, fairness, caring, and citizenship.[2] Other programs have similar lists.

Broadly cast as these lists are, none of them explicitly endorses the virtue of reasonableness, discussed briefly in the Introduction.[3] It may be replied that, properly interpreted, the listed virtues embrace reasonableness (just as, for example, trustworthiness, respect, fairness, and caring embrace honesty as a virtue). However, reasonableness is best seen as a central virtue that can have a moderating influence on other virtues, such as honesty, trustworthiness, fairness, or compassion.

The push for character education in the schools is not new. In the nineteenth century and at least the first half of the twentieth century, it was standardly accepted that this was one of the basic responsibilities of the schools. How these responsibilities might best be fulfilled was then, as it is now, a matter of some controversy. Nevertheless, John Dewey provided advice a century ago that is as valid today as it was then. A strong advocate of character education, Dewey described character in terms of habits. Rejecting the idea that morality is "a set of rules to be applied like drugstore prescriptions or cook-book recipes," Dewey emphasized that moral habits essentially involve reflection, imagination, and good judgment.[4]

For Dewey, developing effective methods of moral inquiry is central to the entire educational endeavor, whether we are talking about history, literature, science, or any other school subject, including morals. Some character education advocates might favor special times being set aside in the school day for moral instruction. However, rather than seeing morality as simply another school subject, we might see it as an aspect, or dimension, of every subject. Thus, the study of history could include reflecting on the moral dimensions of history — of our Constitution, laws, slavery, the treatment of Native Americans, the treatment of women, wars, and so on. The study of literature could include explicit attention to, and critical reflection on, moral themes running through poetry, novels, and short stories. The study of science could include the moral dimensions of engaging in scientific practice, including research and its applications in society.[5]

Dewey is right in insisting that the schools have a responsibility to help children develop such methods of inquiry, even at the elementary school level. Acknowledging this requires respecting children as moral inquirers from the outset. By the time they enter school most children are already rather sophisticated moral inquirers, with strong ideas about what is fair and unfair, kind and cruel, honest and dishonest, and so on. But these ideas need to be much further developed, refined, and applied to contexts they have yet to encounter.

THE KOHLBERGIAN APPROACH

For many, home and church are thought to be the most appropriate sites for moral education; and some may be wary of efforts on the part of the public schools to enter this arena. It is not necessary to resolve these issues here. Regardless of the locus or likely content of the moral education of children, the story of moral development does not end in childhood. One of the strengths of the work of developmental psychologist Lawrence Kohlberg is its realization that moral development is not just about children. Although Kohlberg's theory of moral development is vulnerable to serious criticism, some of his central claims are well worth revisiting in the context of professional ethics.[6]

Kohlbergian accounts of moral development and courses in practical ethics presume that careful reflection can, and should, make a difference to one's ethical perspective.[7] While this reflective process by no means excludes feelings, it cannot be reduced to feelings alone. One of the distinctive marks of Kohlberg's account is its commitment to their being such a thing as moral reasoning and to moral judgment having undeniably cognitive features.[8] Following Jean Piaget's pioneering work in developmental psychology, Kohlberg outlines successive stages of moral development.[9] Each of the six stages of development he describes has cognitive features that cannot plausibly be understood simply as emotive states.

Kohlberg divides his six stages into three levels, each of which contains two stages.[10] The first level is preconventional, with a predominantly self-interested orientation. Stage 1 is marked by a fear of punishment or loss of love and the hope of reward. Stage 2 is often characterized as a back-scratching stage ("You scratch my back and I'll scratch yours"). We realize that some minimal forms of cooperation are necessary in order to get what we want from others. None of us can be wholly self-sufficient. But assistance from others typically comes only if we are willing to reciprocate. So we find that we (usually) need to keep agreements, do our part, and the like.

According to Kohlberg, these two stages are characteristic of children up to about age nine, but they also can play a strong role in adolescence, and even in adulthood.[11] These two stages are highly egocentric.[12] A major challenge for young children is coming to understand that the perspectives of others may be quite different from their own. This may seem intentionally self-serving (egoistic), but it need not be. For example, a young child may offer a present to an older sibling without realizing that the older sibling no longer takes an interest in such things.[13]

In any case, as young children begin to develop some understanding of the different perspectives of others, they can advance to Kohlberg's second level of moral thinking, the conventional level. Stage 3 (the "good boy, good girl" stage) marks a social breakthrough. The child is no longer completely egocentric, making it possible to enter into fuller social relationships of friendship and loyalty, for example. At this stage there is a strong desire for social approval, requiring one to be sensitive to the expectations of others in order to know how to win their acceptance and approval.

Although stage 3 moral reasoning moves beyond the egocentric limitations of stages 1 and 2, it has its own limitations. According to Kohlberg, stage 3 reasoning is not well equipped to deal with situations requiring mediation between two or more individuals whose interests or desires are in conflict. Stage 4 reasoning, characterized as the "law and order" stage, can help mediate such conflicts by appealing to widely accepted rules or laws.

However, reasoning at Kohlberg's second level, whether at stage 3 or 4, remains conventional rather than critical. Both stages are characterized as heteronomous, in that they are marked by pressure to accept uncritically the commonly accepted expectations, standards, or rules of others. Stage 3 "peer pressure" may come in the form of explicit social approval or disapproval. Stage 4 is marked by respect for various types of authority — institutional, governmental, or religious.

To say that one's thinking or behavior is conventional, or conforming, is not necessarily to say that there is anything wrong with it. For example, clothing styles are conventional but typically harmless from a moral point of view. Professional life itself is filled with conventions, most of which, it is hoped, are morally acceptable and some of which are morally desirable, if not necessary. But the moral acceptability of conventions is dependent on what those conventions happen to be; and it cannot be assumed that everything that is conventionally accepted is morally acceptable.

So, the key question for Kohlberg is what is required of us if we are not to settle uncritically for whatever conventions happen to prevail at the moment. He postulates a third level of moral development, a postconventional level. This level is marked by critical reflection on the types of moral reasoning used in the earlier stages. Kohlberg is convinced that this critical perspective ultimately leads one autonomously to base moral judgments on considerations of universal human rights and respect for human dignity, rather than simply self-interest, concern for friends or loved ones, or regard for some particular social or political structure. Stages 5 and 6 are characterized as self-reflective, exhibiting greater independence of mind than the earlier stages, and embracing a more comprehensive and impartial point of view.

Unfortunately, according to Kohlberg, a disturbingly high percentage (80 percent) of even the adult population never gets beyond the conventional stages. This may be largely due to the specific philosophical demands of stages 5 and 6, which require embracing leading elements, first, of social contractarian and utilitarian ethical theories (stage 5) and, finally, of the moral philosophy of Immanuel Kant (stage 6). That is, these two stages are characterized in terms of the acceptance of comprehensive, single-principle ethical theories. Ordinary moral agents seldom, if ever, employ such principles in their moral reasoning. Whether this implies some inadequacy in their moral reasoning is another matter; it is not clear that it does.

Critics complain that the Kohlbergian approach underestimates the role of affect (for example, feeling, emotion, and caring) in moral development, that it overestimates the role of principles of justice, that its stage theory is mistaken in this or that respect, or that its claims to universality are exaggerated. Regardless of how well Kohlbergians might be able to answer these critics, their work seems amply to show that the view that morality is just a matter of how you or I happen to feel about things is mistaken.

An important feature of Kohlberg's work is its explicit acknowledgment that a theory of moral development is not merely descriptive; it is normative. That is, "development" is not to be equated with "change." For Kohlberg, this means that each succeeding moral stage is in important respects a moral improvement over its predecessors. Again, Kohlberg's particular way of putting this is contentious. Yet, a normatively "neutral" account of moral change is simply that — a theory of change rather than development. For Kohlberg this seems to mean that one needs to turn to philosophy for guidance in framing the normative features of moral change. Kohlberg's particular way of doing this makes his theory of development too dependent on utilitarian and Kantian outlooks, and on attempting to resolve the tensions between them.

However, what can easily be lost in this controversy is a more basic distinction central to Kohlberg's thought. James Rest, Muriel Bebeau, Darcia Narvaez, and Stephen Thoma claim that, even if Kohlberg cannot plausibly argue that Kantian thought is developmentally more advanced morally than its philosophical competitors, it is important not to lose sight of the difference between conventional and postconventional moral thinking.[14] Utilitarian, Kantian, social contractarian, as well as a variety of more pluralistic views, they believe, all seem clearly to belong in the postconventional, or critical, domain of morality.

Rest, Bebeau, Narvaez, and Thoma suggest that we loosen up Kohlberg's stage theory in ways that sidestep the major philosophical controversies. It can be conceded that morality is not analyzable into six distinct, invariably sequential stages, that moral reasoning and judgment are only a part of morality, that affect is also important, that morality involves more than justice, and that there is no need to plump for just one central, overarching principle. What should not be given up, they hold, is that there are three importantly different moral schemas, which they label (1) personal interest; (2) maintaining norms; and (3) postconventional.

MORAL SCHEMAS AND PROFESSIONAL ETHICS

We can try to apply these schemas to the subject of professional ethics. The first schema, personal interest, captures much of Kohlberg's first two stages, dominated as they are by self-centered concerns. Although personal interest perspectives certainly enter into the professional domain, it is not clear how they can contribute to a satisfactory professional ethics. This is because the professions are committed to serve others. This by no means requires self-denial, but the basic professional responsibilities are to employers, clients, the public, and fellow professionals. Furthermore, those who enter a profession are joining an already-established practice with principles, rules, and standards not of one's own making. So, the maintaining norms and postconventional schemas can be expected to be highly relevant; and it is to them that I will now turn.

The maintaining norms schema is basically Kohlberg's stage 4. In this schema there is a heavy reliance on established practices, particularly those that help organize and regulate social structures. There is conventionality in another sense: one accepts the norms of these practices without question and as authoritative. Although highly heteronomous, those who operate predominantly within this schema can have a rather sophisticated understanding of societal needs. According to Rest et al. this includes:

- Recognition of the need for norms in order to have a society-wide system of cooperation that provides stability, predictability, safety, and coordination.
- Recognition of the need for rules that apply across society, including strangers as well as friends and acquaintances.

- Recognition of the need for uniform application of rules.
- Recognition of the importance of reciprocity — compliance with rules, with the expectation that others will do likewise.
- A duty orientation in which authorities are afforded unchallenged powers, a view that equates the moral justification of rules with being prescribed by law or the sheer weight of being the established "way of doing things."

The postconventional schema shares the first four features of the maintaining norms schema. However, the duty orientation around unchallenged authorities, laws, and "ways of doing things" is replaced by several other considerations:

- Acceptance of the primacy of criteria for moral evaluation: laws, roles, codes, contracts, and relationships can be set up in a variety of ways; and they must be evaluated, not merely accepted.
- Appeals to positive, sharable ideals: these ideals may be satisfied to varying degrees by existing practices.
- Acceptance of full reciprocity: there is a realization that particular laws, rules, and practices may be biased, favoring some unfairly over others.

From these comparative lists it can be seen that the postconventional schema has a critical dimension absent in the maintaining norms, or conventional, schema.

From the standpoint of professional ethics, it should be evident that the post-conventional schema is preferable to the maintaining norms schema. Both schemas acknowledge the importance of rules, standards, and shared practices. However, those within the postconventional schema accept an additional burden — namely, that of exercising critical, moral judgment. The absence of this critical feature in professionals would be unfortunate in at least two respects. First, it cannot be assumed that existing laws, rules, standards, and practices cover all areas in which professional judgment is needed — or that established norms treat these areas of concern adequately even when they are addressed. This is especially unlikely in areas marked by rapid technological change (for example, medicine and the computer professions). In short, it is exceedingly difficult for established norms and practices to anticipate and provide reliable, specific directives in addressing new problems.

Second, even in relatively stable areas, discretionary judgment is necessary. For example, those who attempt to rely on a professional code of ethics as an algorithm for deciding what to do are likely to be extremely disappointed. Even highly prescriptive codes are rather loosely stated. Although they might contain provisions about conflicts of interest, fidelity to clients or employers, confidentiality, proprietary information, informed consent, or conflicts of interest, none of these terms is defined with sufficient clarity or precision to make professional judgment unnecessary; and novel cases that challenge precedent are always possible.

Fortunately, according to the research of Rest and his associates, a much higher proportion of the adult population operates within the postconventional schema than Kohlberg's original theory suggested. Kohlberg repeatedly emphasized how few adults ever move into his stages 5 and 6 (no more than 20 percent). This may be, in part, because of the narrowness of the criteria he used (namely, the requirement that one's reasoning reflect one or more of Kohlberg's favored comprehensive philosophical theories of morality). In any case, Rest and his associates have much more flexible criteria; and, separable as these criteria are from commitment to utilitarian, Kantian, or some other comprehensive, single principle moral theory, they seem to do much greater justice to the critical capacity of professionals in particular and ordinary moral agents in general.

FROM THEORY TO PRACTICE: PROBLEMS IN APPLYING THE SCHEMAS

While there are, in principle, important differences between the maintaining norms and postconventional schemas, we might nevertheless ask what this comes to in practice. This is because, in particular circumstances, the reasons for judgments in the maintaining order schema may be able to hold their own in the postconventional schema as well. We should expect this, since the postconventional schema embraces rather than repudiates much of the maintaining order schema.

This is illustrated in, for example, the teaching of U.S. history and government. Much of the content of this teaching is about long-standing social and political conventions. At the same time, it seems that, at least in principle, there is much in the teaching of history and government in the schools that reinforces students adopting a postconventional schema. For example, U.S. history books discuss the American Revolution, the Civil War and slavery, child labor laws, and women's acquisition of the right to vote. In fact, the U.S. Constitution can be understood both as providing a basis for our federal government and as a critical tool for evaluating existing laws, practices, and institutions.

Robert Fullinwider observes that learning moral conventions *itself* involves acquiring critical tools for evaluating conventions and practices: "*Criticism and convention go together.* The power and force of social criticism generally reside precisely in its imaginative application and extension of well-known precepts or paradigm cases or familiar critical practices."[15] Fullinwider's observation may be more obviously applicable in democratic societies that have a robust tradition of social and political criticism and whose history is one of critical (and not merely violent) struggle; but the United States does not stand alone as such a society.

This raises the question of whether, especially in a democratic society, the learning of conventions is so distinct from critical evaluation that we can in particular cases reliably determine whether it is a conventional or a postconventional schema that is operative. Conceptually we can make a distinction between an uncritical attitude toward norms and a critical attitude toward norms. But developmentally it seems that coming to recognize the importance of norms might, at least in democratic societies, go hand in hand with the acquisition of certain critical thinking skills. And even when some particular norms are uncritically accepted, it seems that we have the capacity to stand back and critically evaluate them, even if we do not choose to do so.[16]

IMPLICATIONS FOR PROFESSIONAL ETHICS

The practical difficulty of distinguishing clearly between conventional and postconventional schemas is especially serious in professional ethics, since those entering the professions are entering a domain of practice whose norms and expectations are typically rather well established. Many of these norms and expectations are enshrined in professional codes of ethics, which themselves typically are the product of the joint deliberation of leading members of the profession and which have been adopted by the profession as a whole. Those who join a given profession are expected to commit themselves to the provisions of its code of ethics.

Thus, professional ethics embraces norms that are "conventional" within the practice of the profession in question. Still, what is accepted as right is not necessarily actually right. As noted in chapter 6, professional codes of ethics are not static documents. But even if a code is relatively unchanging, it is not simply an algorithm for decision making. It must be interpreted and applied — which calls for independent judgment on the part of the professional. Professionals must deal with unprecedented circumstances. Reform of existing rules and practices is sometimes needed. So, the responsible professional needs to retain some degree of autonomy and capacity to critically evaluate ongoing practices.

At the same time, professional ethics is not an ethics for each individual professional simply to conjure up. Ethics in a given profession applies to a specific group of persons, its members, and each profession has a history that those entering the profession are expected to assimilate and take seriously. Appealing to this history and relying on a profession's code of ethics for guidance might well be classified as conventional thinking. Yet, some deference to this history and its conventions is made with good reason — but it need not be mindless or "conformist" in any way that detracts from the moral maturity of the professional. In fact, insofar as membership in such a profession is voluntary, it could be said that acceptance of the code is also voluntary — and, in that sense, autonomously undertaken. And as a moral commitment it should inform the moral stance of the professional. So, it is "conventional" in a way that does not easily fit the maintaining norms schema.

When a professional appeals to provisions in the profession's code of ethics as a basis for making a decision, is this a maintaining norms posture or something else? We cannot tell unless we also have insight into the professional's general moral stance. Did the professional exercise critical judgment in (a) deciding to commit to the code and (b) agreeing to respect it even when perhaps disagreeing with parts of it? If so, then we seem to have a combination of critical thinking and professional integrity (sticking to one's commitments).

Additional connections between critical thinking and conventional professional practice can be seen when we notice the extent to which particular cases calling for moral judgment are appropriately discussed in terms of "thick" concepts of a particular profession rather than abstract principles of the sort Kohlberg called on in his original characterization of stages 5 and 6. Bebeau and Thoma point out that the ethical problems in professional life are more frequently cast at what they call an "intermediate level" of theoretical analysis than at the more general and abstract level of theory Kohlberg invokes at his postconventional level.[17] Thus, problems related to confidentiality, informed consent, safety, loyalty, reliability, conflicts of interest, and the like are typically the main subjects of analysis rather than utilitarianism, Kantianism, or some large-scale, abstract theory of morality.

These more context-bound concepts are likely to be featured in professional codes of ethics, but without sufficient explanation. (Hence, Bebeau and Thoma characterize the codes as being at a more concrete level than "intermediate" concepts.) However, it is these concepts that point us in the direction of the particular kinds of responsibilities professionals have. This may all sound rather conventional, but that should not be taken to imply simple deference to authority or the "way things are done." Those who frame the codes for a given profession help establish the "conventions," but they are not necessarily using only conventional forms of reasoning when they do this — nor are members of a profession when they commit themselves to and appeal to the code.

It is interesting to note that Bebeau and Thoma acknowledge that it is unclear just how the three neo-Kohlbergian schemas relate to either intermediate level concepts or professional codes of ethics: "We do not know whether or not intermediate concepts, the second level of representation, follow a general developmental sequence, nor do we make the claim that the most concrete level (knowledge about professional codes) follows a developmental sequence."[18] Nevertheless, they suggest that the adequacy of code-driven prescriptions be evaluated in terms of their "coherence with the more general intermediate concepts and principles."[19] Intermediate concepts and principles themselves can, they say, be evaluated in terms of their coherence with more general principles of justice or utility, which presumably are featured in the postconventional schema. Thus, Bebeau and Thoma seem to think that, in the end, full justification requires wrestling with the sorts of principles Kohlberg invokes in his two highest stages.

However, this invites a return to the philosophical disputes that critics of Kohlberg have long raised. Why, they may ask, do we need to check on the "coherence" of analyses at the "intermediate" level with abstract principles of justice or utility? This is, of course, a philosophical position one might wish to defend. But, as philosophers such as Bernard Gert, James Wallace, William Whewell, and Thomas Reid might well respond, "intermediate" concepts and principles can hold their own without necessary reliance on "higher," or more general, principles. An advantage of the initial characterization of the postconventional schema by Rest et al. is its abandonment of Kohlberg's dependence on these "higher," or more general, principles.

There seems to be little reason to doubt that even relatively young children are capable of postconventional thinking about "intermediate" concepts and principles about such things as sharing, being fair, promising, and lying without having to invoke "higher," more general, principles of justice or utility. The same should be true for students in professional programs, as Bebeau and Thoma say of dentistry.

Rest et al. indicate that, judged by their three-level neo-Kohlbergian schemas, a much higher percentage of adults engage in postconventional moral thinking. Paying closer attention to how students can critically reflect on "intermediate" level concepts and principles without necessarily relating them to "higher," more general, principles should confirm this. The fact that determining the lines between conventional and postconventional thinking at this level is difficult does not diminish the importance of trying to promote the latter. Evidence of earlier and more abundant examples of postconventional thinking in children should encourage those who teach courses in professional ethics to proceed on the assumption that their students are quite capable of such thinking in the context of the professions for which they are preparing.

It may be tempting to think that, unless we are probing for the ultimate foundations of morality, we are not really engaging in postconventional, or critical, thinking. However, as we have already noted, philosopher Henry Sidgwick went to great pains in his *Practical Ethics* to show that this is not so.[20] Eschewing efforts to "get to the bottom of things," Sidgwick advised his late-nineteenth-century Ethical Society of Cambridge (which had a diverse professional composition) to concentrate on clarifying and refining the common ground they shared so that they might make genuine progress in addressing and resolving the moral challenges of the day. The history of philosophical and theological efforts to "get to the bottom of things," he thought, is a history of endless controversy — despite the fact that there is widespread agreement on "middle axioms" supported by common sense.[21] Our task is to use our shared morality somehow to navigate through differences in our complicated everyday world, as well as through those junctures where our more "foundational" differences threaten to block the possibility of reasonable compromise.[22] This difficult process cannot fairly be described within the maintaining norms schema; seeking to clarify and refine shared standards and use them in resolving moral problems may require a great deal of careful, critical thinking.

Kohlberg's theory of moral development concentrates on moral reasoning. It assumes that if we can determine how people reason their way through moral dilemmas, this will provide us with reliable insight into how moral reasoning proceeds in situations that do not present us with dilemmas. James Rest's Defining Issues Test seems to be based on the same assumption. However, this assumption can be questioned. Moral reasoning is employed in rather straightforward, easy to resolve cases, difficult but resolvable cases, cases filled with ambiguities and uncertainties (about the facts, future consequences, and the like), otherwise intractable cases that are amenable to acceptable compromise resolutions among the disputants, and genuine dilemmas. The critical thinking tasks for these different kinds of cases are likely to be quite varied — including, for example, the careful collection and organization of relevant facts while guarding against bias and hasty judgment, uncovering hidden assumptions, clarifying key concepts, carefully comparing and contrasting the current case with previous ones, dealing effectively and fairly with disagreement, and attempting to prioritize conflicting values.

However, as Rest is careful to point out, moral development involves more than the development of moral judgment and reasoning. Kohlberg's account slights three other essential components of moral development: moral sensitivity, motivation, and character. Interestingly, these additional components also play an important role in the development of moral judgment and reasoning. All of this calls for the exercise of critical thinking skills that can be employed in moral reflection. Such skills are best thought of as dispositions which, when well developed, are features of one's moral character. Insofar as such dispositions are essential for the responsible conduct of professionals, it is appropriate to emphasize their importance in the moral education of children, many of whom will end up being tomorrow's professionals and all of whom will find themselves depending heavily on the services they provide. However, as I have tried to indicate throughout this book, reflection on these dispositions should be an important part of the continuing education of adults as well as of children.

CONCLUDING THOUGHTS

The Hastings Center goals for teaching ethics in higher education are essentially forward-looking. For those entering the professions, they are an invitation to reflect on the sorts of ethical challenges that lie ahead in the hope that this will better prepare them to deal with them when they actually arise. This book has been written with these goals in mind. Much of the literature of professional ethics is backward-looking, seeking ways of explaining what has gone wrong and who is to blame. Of course, this is an important task for those who would look forward in the hope that such mistakes will not be repeated. It has been a task of this book to show that professional responsibility is not simply a matter of avoiding or preventing wrongdoing. It also involves "rightdoing," a concept that serves as a useful complement to wrongdoing in providing us with a more comprehensive picture of what professional responsibility can involve. As with wrongdoing, if we are concerned about rightdoing we can focus on specific activities or matters of character; and they can be considered together in relation to each other.

In the end, professional ethics must address questions about ethical principles, rules of practice, justification, good judgment, and decision making. However, as we have seen, it must also address questions about character, perception, and imagination. When it does, it becomes clear that what is required is the integration of ethical values and professional expertise, such that, in the midst of professional practice, the perceptions, imaginings and, finally, judgments of professionals reflect their blending in responsible practice. There are times when it is important for professionals to pause reflectively and ask whether what they are contemplating doing is ethically justifiable. As a subject of study, professional ethics needs to examine ways in which such questions might best be answered. However, equally important are the dispositions and values reflected in the very ways professionals come to perceive problems and possibilities in the first place. Professional ethics needs to pose for professionals the questions Lawrence Blum poses for all of us: "How do agents come to perceive situations in the way that they do? How does a situation come to have a particular character *for* a particular moral agent?" Furthermore, it needs to take seriously William F. May's question: "What do professionals do when no one is watching?" — for, as we have noted, usually no one is.

Notes

CHAPTER 1: INTRODUCTION

1 Henry Sidgwick, *Practical Ethics,* ed. Sissela Bok (New York: Oxford University Press, 1998), p. 5.

2 This particular strip appeared in the *Kalamazoo Gazette* and other newspapers on September 1, 1975.

3 It is also commonly referred to as "applied ethics." I choose to avoid this expression, as it suggests a controversial relationship between theory and practice, namely, that ethical theory has priority. "Practical ethics" leaves open the question of what, if anything, takes priority.

4 See, e.g., Thomas Reid, *Practical Ethics,* ed. Knud Haakonssen (Princeton, NJ: Princeton University Press, 1990); William Whewell, *Elements of Morality,* vols. I and II, 4th ed. (London: Cambridge University Press, 1864); Sidgwick, *Practical Ethics.*

5 For examples, see Daniel Callahan and Sissela Bok, eds., *Ethics Teaching in Higher Education* (New York: Plenum, 1980), as well as the many monographs in specific areas of the curriculum.

6 For a good discussion of these goals, see Daniel Callahan, "Goals in the Teaching of Ethics," in Callahan and Bok, eds., *Ethics Teaching in Higher Education,* pp. 61–74.

7 William F. May, "Professional Virtue and Self-Regulation," in *Ethical Issues in Professional Life,* ed. Joan Callahan (New York: Oxford University Press, 1988), p. 408.

8 Michael Bayles, *Professional Ethics,* 2nd ed. (Belmont, CA: Wadsworth, 1989), chap. 1, "Problems of Professions."

9 Ibid., p. 8.

10 The issues raised in this paragraph are the subject of chapter 2.

11 Like most current writers in ethics, I am making no substantive distinction between the words "moral" and "ethical."

12 Michael S. Pritchard, *Reasonable Children* (Lawrence: University Press of Kansas, 1996).

13 Lawrence Splitter and Ann Margaret Sharp, *Teaching Better Thinking: The Classroom Community of Inquiry* (Melbourne: Australian Center for Educational Research, 1995), p. 6.

14 W. H. Sibley, "The Rational and the Reasonable," *Philosophical Review* 62 (1953): 557. In light of common morality's apparent plurality of rules and principles, perhaps Sibley's last sentence needs some qualification. But the basic thrust of his position remains unaffected.

15 Max Black, "Reasonableness," in *Education and the Development of Reason,* ed. R. F. Dearden, P. H. Hirst, and R. S. Peters (London: Routledge and Kegan Paul, 1972), p. 202.

16 Albert Jonsen and Stephen Toulmin, *The Abuse of Casuistry* (Berkeley: University of California Press, 1988).

17 The following discussion of Sidgwick draws from my "Sidgwick's *Practical Ethics,*" in *International Journal of Applied Philosophy* 12, no. 2 (1998): 147–151.

18 Henry Sidgwick, *The Methods of Ethics,* 7th ed. (London: Macmillan, 1963). The 1st edition was published in 1874; the 6th and 7th editions were published after Sidgwick's death in 1900. Utilitarianism is popularly characterized as advocating pursuit of "the greatest good for the greatest number" as its first principle. However, as Sidgwick's own detailed analysis indicates, just how this principle should be interpreted is a matter of some subtlety and controversy.

19 Sidgwick, *Practical Ethics,* p. 35.

20 Ibid., p. 6.

21 Ibid., p. 5.

22 Sidgwick, *Methods of Ethics,* pp. 473–474.

23 Sidgwick, *Practical Ethics,* p. 32.

24 Ibid., p. 33.

25 Ibid.

26 Ibid., p. 35.

27 Thomas Reid, *On the Active Powers of the Mind in Philosophical Works,* vol. II, with notes by Sir William Hamilton (Hildesheim: Georg Olms Verlagsbuchhandlung, 1997), p. 594.

28 Ibid., p. 643.

29 Ibid.

30 Ibid., p. 642.

31 Thomas Reid, *Practical Ethics,* ed. Knud Haakonssen (Princeton, NJ: Princeton University Press, 1990), p. 110.

32 Ibid.

33 See Alan Donagan's "Sidgwick and Whewellian Intuitionism," in *Essays on Henry Sidgwick,* ed. Bart Schultz (New York: Cambridge University Press, 1992), pp. 123–142, for a vigorous defense of Whewell. Donagan argues that Sidgwick vastly underestimated the subtlety of Whewell's casuistry. He also argues that Sidgwick's reasoned explanation of his decision to resign his academic position at Trinity College in Cambridge seems not to be utilitarian.

34 This is likely closely related to his strikingly different views of philosophy of science from those who use physics as their primary model of a science. Interestingly, there is renewed interest today in Whewell's philosophy of science.

35 From the preface to vol. I of Whewell's *Elements of Morality,* p. vii.

36 Here Aristotle rather than Plato seems to provide the better model of inquiry.

CHAPTER 2: PRACTICAL ETHICS

1 Plato, *Euthyphro,* in *The Trial and Death of Socrates,* translated by G. M. A. Grube (Indianapolis, IN: Hackett Publishing, 1975), p. 6.

2 Ibid.

3 Ibid.

4 Ibid., p. 9.

5 Ibid., p. 10.

6 Ibid., p. 12.

7 Ibid., p. 20.

8 Ibid.

9 Socrates recounted an instance of his disobedience in *Apology*, in *Trial and Death of Socrates*, p. 34. Given an order to do something he regarded as unjust, Socrates resisted even at the possible price of being put to death for refusing. He commented that "government, powerful as it was, did not frighten me into any wrongdoing."

10 Ibid., p. 26.

11 Ibid.

12 It is noteworthy that Sidgwick says this in his *Methods of Ethics*, which is such a quest.

13 Bernard Gert, *Common Morality: Deciding What to Do* (New York: Oxford University Press), 2004.

14 Ibid., p. 125.

15 Ibid., preface, v.

16 Ibid., preface, vii.

17 Ibid., preface, x.

18 Ibid., pp. 4–5.

19 Ibid., p. 9.

20 Ibid., p. 20.

21 Gert does not discuss the possibility of adding another layer to the structure of his system: i.e., having two basic rules — not harming and not violating trust — with his ten rules serving as corollaries. Perhaps he would say that adding this layer would not aid our practical reasoning, as we would still need to focus on the more specific kinds of harms in any given case.

22 Ibid., p. 46.

23 Ibid., p. 34.

24 Ibid., p. 76.

25 To cruelty we might add indifference, callousness, or other vices that betray a lack of concern for harms caused, even if there is no cruelty.

26 Ibid., p. 77.

27 Martin Benjamin usefully explores the possibility of compromising without compromising one's integrity in *Splitting the Difference: Compromise and Integrity in Ethics and Politics* (Lawrence: University Press of Kansas, 1990).

28 An explicit endorsement of the notion of universalizability can be found in Sidgwick's *Methods of Ethics*. Reid's endorsement is cited in what follows above in the main text. For detailed treatments of the idea of universalizability, see, for example, Kurt Baier, *The Moral Point of View* (Ithaca, NY: Cornell University Press, 1958), chap. 8; Marcus G. Singer, *Generalization in Ethics* (New York: Knopf, 1961), chap. 2; or any of the ethical writings of R. M. Hare. Gert (*Common Morality*, pp. 9–10) says that the notion of universalizability is employed in justifying exceptions to his moral rules: "There is universal agreement that what counts as an adequate justification for one person to break a moral rule also counts as a justification for all other persons when the violation has all of the same morally relevant features."

29 Reid, *Active Powers of the Mind*, p. 639. Italics in original.

30 Unfortunately, much of the work of developmental psychologist Lawrence Kohlberg (to be discussed later) is marred by the failure to distinguish these two levels of impartiality. Kohlberg's highest level of morality seems to require impartiality at both levels. In his famous Heinz dilemma, Kohlberg insists that, in order to be operating at the highest moral level, Heinz should be as willing to steal a drug to save the life of a total stranger as that of his own wife.

31 This discussion of the Golden Rule is based on James Jaksa and Michael S. Pritchard, *Communication Ethics: Methods of Analysis,* 2nd ed. (Belmont, CA: Wadsworth, 1994), pp. 101–104.

32 Gert, *Common Morality,* p. vii. He details his criticisms in "Morality vs. Slogans," *Publications of the Center for the Study of Ethics in Society* (Kalamazoo: Western Michigan University, 1989).

33 Richard Whately, "Critique of the Golden Rule," in Marcus G. Singer, ed., *Morals and Values* (New York: Scribners, 1977). It should be noted that Whately did not himself agree with these objections, although he did think that we must concede that the Golden Rule is much less powerful than its supporters typically suppose.

34 "Defense of the Golden Rule," in Singer, *Morals and Values,* pp. 115–129. This article, originally published in *Philosophy* in 1963, is reprinted in Marcus G. Singer, *The Ideal of a Rational Morality* (New York: Oxford University Press, 2002), pp. 264–283; and it is supplemented with an illuminating set of additional notes and comments (pp. 284–292).

35 Sissela Bok, *Lying: Moral Choice in Public and Private Life* (New York: Vintage Books, 1999), p. 28.

CHAPTER 3: TRUST AND TRUTHFULNESS

1 Adam Smith, *An Inquiry into the Nature and Causes of the Wealth of Nations,* ed. Edwin Canaan (New York: Modern Library, 1937).

2 Annette Baier, "Trust and Anti-Trust," in her *Moral Prejudices* (Cambridge, MA: Harvard University Press, 1995), p. 116.

3 Ibid., pp. 116–117.

4 Ibid., p. 117.

5 Ibid., p. 118.

6 This paragraph is adapted from chap. 2, "A Crisis of Confidence?" in Jaksa and Pritchard, *Communication Ethics,* p. 35.

7 The trends since 1976 are available from the Gallup Poll News Service and can be found at http://www.gallup.com/poll.

8 This is according to the November 10–21, 2004, Gallup Poll.

9 Bok, *Lying: Moral Choice in Public and Private Life,* p. 31.

10 Thomas Reid, *An Inquiry into the Human Mind on the Principles of Common Sense,* ed. Derek Brookes (University Park: Pennsylvania State University Press, 1997), p. 193.

11 Ibid.

12 Ibid., p. 194.

13 Ibid., p. 193.

14 Ibid.

15 Ibid., p. 194.

16 Ibid.

17 James Wallace, *Ethical Norms, Particular Cases* (Ithaca, NY: Cornell University Press, 1996), p. 100.

18 Ibid., p. 38.

19 Ibid., p. 16.

20 For a discussion of how quickly and insightfully a group of ten-year-olds can generate examples illustrating the sorts of conflicts Wallace identifies under the rubric of *justice,* see my *Reasonable Children,* pp. 165–167.

21 Ronald Dworkin, *Taking Rights Seriously* (Oxford: Oxford University Press, 1977), p. 133.

22 Wallace, *Ethical Norms, Particular Cases,* p. 43, quoted from Dewey.

23 Of course, being honest does not by itself mean that one can be relied on to exercise good judgment or to complete tasks competently.

24 Wallace, *Ethical Norms, Particular Cases,* p. 101.

25 Ibid., p. 101.

26 Ibid., p. 99.

27 Ibid., pp. 14–18.

28 Ibid., p. 22.

29 Ibid., p. 93.

30 Stephen Klaidman and Tom L. Beauchamp, *The Virtuous Journalist* (New York: Oxford University Press, 1987), p. 33.

31 Ibid., p. 155. Trust, they say, also can be harmed by reporters who are careless, exercise poor judgment, fail to respect confidentiality, or show little concern for whether their stories hurt people.

32 Code of Professional Conduct of the American Institute of Certified Public Accountants (AICPA), section 54, article III: Integrity, .01.

33 Ibid., section 54, article III: Integrity, .02.

34 Ibid., section 55, article IV: Objectivity and Independence, .01.

35 Ibid., section 100— Independence, Integrity, and Objectivity: .01 Rule 102— Integrity and Objectivity.

36 Ibid., Interpretations under Rule 102— Integrity and Objectivity, .01: Rule 201— General Standards, D. *Sufficient Relevant Data.*

37 For discussions of these and other prominent cases of accounting misconduct, see Ronald F. Duska and Brenda Shay Duska, *Accounting Ethics* (Oxford: Blackwell Publishing, 2003).

38 Wallace, *Ethical Norms, Particular Cases,* p. 94.

39 Ibid., p. 95.

40 Ibid.

41 Ibid., p. 96.

42 Ibid.

43 Ibid.

44 Or, if he is also committed to truthfulness in other activities as well, this is to be understood as commitment to a set of "technical" norms applicable in these practices — but not to a *moral* norm of truthfulness that cuts across these practices.

45 Wallace, *Ethical Norms, Particular Cases,* p. 96.

46 For a brief discussion of problems in defining "research misconduct," see *On Being a Scientist: Responsible Conduct in Research,* prepared by the Committee on Science,

Engineering, and Public Policy and sponsored by the National Academy of Sciences, the National Academy of Engineering, and the Institute of Medicine (Washington, DC: National Academy Press, 1995), pp. 15–17.

47 Wallace, *Ethical Norms, Particular Cases*, pp. 71–76.

48 Ibid., p. 93.

49 Ibid., p. 96.

50 Ibid., p. 79.

51 For a good discussion of what is involved in noticing these factors, see Lawrence Blum's *Moral Perception and Particularity* (New York: Cambridge University Press, 1994). Chap. 3, "Moral Perception and Particularity," discusses the idea of moral *salience.*

CHAPTER 4: GOOD JUDGMENT

1 See, for example, #2 under I. Fundamental Canons in the National Society for Professional Engineers (NSPE) Code of Ethics for Engineers. Similar wording is found in most of the codes of the major engineering societies.

2 A more detailed presentation of this case is in Charles E. Harris Jr., Michael S. Pritchard, and Michael J. Rabins, *Engineering Ethics: Concepts and Cases*, 3rd ed. (Belmont, CA: Wadsworth, 2005), p. 347. This account is based on Molly Galvin, "Unlicensed Engineer Receives Stiff Sentence," *Engineering Times* 16, no. 10 (October 1994): 1, 6.

3 This account is based on Eugene Braunwald, "Cardiology: The John Darsee Experience," in David J. Miller and Michel Hersen, eds., *Research Fraud in the Behavioral and Biomedical Sciences* (New York: John Wiley, 1992), pp. 55–79. For further discussion of honesty and deception in research, including both the Darsee case and the Robert A. Millikan case discussed below, see Harris, Pritchard, and Rabins, *Engineering Ethics*, pp. 132–134.

4 "Conduct Unbecoming," *Sunday New York Times Magazine*, October 29, 1989, p. 41.

5 For a discussion of research misconduct, see Nicholas Steneck, *Office of Research Integrity: Introduction to Responsible Conduct of Research* (Washington, DC: Office of Research Integrity, 2004).

6 Much of what follows is from my article, "Bribery: The Concept," *Science and Engineering Ethics* 4 (1998): 281–286.

7 Bok, *Lying: Moral Choice in Public and Private Life.*

8 See, for example, John Danley, "Toward a Theory of Bribery," *Business and Professional Ethics Journal* 2 (1984): 19–39.

9 Thomas Carson, "Bribery," in *Encyclopedia of Ethics*, ed. Lawrence C. Becker and Charlotte Becker (New York: Garland Press, 1992), p. 98.

10 Richard DeGeorge, *Competing with Integrity* (New York: Oxford University Press, 1993), p. 198.

11 Ibid., pp. 99–100.

12 Scott Turow, "What's Wrong with Bribery," in *Business Ethics*, ed. W. Michael Hoffman and Robert E. Frederick, 3rd ed. (New York: McGraw-Hill, 1995), pp. 536–538.

13 Ibid., p. 537.

14 Ibid., p. 538.

15 DeGeorge, *Competing with Integrity*, p. 10.

16 Ibid., p. 115.

17 Turow, "What's Wrong with Bribery," p. 538. Turow's specific example is bribing a Nazi guard to facilitate escape.

18 For my earliest attempts, see "Conflicts of Interest: Conceptual and Normative Issues," *Academic Medicine* 71, no. 12 (December 1996): 1305–1313; and Sandra Borden and Michael S. Pritchard, "Conflict of Interest in Journalism," in Michael Davis and Andrew Stark, eds., *Conflicts of Interest in the Professions* (New York: Oxford University Press, 2001), 73–91.

19 Michael Davis, "Conflict of Interest," *Business and Professional Ethics Journal* 1 (Summer 1982): 17–28. His most recent discussion is in his introduction for Davis and Stark, eds., *Conflicts of Interest in the Professions*.

20 Neil Luebke, "Conflict of Interest as a Moral Category," *Business and Professional Ethics Journal* 6 (Spring 1987): 66–81.

21 Kevin McMunigal, "Rethinking Attorney Conflict of Interest Doctrine," *Georgetown Legal Ethics* 5 (1992): 844–847.

22 In Davis and Stark, eds., *Conflicts of Interest in the Professions*, p. 9. For Davis, the obligation in question is to exercise reliable judgment in behalf of another.

CHAPTER 5: PROFESSIONAL INTEGRITY

1 Stephen Carter, *Integrity* (New York: Basic Books, 1996), p. 7.

2 Ibid.

3 Ibid., p. 29.

4 Ibid., p. 27.

5 Ibid., p. 7.

6 See, for example, the Preamble to the Code of Professional Conduct of the American Institute of Certified Public Accountants: "The principles call for an unswerving commitment to honorable behavior, even at the sacrifice of personal advantage." Cited in Duska and Duska, *Accounting Ethics*, p. 201.

7 Damien Cox, Marguerite La Caze, and Michael P. Levine, *Integrity and the Fragile Self* (Burlington, VT: Ashgate, 2003), p. 103.

8 Ibid.

9 Ibid., p. 104.

10 Ibid.

11 Ibid.

12 Plato, *The Republic*, trans. G. M. A. Grube (Indianapolis, IN: Hackett Publishing, 1974), p. 32.

13 Ibid.

14 Gareth Matthews reports an interesting question posed by a fifth grader with whom he shared the Ring of Gyges story. If you were trying to steal a TV, Adam wondered, "would that become invisible just because you were carrying it, or would people see a TV set float across the room and out the door?" (p. 6). This sort of question, says Matthews, raises a set of other questions that may cast into doubt the invulnerability such a ring might provide its bearer. See Gareth Matthews, "*The Ring of Gyges:* Plato

in Grade School," *International Journal of Applied Philosophy* 14, no. 1 (Spring 2000): 3–11.

15 Immanuel Kant, *Kant's Critique of Practical Reason,* trans. Thomas Kingsmill Abbott (London: Longmans, Green, 1889), pp. 124–125. Cited in Emma Rothschild, "Condorcet and Adam Smith on Education," in Amelie Oksenberg Rorty, ed., *Philosophers on Education* (Routledge: New York, 2000), 213.

16 David Hume, "Enquiry Concerning the Principles of Morals," in *Hume's Enquiries,* ed. Paul Nidditch (Oxford: Clarendon Press, 1975), pp. 282–283.

17 Ibid.

18 Ibid.

19 Of course, sensible knaves are not alone in this. In general, it can be quite challenging to muster up the courage to acknowledge mistakes, even mistakes that are in some sense excusable.

20 This may go some distance in explaining why, for decades, national surveys have consistently indicated that the public's confidence in the honesty and ethics of professionals is so low.

21 Martin Hollis, *Trust within Reason* (New York: Cambridge University Press, 1998), p. 13.

22 This story is based on an article that appeared in the *Seattle Times,* July 24, 2000.

23 Wilson's suggestion that there is more reason to strip someone of his or her degree in a professional area than in history is a bit puzzling. The thought may be that, in the professions, having earned one's credentials is a necessary element of trustworthiness. At the same time, Lewis's credibility as an author and historian may rest at least in part on the credibility of the claim that he had earned his Ph.D.

24 R. Johnson, "Inside Job," *Wall Street Journal,* January 19, 1988, p. 1.

25 Ibid., p. 12.

26 Ibid., p. 1.

27 Ibid., p. 12.

28 Ibid.

29 Ibid. This is a quote of a remark by Robert C. Smith, vice president of investor relations.

30 Mike Martin, *Meaningful Work: Rethinking Professional Ethics* (Lawrence: University Press of Kansas, 2000), p. 173.

31 Ibid. Social psychologist Irving Janis's important work on group dynamics seems to focus primarily on social explanations of wrongdoing. However, his more positive account of how groups can resist the shortcomings of "groupthink" seems to presuppose that certain qualities of character on the part of individual members of groups can make a crucial difference (e.g., the commitment to developing and sustaining independent, critical judgment even in the face of pressure to go along with others and the courage to speak up in opposition to apparent consensus). See Irving Janis, *Groupthink,* 2nd ed. (Boston: Houghton Mifflin, 1982).

32 Ibid.

33 *Gilbane Gold* (1989), National Society for Professional Engineers, 1420 King Street, Alexandria, VA 22314.

34 For a critical discussion of this shortcoming, see Michael Pritchard and Mark Holtzapple's "Responsible Engineering: *Gilbane Gold* Revisited," *Science and Engineering Ethics* 3, no. 2 (1997): 217–230.

35 For 3M's own account of its Pollution Prevention Pays (3P) program, see its Web site at http://www.mmm.com/profile/envt/3p.html.

36 See David Lorge Parnas, "SDI: A Violation of Professional Responsibility," in Deborah Johnson, ed., *Ethical Issues in Engineering* (Englewood Cliffs, NJ: Prentice-Hall, 1991), pp. 15–25. The account that follows is adapted from my discussion in "The Responsible Professional," in *Responsible Communication: Ethical Issues in Business, Industry, and the Professions,* edited by James A. Jaksa and Michael S. Pritchard (Cresskill, NJ: Hampton Press, 1966), pp. 146–148.

37 Ibid., p. 17.

38 Ibid., p. 15.

39 Ibid., p. 25.

40 Ibid.

41 Ibid., pp. 23–24.

42 Akira Kurosawa, *Ikiru* (the movie script for *To Live*), edited by Donald Richie (New York: Simon and Schuster, 1968).

43 Hume, *Enquiry Concerning the Principles of Morals,* p. 283.

CHAPTER 6: BASIC DUTIES AND CODES OF ETHICS

1 J. O. Urmson, "Saints and Heroes," in *Essays in Moral Philosophy,* ed. A. I. Melden (Seattle: University of Washington Press, 1958), p. 205.

2 Gert, *Common Morality,* p. 50.

3 Ibid., p. 53.

4 The next few paragraphs are adapted from my "Engineering Ethics," in R. G. Frey and Christopher Heath Wellman, eds., *A Companion to Applied Ethics* (Oxford: Blackwells, 2003), pp. 620–632.

5 John Ladd, "The Quest for a Code of Professional Ethics," in *AAAS Professional Ethics Project: Professional Ethics Activities of the Scientific and Engineering Societies,* ed. Rosemary Chalk, Mark S. Frankel, and Sollie B. Chafer (Washington, DC: American Association for the Advancement of Science, 1980), pp. 154–159; Heinz Luegenbiehl, "Codes of Ethics and the Moral Education of Engineers," *Business and Professional Ethics Journal* 2, no. 4: 41–61. Both articles are reproduced in Johnson, *Ethical Issues in Engineering.*

6 Steven Unger, *Controlling Technology: Ethics and the Responsible Engineer,* 2nd ed. (New York: Holt, Rinehart and Winston, 1994); Michael Davis, *Thinking Like an Engineer* (New York: Oxford University Press, 1998), chap. 4.

7 In recent years those who have this specialization have come to be called "ethicists." Although "moral" and "ethical" are commonly treated as more-or-less synonymous (as they are in this book), "moralist" and "ethicist" are not.

8 Cass Sunstein, "Agreement without Theory," in Cass Sunstein, *Deliberative Politics,* ed. Stephen Macedo (New York: Oxford University Press, 1999), pp. 123–150.

9 Ibid., p. 123.

10 Amy Gutmann and Dennis Thompson, *Democracy and Disagreement* (Cambridge, MA: Harvard University Press, 1996).

11 Ibid., p. 124.

12 Jonsen and Toulmin, *Abuse of Casuistry.*

13 Ibid., p. 17.

14 *The Belmont Report: Ethical Principles and Guidelines for Protection of Human Subjects of Biomedical and Behavioral Research,* Publication No. OS 78-0012 (Washington, DC: Department of Health, Education, and Welfare, 1978).

15 Ibid., pp. 1–2.

16 Sunstein, *Deliberative Politics,* p. 124.

17 The next several pages are adapted from my article, "Engineering Ethics," in Frey and Wellman, *A Companion to Applied Ethics,* pp. 620–632.

18 H. W. Clausen, "Procedure in Developing Ethical Standards Adopted by the American Association of Engineers," *Annals of the American Academy of Political and Social Science* 101 (1922): 90.

19 Ibid., p. 92.

20 Ibid.

21 C. F. Taeusch, *Professional and Business Ethics* (New York: Henry Holt, 1926), p. 101.

22 See Jonsen and Toulmin, *Abuse of Casuistry.* See also David Boeyink, "Casuistry: A Case-Based Method for Journalists," *Journal of Mass Media Ethics* (Summer 1992): 112–113, for a similar account of how a local newspaper developed its code of ethics.

23 Board of Ethical Review, National Society of Professional Engineers (1965–2000), *Opinions of the Board of Ethical Review,* volumes 1– 8 (Arlington, VA: NSPE Publications), various dates.

24 Jonsen and Toulmin, *Abuse of Casuistry,* chap. 17.

25 This theme will be developed more fully in chapter 9.

26 Benjamin, *Splitting the Difference.*

27 I wish to thank Insoo Hyun for pointing this out to me.

28 Sunstein, *Deliberative Politics,* p. 128.

29 Ibid., p. 125.

30 Ibid., p. 126.

31 Ibid., p. 134.

32 Ibid., p. 125.

33 Ibid., p. 131.

34 Ibid., p. 132.

35 Ibid., p. 145.

CHAPTER 7: GOOD WORKS

1 J .O. Urmson, "Hare on Intuitive Moral Thinking," in *Hare and Critics,* ed. Douglas Seanor and N. Fotion (Oxford: Clarendon Press, 1988), p. 168.

2 Since first publishing my "Good Works" article (*Professional Ethics* 1, nos. 1–2 [Spring/Summer 1992]: 155–177), the expression "good works" has taken hold somewhat in engineering ethics literature. It is used extensively in all three editions (1995, 2000, 2005) of Harris, Pritchard, and Rabins, *Engineering Ethics.* My special interest in engineering ethics may explain my peculiar attraction to this expression, in preference to, for example, "good deeds." In one of its senses, "works" refers to engineer-

ing structures. In another it connotes "succeeds." "Good works" plays on this ambiguity. However, "good deeds" might also be serviceable insofar as it suggests that character as well as outcome is involved. In any case, I use "good works" only as shorthand for referring to a complex variety of notions, rather than as a technical expression.

3 Herbert Fingarette, *On Responsibility* (New York: Basic Books, 1967), p. 146.

4 Philip Hallie, *Lest Innocent Blood Be Shed* (Kansas City, MO: Harrow, 1979).

5 Ibid., p. 161.

6 Ibid., p. 21.

7 I discuss these differences more fully in my *On Becoming Responsible* (Lawrence: University Press of Kansas, 1991), chap. 9, pp. 160–180.

8 Certainly a great many residents were brave, even if not heroic. But it may be that many others were neither, even though they lent support. For example, it is not clear that the many children who lent support were as aware of the dangers to themselves as they were of the dangers to those they protected. Nevertheless, the support they provided does not seem to be fully captured by the notion of basic duty.

9 This is not offered as a definition of "profession," or as a set of necessary and sufficient conditions. For a more comprehensive statement of the salient features (but still no definition), see Bayles, *Professional Ethics*, pp. 7–13.

10 Personal communication with statistician Michael Stoline, my colleague at Western Michigan University.

11 This is a fictional example but representative of actual faculty members who can be found on any college or university campus.

12 This is based on Dr. Robert A. Berenson's account of one of his challenges as a physician: Robert A. Berenson, "A Physician's Reflections," *Hastings Center Report* 19, no. 1 (January/February 1989): 12–15.

13 This is one of seven individuals featured in *Quintessence International* as moral exemplars in dentistry. James T. Rule and Muriel J. Bebeau discuss John E. Echternacht's professional career and personal values in great detail in *Quintessence International* 31, no. 9 (2000): 673–683. They discuss the other six exemplars in subsequent issues.

14 It is not plausible for *us* to say this. They might say this of *themselves*, however. For a discussion of the distinction between first and third person perspectives, see chap. 9, "Personal Morality," in my *On Becoming Responsible*.

15 John Ladd, "Bhopal: An Essay on Moral Responsibility and Civic Virtue," *Journal of Social Philosophy* 22, no. 1 (Spring 1991): 73–91.

16 Ibid., p. 82.

17 Ibid., p. 88.

18 Ibid.

19 Ibid.

20 Ibid., p. 78.

21 Ibid., p. 90.

22 Accreditation Board for Engineering and Technology, *Fifty-third Annual Report*, 1985, 98.

23 See http://www.abet.org/EAC/each2000.html.

24 Two notable exceptions are Edmund Tsang, "Why Service Learning? And How to Integrate It into a Course in Engineering," and Rand Decker, "Professional Activism: Building from Service-Learning, Reconnecting Community, Campus and Alumni through Acts of Service," both in Kathryn Ritter-Smith and John Saltmarsh, eds.,

When Community Enters the Equation: Enhancing Science, Mathematics and Engineering Education through Service-Learning (Providence, RI: Campus Compact, Brown University, 1998).

25 I have made an initial effort in my "Professional Responsibility: Focusing on the Exemplary," *Science and Engineering Ethics* 4 (1998): 215–233.

26 In November 1996 the ASCE Board of Direction adopted the following as its definition of "sustainable development": "Sustainable Development is the challenge of meeting human needs for natural resources, industrial products, energy, food, transportation, shelter, and effective waste management while conserving and protecting environmental quality and the natural resource base essential for future development."

27 Campus Compact supports the development of service-learning programs throughout the country. For an early statement of its efforts, see Timothy Stanton, *Integrating Public Service with Academic Study* (Providence, RI: Campus Compact, Brown University, 1989). For recent applications of Campus Compact objectives to science, mathematics, and engineering education, see Ritter-Smith and Saltmarsh, eds., *When Community Enters the Equation*.

28 *Calvin and Hobbes,* by Bill Watterson, in *Kalamazoo Gazette,* December 23, 1990.

29 See Frederick C. Cuny, *Disasters and Development* (New York: Oxford University Press, 1983), edited by Susan Abrams for Oxfam America; and Frederick C. Cuny, with Richard B. Hill, *Famine, Conflict, and Response* (West Hartford, CT: Kumarian Press, 1999). For further discussion of Cuny's relief efforts, see my "Professional Responsibility: Focusing on the Exemplary" and the Moral Leaders section of the Center for Ethics in Science in Engineering: http://onlineethics.org.

30 Two other sources that might be helpful are Sarah Kuhn, "Engineering Students Encounter Social Aspects of Production," *Science and Engineering Ethics* 4 (1998): 457–472; and Eugene Schlossberger, "The Responsibility of Engineers, Appropriate Technology, and Lesser Developed Nations," *Science and Engineering Ethics* 3 (1997): 317–326.

CHAPTER 8: WORKING TOGETHER

1 Margaret Gilbert, "Walking Together: A Paradigmatic Social Phenomenon," in *Living Together* (Lanham, MD: Rowman and Littlefield, 1996), pp. 184–187. I thank Rachelle Hollander for bringing the work of Margaret Gilbert to my attention in her forthcoming "Professional Responsibilities in Scientific and Engineering Research," in *Science, Technology, and Society,* edited by Sal Restive (New York: Oxford University Press, forthcoming).

2 At the outset of her attempt to explain how the concept of a social group involves this idea, Gilbert quotes sociologist George Simmel: "Sociation ranges all the way from the momentary getting together for a walk to founding a family . . . from the temporary aggregation of hotel guest to the intimate bonds of a medieval guild" (Gilbert, *Living Together,* p. 178). The Simmel passage is cited from Georg Simmel in D. N. Levine, ed., *Georg Simmel: On Individuality and Social Forms* (Chicago: University of Chicago Press, 1908/1971), p. 24. Gilbert sees the key elements in taking a walk together as central to much of political philosophy. I am more interested here in its possible

application to professionals working together in groups, bringing it closer, perhaps, to Simmel's understanding of medieval guilds.

3 Gilbert, *Living Together*, p. 184.

4 Ibid., p. 185.

5 Ibid.

6 Ibid.

7 Ibid., p. 188.

8 Ian McEwan, *Enduring Love* (New York: Anchor Books, 1997). I thank Martin Benjamin for bringing this novel to my attention.

9 Ibid., p. 11.

10 Ibid., p. 14.

11 Ibid., p. 15.

12 Ibid.

13 Ibid.

14 Ibid.

15 Ibid., pp. 16–17.

16 Martin Benjamin, *Philosophy and This Actual World* (Lanham, MD: Rowman and Littlefield, 2003), p. 101.

17 Here it is assumed that consensus is not attainable. With compromise one retains disagreement with the view one ultimately settles for; it is just that one can "live with it." Benjamin's question is how one can settle for something in this way without also compromising one's integrity. Consensus, too, can raise questions of integrity (if, for example, it is suspected that one has simply "caved in"); but here there is no disagreement with the view one ultimately settles for. For a good discussion of the distinction between consensus and compromise, and of problems in "deciding together," see Jonathan Moreno, *Deciding Together: Bioethics and Moral Consensus* (New York: Oxford University Press, 1995).

18 Ibid., p. 125.

19 John Rawls, *Political Liberalism* (New York: Columbia University Press, 1993), p. 37.

20 Benjamin, *Philosophy and This Actual World*, p. 133.

21 Ibid.

22 Benjamin, *Splitting the Difference*, p. 5.

23 Benjamin discusses this example in chap. 2, "Moral Compromise," of *Splitting the Difference*. This account that follows is adapted from Jaksa and Pritchard, *Communication Ethics*, pp. 150–151.

24 Ibid., p. 25.

25 Benjamin, *Philosophy and This Actual World*, p. 138.

26 Ibid., p. 141.

27 Ibid.

28 Ibid., p. 135. There is no guarantee, of course, that a compromise solution can be worked out in particular cases. Regarding human embryo research, Benjamin suggests the following possibility: Research is to be permitted only for the first fourteen weeks from fertilization (the formation of the primitive streak). Is this enough for those who feel strongly that there should be a more permissive policy? Can it be accepted without loss of integrity by those who feel strongly that no human embryo research should be undertaken? Benjamin leaves these questions for the reader.

29 Irving Janis, *Groupthink*. The account that follows is adapted from Jaksa and Pritchard, *Communication Ethics*, pp. 151–157.

30 This film, produced by CRM Films in 1975, has now been replaced by CRM's video-cassette *Groupthink*, which features the 1986 Challenger space-shuttle disaster as its case study. Although the original film is no longer available, Janis's analysis remains useful.

31 Ibid.

32 Rogers Commission, *Report to the President by the Presidential Commission on the Space Shuttle Challenger Accident*, June 6, 1986 (Washington, DC).

33 This account is based on personal communication with the author and on a public presentation he made at Western Michigan University in 1993. Widely discussed, whistleblowing is a very important topic but will not be pursued further in this book. For the author's current views on this topic, see Harris, Pritchard, and Rabins, *Engineering Ethics*, pp. 197–206.

34 Michael Davis discusses alternative strategies in his "Avoiding the Tragedy of Whistle-blowing," *Business and Professional Ethics Journal* 8, no. 4 (1989): 3–19.

CHAPTER 9: DISPOSITIONS, PERCEPTION, AND IMAGINATION

1 This chapter draws heavily from my "Perception and Imagination in Engineering Ethics," *International Journal of Engineering Education*, Vol. 21, No, 3, April 2005. Here I focus on engineering. But similar comments about character, perception, and imagination apply to other professions as well.

2 May, "Professional Virtue and Self-Regulation," p. 408.

3 Ibid.

4 For a discussion of some of the results of this project, see Michael S. Pritchard, "Professional Responsibility: Focusing on the Exemplary," *Science and Engineering Ethics* 4, no. 2 (1998): 215–233. This was supported by National Science Foundation Grant #SBR-930257.

5 My account is based on Joseph Morgenstern's excellent "The Fifty-Nine Story Crisis," in the *New Yorker*, May 29, 1995, 45–53.

6 Ibid., p. 48.

7 Ibid.

8 Ibid.

9 This might be compared with a remark once made by a sports announcer in reaction to a spectacular golf shot by Tiger Woods in the third round of the 2001 PGA golf championship. After Woods hit his shot through a narrow opening in the trees, 143 yards to the green, and landed it 18 feet from the cup, the announcer commented: "Luck is just preparation for an opportunity."

10 W. Gale Cutler, "When 'Johnny' Won't Read," *Research.Technology.Management* (September/October 1988), p. 53. This is one of a series of fictional case studies designed by Cutler to encourage reflection on engineering ethics.

11 Taken from the IEEE Code of Ethics as approved by the IEEE Board of Directors, August 1990: http://swww2.ieee.org/about/whatis/code.html.

12 I explore the idea of exemplary engineering practice in "Professional Responsibility: Focusing on the Exemplary." Although not an example from engineering, the Fran Kelsey example is also discussed in this article.

13 William Grigg, "The Thalidomide Tragedy — 25 Years Ago," *FDA Consumer*, February 1987, pp. 14–17.

14 I first explored the idea that one might be "prepared to be lucky" in discussing the case of engineer William LeMessurier in my "Responsible Engineering: The Importance of Character and Imagination," *Science and Engineering Ethics* 7, no. 3 (2001). I draw from and extend that analysis further in the discussion of LeMessurier below.

15 Eugene S. Ferguson, *Engineering and the Mind's Eye* (Cambridge, MA: MIT Press, 1992), p. 39.

16 Blum, *Moral Perception and Particularity.* See especially chap. 3, pp. 30–61.

17 Ibid., p. 30.

18 Ibid.

19 Ibid., p. 32.

20 Richard DeGeorge opens his *Business Ethics,* 5th ed. (New York: Prentice-Hall, 1999), pp. 3–5, with this case.

CHAPTER 10: MORAL DEVELOPMENT

1 My book *Reasonable Children* is an extended defense of the inclusion of moral education in the schools. There I argue that the Hastings Center goals for moral education in higher education can also be employed in suitable ways even at the elementary school level. Here the focus will be on those aspects of moral education that might later prove to be relevant for professional life.

2 Character Counts is a coalition effort by the Josephson Institute of Ethics that has gained widespread support from national educational organizations, national youth development and service organizations, national community service and civic organizations, national community organizations, and regional educational organizations. See http://www.charactercounts.org.

3 I explore reasonableness as a basic goal of moral education in the schools in *Reasonable Children.*

4 John Dewey, *Reconstruction in Philosophy,* in Jo Ann Boydston, ed., *John Dewey: The Middle Works, 1899–1924,* vol. 12 (Carbondale: Southern Illinois University Press, 1991), p. 177, cited in Wallace, *Ethical Norms, Particular Cases,* p. 43.

5 Environmental chemist Theodore Goldfarb (SUNY–Stony Brook) and I have written an instructional text, *Ethics in the Science Classroom,* for middle and high school teachers who wish to integrate ethics into their regular science classes. This text is accessible in the Education section of the Online Center for Ethics in Science and Engineering at http://onlineethics.org/. It can also be accessed at http://www.wmich.edu/ethics/.

6 The next several pages are based on my "Kohlbergian Contributions to Educational Programs for the Moral Development of Professionals," in *Educational Psychology Review* 11, no. 4 (1999): 397–411.

7 For extended discussions of the special relevance of Kohlbergian accounts of moral development to the professions, see James Rest and Darcia Narvaez, eds., *Moral Development in the Professions* (Hillsdale, NJ: Lawrence Erlbaum Associates, 1994). Of course, not all courses in professional ethics presume the soundness of Kohlbergian accounts of moral development.

8 See, for example, Lawrence Kohlberg, *The Philosophy of Moral Development: Moral Stages and the Idea of Justice,* vol. 1 of *Essays on Moral Development* (San Francisco: Harper and Row, 1981).

9 Jean Piaget, *The Moral Judgment of the Child* (New York: Free Press, 1965).

10 This brief summary of Kohlberg's account is based on my account in Jaksa and Pritchard, *Communication Ethics: Methods of Analysis,* pp. 95–97. The intent here is not to encourage the acceptance of Kohlberg's theory, which has been subjected to very serious criticism. See, for example, Carol Gilligan, *In a Different Voice: Psychological Theory and Women's Development* (Cambridge, MA: Harvard University Press, 1982); Martin Hoffman, *Empathy and Moral Development: Implications for Caring and Justice* (Cambridge, UK: Cambridge University Press, 2000); John C. Gibbs, *Moral Development and Reality: Beyond the Theories of Kohlberg and Hoffman* (London: Sage Publications, 2003); and my own *On Becoming Responsible* and *Reasonable Children.*

11 Lawrence Kohlberg, "Moral Stages and Socialization," in *The Psychology of Moral Development: The Nature and Validity of Moral Stages,* vol. 2 of *Essays on Moral Development* (San Francisco: Harper and Row, 1983), p. 173.

12 Piaget and Kohlberg fail to mention a possibly significant difference between egoistic and egocentric thinking. The egocentric child fails to understand differences between his or her own perspective and that of others. However, it does not follow from this that the child is only self-interested (egoistic). He or she may want genuinely to please another but simply not know how to do so.

13 Although Kohlberg stresses the cognitive limitations of these two stages, it would seem that Hume's sensible knave or Kant's prudent steward would not have cognitive shortcomings of the sort that Piaget and Kohlberg have in mind, however impoverished their affective development may seem.

14 See James Rest, Muriel Bebeau, Darcia Narvaez, and Stephen Thoma, "A Neo-Kohlbergian Approach: The DIT and Schema Theory," *Educational Psychology Review* 11, no. 4 (1999): 291–324. See also James Rest, Muriel Bebeau, Darcia Narvaez, and Stephen Thoma, *Postconventional Moral Thinking* (Mahwah, NJ: Lawrence Erlbaum Associates, 1999).

15 Robert Fullinwider, "Moral Convention and Moral Lessons," *Social Theory and Practice* 15, no. 3 (1989): 333.

16 For some complications this might pose for the ability of Rest's Defining Issues Test (DIT) to distinguish responses that reflect conventional versus postconventional schemas, see my "Kohlbergian Contributions to Educational Programs for Moral Development," pp. 400–404.

17 Muriel Bebeau and Stephen J. Thoma, " 'Intermediate' Concepts and the Connection to Moral Education," *Educational Psychology Review* 11, no. 4 (1999): 343–360.

18 Ibid., p. 349.

19 Ibid., p. 348.

20 Sidgwick, *Practical Ethics.*

21 For a more recent effort to seek common moral ground without agreement on "foundational" philosophical or theological matters, see Sissela Bok, *Common Values* (Columbia, MO: University of Missouri Press, 1995).

22 For an illuminating discussion of the role of critical thinking in achieving compromises that leave one's moral integrity intact, see Benjamin, *Splitting the Difference*.

Selected Bibliography

Baier, Annette. *Moral Prejudices.* Cambridge, MA: Harvard University Press, 1995.

Bayles, Michael. *Professional Ethics.* 2nd ed. Belmont, CA: Wadsworth, 1989.

Bebeau, Muriel, and Stephen J. Thoma. " 'Intermediate' Concepts and the Connection to Moral Education." *Educational Psychology Review* 11, no. 4 (1999): 343–360.

Benjamin, Martin. *Philosophy and This Actual World.* Lanham, MD: Rowman and Littlefield, 2003.

_____. *Splitting the Difference: Compromise and Integrity in Ethics and Politics.* Lawrence: University Press of Kansas, 1990.

Black, Max. "Reasonableness." In *Education and the Development of Reason,* edited by R. F. Dearden, P. H. Hirst, and R. S. Peters, 194–207. London: Routledge and Kegan Paul, 1972.

Blum, Lawrence. *Moral Perception and Particularity.* New York: Cambridge University Press, 1994.

Bok, Sissela. *Lying: Moral Choice in Public and Private Life.* New York: Vintage Books, 1999.

Callahan, Daniel, and Sissela Bok, eds. *Ethics Teaching in Higher Education.* New York: Plenum, 1980.

Carson, Thomas. "Bribery." In *Encyclopedia of Ethics,* edited by Lawrence C. Becker and Charlotte Becker. New York: Garland Press, 1992.

Carter, Stephen. *Integrity.* New York: Basic Books, 1996.

Cox, Damien, Marguerite LaCaze, and Michael P. Levine. *Integrity and the Fragile Self.* Burlington, VT: Ashgate, 2003.

Cuny, Frederick C. *Disasters and Development.* New York: Oxford University Press, 1983.

Danley, John. "Toward a Theory of Bribery." *Business and Professional Ethics Journal* 2 (1984): 19–39.

Davis, Michael. "Avoiding the Tragedy of Whistleblowing." *Business and Professional Ethics Journal* 8 (1989): 3–19.

_____. "Conflict of Interest." *Business and Professional Ethics Journal* 1 (1982): 17–28.

_____. *Thinking Like an Engineer.* New York: Oxford University Press, 1998.

Davis, Michael, and Andrew Stark, eds. *Conflicts of Interest in the Professions.* New York: Oxford University Press, 2001.

DeGeorge, Richard. *Business Ethics.* 5th ed. New York: Prentice-Hall, 1999.

_____. *Competing with Integrity.* New York: Oxford University Press, 1993.

Donagan, Alan. "Sidgwick and Whewellian Intuitionism." In *Essays on Henry Sidgwick,* edited by Bart Schultz, 123–142. New York: Cambridge University Press, 1992.

Duska, Ronald F., and Brenda Shay Duska. *Accounting Ethics.* Oxford: Blackwell Publishing, 2003.

Dworkin, Ronald. *Taking Rights Seriously.* Oxford: Oxford University Press, 1977.

Ferguson, Eugene S. *Engineering and the Mind's Eye.* Cambridge, MA: MIT Press, 1992.

Fingarette, Herbert. *On Responsibility.* New York: Basic Books, 1967.

Frey, R. G., and Christopher Heath Wellman, eds. *A Companion to Applied Ethics.* Oxford: Blackwells, 2003.

Fullinwider, Robert. "Moral Convention and Moral Lessons." *Social Theory and Practice* 15, no. 3 (1989): 321–337.

Gert, Bernard. *Common Morality: Deciding What to Do.* New York: Oxford University Press, 2004.

———. "Morality vs. Slogans." *Publications of the Center for the Study of Ethics in Society.* Kalamazoo: Western Michigan University, 1989.

Gibbs, John C. *Moral Development and Reality: Beyond the Theories of Kohlberg and Hoffman.* London: Sage Publications, 2003.

Gilbert, Margaret. *Living Together.* Lanham, MD: Rowman and Littlefield, 1996.

Gilligan, Carol. *In a Different Voice: Psychological Theory and Women's Development.* Cambridge, MA: Harvard University Press, 1982.

Gutmann, Amy, and Dennis Thompson. *Democracy and Disagreement.* Cambridge, MA: Harvard University Press, 1996.

Harris, Charles E., Jr., Michael J. Rabins, and Michael S. Pritchard. *Engineering Ethics: Concepts and Cases.* 3rd ed. Belmont, CA: Wadsworth, 2005.

Hoffman, Martin. *Empathy and Moral Development: Implications for Caring and Justice.* Cambridge, UK: Cambridge University Press, 2000.

Hollis, Martin. *Trust within Reason.* New York: Cambridge University Press, 1998.

Hume, David. "Enquiry Concerning the Principles of Morals." In *Hume's Enquiries,* edited by Paul Nidditch. Oxford: Clarendon Press, 1975.

Jaksa, James, and Michael S. Pritchard. *Communication Ethics: Methods of Analysis.* 2nd ed. Belmont, CA: Wadsworth, 1994.

Janis, Irving. *Groupthink.* 2nd ed. Boston: Houghton Mifflin, 1982.

Johnson, Deborah, ed. *Ethical Issues in Engineering.* Englewood Cliffs, NJ: Prentice-Hall, 1991.

Jonsen, Albert, and Stephen Toulmin. *The Abuse of Casuistry.* Berkeley: University of California Press, 1988.

Kant, Immanuel. *Kant's Critique of Practical Reason,* translated by Thomas Kingsmill Abbott. London: Longmans, Green, 1889.

Klaidman, Stephen, and Tom L. Beauchamp. *The Virtuous Journalist.* New York: Oxford University Press, 1987.

Kohlberg, Lawrence. *The Philosophy of Moral Development: Moral Stages and the Idea of Justice.* Vol. 1 of *Essays on Moral Development.* San Francisco: Harper and Row, 1981.

———. *The Psychology of Moral Development: The Nature and Validity of Moral Stages.* Vol. 2 of *Essays on Moral Development.* San Francisco: Harper and Row, 1983.

Luebke, Neil. "Conflict of Interest as a Moral Category." *Business and Professional Ethics Journal* 6 (1987): 66–81.

Martin, Mike. *Meaningful Work: Rethinking Professional Ethics.* Lawrence: University Press of Kansas, 2000.

Matthews, Gareth. "*The Ring of Gyges:* Plato in Grade School." *International Journal of Applied Philosophy* 14, no. 1 (2000): 3–11.

May, William F. "Professional Virtue and Self-Regulation." In *Ethical Issues in Professional Life,* edited by Joan Callahan, 408–411. New York: Oxford University Press, 1988.

McEwan, Ian. *Enduring Love*. New York: Anchor Books, 1997.

Miller, David J., and Michel Hersen, eds. *Research Fraud in the Behavioral and Biomedical Sciences*. New York: John Wiley, 1992.

Morgenstern, Joseph. "The Fifty-Nine Story Crisis." *New Yorker*, May 29, 1995, pp. 45–53.

Plato. *The Republic*, translated by G. M. A. Grube. Indianapolis, IN: Hackett Publishing, 1974.

_____. *The Trial and Death of Socrates*, translated by G. M. A. Grube. Indianapolis, IN: Hackett Publishing, 1975.

Pritchard, Michael S. "Good Works." *Professional Ethics* 1, nos. 1–2 (Spring/Summer 1992): 155–177.

_____. "Kohlbergian Contributions to Educational Programs for the Moral Development of Professionals." *Educational Psychology Review* 11, no. 4 (1999): 397–411.

_____. *On Becoming Responsible*. Lawrence: University Press of Kansas, 1991.

_____. "Professional Responsibility: Focusing on the Exemplary." *Science and Engineering Ethics* 4 (1998): 215–233.

_____. *Reasonable Children*. Lawrence: University Press of Kansas, 1996.

_____. "Sidgwick's *Practical Ethics*." *International Journal of Applied Philosophy* 12, no. 2 (1998): 147–151.

Rawls, John. *Political Liberalism*. New York: Columbia University Press, 1993.

Reid, Thomas. *An Inquiry into the Human Mind on the Principles of Common Sense*. Edited by Derek Brookes. University Park: Pennsylvania State University Press, 1997.

_____. *On the Active Powers of the Mind in Philosophical Works*. Vol. II, with notes by Sir William Hamilton. Hildesheim: Georg Olms Verlagsbuchhandlung, 1997.

_____. *Practical Ethics*. Edited by Knud Haakonssen. Princeton, NJ: Princeton University Press, 1990.

Rest, James, Muriel Bebeau, Darcia Narvaez, and Stephen Thoma. *Postconventional Moral Thinking*. Mahwah, NJ: Lawrence Erlbaum Associates, 1999.

Rest, James, and Darcia Narvaez, eds. *Moral Development in the Professions*. Hillsdale, NJ: Lawrence Erlbaum Associates, 1994.

Ritter-Smith, Kathryn, and John Saltmarsh, eds. *When Community Enters the Equation: Enhancing Science, Mathematics and Engineering Education through Service-Learning*. Providence, RI: Campus Compact, Brown University, 1998.

Sibley, W. H. "The Rational and the Reasonable." *Philosophical Review* 62 (1953): 554–560.

Sidgwick, Henry. *The Methods of Ethics*. 7th ed. London: Macmillan, 1963.

_____. *Practical Ethics*. Edited by Sissela Bok. New York: Oxford University Press, 1998.

Singer, Marcus G. *The Ideal of a Rational Morality*. New York: Oxford University Press, 2002.

_____, ed. *Morals and Values*. New York: Scribners, 1977.

Smith, Adam. *An Inquiry into the Nature and Causes of the Wealth of Nations*. Edited by Edwin Canaan. New York: Modern Library, 1937.

Splitter, Lawrence, and Ann Margaret Sharp. *Teaching Better Thinking: The Classroom Community of Inquiry*. Melbourne: Australian Center for Educational Research, 1995.

Steneck, Nicholas. *Office of Research Integrity: Introduction to Responsible Conduct of Research*. Washington, DC: Office of Research Integrity, 2004.

Sunstein, Cass. "Agreement Without Theory," *Deliberative Politics*. Edited by Stephen Macedo. New York: Oxford University Press, 1999, 123–150.

Taeusch, C. F. *Professional and Business Ethics*. New York: Henry Holt, 1926.

Turow, Scott. "What's Wrong with Bribery?" In *Business Ethics,* edited by W. Michael Hoffman and Robert E. Frederick. 3rd ed. New York: McGraw-Hill, 1995.

Unger, Steven. *Controlling Technology: Ethics and the Responsible Engineer.* 2nd ed. New York: Holt, Rinehart and Winston, 1994.

Urmson, J. O. "Hare on Intuitive Thinking." In *Hare and Critics,* edited by Douglas Seanor and N. Fotion. Oxford: Clarendon Press, 1988.

———. "Saints and Heroes." In *Essays in Moral Philosophy,* edited by A. I. Melden. Seattle: University of Washington Press, 1958.

Wallace, James. *Ethical Norms, Particular Cases.* Ithaca, NY: Cornell University Press, 1996.

Whewell, William. *Elements of Morality.* Vols. I and II. 4th ed. London: Cambridge University Press, 1864.

Index

AAE (American Association of
  Engineers), 90–92
ABET (Accreditation Board for
  Engineering and Technology), 109,
  175nn22–23
Abuse of Casuistry (Jonsen and Toulmin),
  7, 12, 166n16, 174n12
Accountants as professionals, 69
code of ethics for, 45, 169nn32–36, 171n6
Accreditation Board for Engineering and
  Technology (ABET), service-
  learning and, 109, 175–176n24,
  175nn22–23
Advertising, codes of ethics and, 43
Altruism, 30, 120
American Association of Engineers
  (AAE), 90–92
American Society of Civil Engineers
  (ASCE), service-learning and,
  110–111
Applied ethics. *See* Practical ethics
Aristotle, inquiry method of, 13, 166n36
ASCE (American Society of Civil
  Engineers), 110–111
Attorneys as professionals, 40–41, 69,
  171n20
code of ethics for, 41, 61, 171n21

Baier, Annette, 33–35, 168n2
Bayles, Michael, 4, 165nn8–9, 175n9
Beauchamp, Tom L., 44–45, 169nn30–31
Bebeau, Muriel
  on ethical problems in professional
    life, 161–162, 180nn17–19
  on moral thinking, 156–157, 159,
    180n14, 180n16

Behavioral research, ethics and, 89,
  174nn12–15
Belmont Report, The (U.S. Dept. of
  HEW), 89, 174nn14–15
Benjamin, Martin
  on compromise, 122–125, 177n20–28,
    177nn17–18
  on resolving personal conflicts, 120,
    121, 177n16
BER (Board of Ethical Review), 92–93,
  94–95, 174n23
Bhopal, India, disaster, 108, 175nn19–20
Biomedical research, human subjects in,
  89, 113, 174nn12–15
Black, Max, 7, 165n15
Blum, Lawrence, on moral perception,
  145–148, 150, 164, 179nn16–19
Board of Ethical Review (BER), 92–93,
  94–95, 174n23
Boisjoly, Roger, whistleblowing by,
  131–132, 178nn32–33
Bok, Sissela, 181n21
  Golden Rule support by, 31,
    168n35
  on trust and truthfulness, 36–37, 40,
    168n10
Braunwald, Eugene, 53
Bribery, 54–60, 133
  consequences of, 57
  extortion compared to, 56–57, 59, 60
  prohibitions against, 58–59
  Socrates and, 54–55, 115
Business ethics, 173n5
  bribery and, 56–59, 133, 171nn15–17
  customers and, 82, 149, 179n20
  honesty in, 36, 48

Business ethics, *continued*
    mixed conscience in, 77–79, 127,
      172nn24–29
    nonseparation of, and engineering
      ethics, 95–96

Callousness, 167n25
Calvin and Hobbes (comic strip), 59–60,
    111
Cambridge Ethical Society, England, 8,
    163
Campus Compact (organization), 111,
    175–176n24, 176n27
Caring, 153
Carson, Thomas, 56, 170n9
Carter, Stephen, 67–68, 171nn1–5
Cartoons, 1, 14, 35–36, 59–60, 165n2
Casuistry, 7, 11–12, 166n16
method of, 91, 94–95, 174n22
Center for Academic Integrity, 76,
    172n23
Challenger disaster, 130–132, 178nn32–33
Character
    development of, 152–153, 179n2
    explanation of, 79–81
    tests of, 3–4, 69–71, 80–81, 134, 164
Character Counts (organization), 153,
    179n2
Cheating, 23, 24, 76–77
Children
    independent thinking in, 39–40,
      169n21
    Kohlbergian stages characteristic of,
      155, 180n13
    moral education of, 25, 38, 39–40, 43,
      152, 163–164
    reasonableness promoted in, 6,
      165nn12–13
Citicorp Center, Manhattan, structural
    design of, 138–141
Citizenship, 153
Civic-mindedness, 137
Clausen, H. W., 90–92, 174nn18–20
Codes of ethics, 85–99
    agreement despite differences about,
      87–90, 173nn7–10, 173nn11–16

basic duties and, 85, 173nn1–3
construction of, 90–92, 173nn17–22
ideas of, 60, 85–87, 173nn4–6
limitations of, 94–97, 173nn24–26
revision of, 92–93, 173n23
theoretical ambitions, 97–99,
    173nn27–35
See also under specifics, e.g.,
    Accountants as professionals, code
    of ethics for; Engineers as
    professionals, codes of ethics for
Collegiality, 53
Commitment, 137
    professional integrity and, 69, 83, 84,
      116–117, 177nn3–5
Common Morality (Gert), 21–25, 167n13,
    167n28, 181n21
    basic duties in, 85, 107–109, 173nn2–3
    definition of, 22, 167n17
    moral rules in, 22–25, 167nn18–21
Common sense
    principles of, 37, 168n10
    Sidgwick and morality of, 8–11, 21, 163,
      166n19 (*see also Common Morality*
      (Gert))
Communication skills, 137, 151–152
Compassion, 153
Competence, 51–52, 137, 151–152
Compromise, 26, 137, 167n27
    circumstances of, 124, 126, 177n25
    critical thinking and, 163, 181n22
    integrity and, 122, 125, 177n17,
      177nn27–28
    working together and, 122–125, 177n17,
      177n28
Conflicts of interest
    codes of ethics and, 60
    judgment and, 62–66, 119, 120
    standard view of, 61, 62
Conscience, 94
    bad, and integrity, 75–77
    good, and integrity, 81–82
    mixed, and integrity, 77–79
Conscientiousness, 25
Contracts, 33–35, 168n2
Cooperation, 118–122, 137, 154

Courage, 137
Cox, Damien, on integrity, 68–69,
    171nn7–11
Credulity, 37–38
Critical thinking
    compromise and, 163, 181n22
    as groupthink antidote, 129–130
    moral schemas and, 159–160
    as postconventional thinking, 158,
        162
    Sidgwick on, 163–164, 180n20
Crito (Plato), 20, 114
    Socrates and, 18–19, 54–55, 97–98, 115
Cruelty, 24, 167n25
Cuny, Frederick, 112, 175nn29–30

Darsee, John, 52–53, 54, 170nn3–4
Davis, Michael, on conflicts of interest,
    61, 62, 64, 171n19, 171n22
Deceitfulness, 23, 25
Decision making, 7, 164
    bad, and historical fiascoes, 128, 130
    moral perception and, 145–146
    working together and, 124, 126–127
Defining Issues Test (DIT), 163,
    180nn14,16
DeGeorge, Richard, on bribery, 56–58,
    170nn10–11, 171nn15–16
Democratic values
    reasonable pluralism, 123, 125, 126,
        177n22, 177n26, 177nn19–20
    social and political criticism, 159–160
Dependability, 25
Dewey, John, on methods of inquiry, 40,
    41, 153–154, 179n4
Disagreement. *See* Dissent
Disasters
    aversion of, 139–140, 142
    industrial accidents in, 108,
        175nn19–20
    relief efforts after, 109, 112, 175n29
    space shuttle, 130–132, 178nn32–33
    structural roof collapse, 143, 179n15
Dishonesty, 25
Disobedience, 18, 167n9
Dispositions, settled, 136–138

Dissent, 26
    reasonable, as possibility, 50, 123–124,
        177nn19–21
    working together and, 130–132
DIT (Defining Issues Test), 163,
    180nn14,16
Doctors as professionals, 69, 85, 105,
    173n1
    medical specialties and, 49, 51
Doonesbury (comic strip), 1, 165n2
Duty, 85, 100–104, 138, 140–141, 142,
    175nn3–8
Dworkin, Ronald, 39–40, 169n21

Educators as professionals, 69, 76, 85,
    105–106, 172n23, 173n1
Egocentric thinking, 30, 155, 157
Elements of Morality (Whewell), 12–13,
    166n34, 166nn35–36
Enduring Love (McEwan), 118–122,
    177nn8–15
Engineers as professionals
    codes of ethics for, 52, 90–92, 95–96,
        110–111, 135–136, 142, 170n1,
        173nn5–6, 178n11
    environment and, 80–81, 94–95, 111,
        172nn33–34, 173n35, 176n26
    integrity and, 69, 96
    moral norms and, 42–43
    preparation of, 109–112, 141–145,
        175–176n24, 175nn22–23,
        176nn25–30, 178n9
    responsibilities of (*see* Professional
        responsibility)
    societies for, 90–93, 94–95, 96, 142,
        174n23
    whistleblowing by, 131–132, 178nn32–33
Environmental enhancement, 94–95, 111,
    176n26
Environmental pollution, 80–81, 108,
    172nn33–34, 173n35, 175nn19–20
Ethicists, 87–88, 173n7
Ethics, 31, 165n11
    higher education goals for, 2, 164,
        165n6
    priorities and, 63, 68, 91–92

Ethics, *continued*
    See also Business ethics; Codes of
      ethics; Practical ethics;
      Professional ethics
Euthyphro (Plato), 20, 98, 114, 166n1
    Socrates and, 15–18, 115
Extortion, 56–57, 59, 60

Fairness, 17–18, 25, 39–40, 57, 153
Feith, Mark, mixed conscience and,
    77–79, 172nn24–29
Ferguson, Eugene, on structural
    engineering, 143, 179n15
Foreign Corrupt Practices Act (FCPA),
    58–59, 60

Gert, Bernard, 162
    common morality and basic duties,
      85, 107–109, 173nn2–3
    critique of Golden Rule by, 29,
      168n32
    moral rules of, 22–25, 167n21
    works by, 21–22, 167n13
Gilbane Gold (video), 80, 172nn33–34
Gilbert, Margaret, on plural subjects,
    116–117, 176–177n2, 176n1, 177nn3–7
Golden Rule
    critiques of, 29, 168nn32–33
    in practical ethics, 28–31, 168nn31–35
    support for, 29–31, 168nn34–35
Good works, 100–112, 174–175n2
    as beyond duty by ordinary people,
      100–104, 175nn3–8
    positive shift from basic duties to,
      107–109, 134, 175nn15–21
    in professional life, 104–107, 175nn9–14
    service-learning as, 109–112,
      175–176n24, 175nn22–23,
      176nn25–30
Great Britain. Warnock Committee,
    124–125
Group Dynamics (film), 128–130,
    178n30
Groupthink, 127–130
Gutmann, Amy, 88, 173n10, 174n11

Hallie, Philip, 102–104, 175nn4–6
Harmfulness, 57
    industrial accidents and, 108,
      175nn19–20
    justification and, 23, 119–120
    morality and, 147, 167n21, 167n25
    professionals and, 45, 169n31, 169n37
Hartford Civic Center, Connecticut,
    disaster, 143, 179n15
Hastings Center, Briarcliff, New York
    goals for teaching practical ethics and,
      2, 5–6, 164, 165n6, 179n1
Heinz dilemma, 168n30
Hollis, Martin, 75, 172n21
Honesty, 153
    as moral virtue, 25, 137
    as policy or principle, 35–37
    trust and truthfulness in, 40, 172n20
HSIRBs (Human Subject Institutional
    Review Boards), 89, 113, 174nn12–15
Human subjects
    biomedical research and, 89, 113,
      174nn12–15
    embryos in research, 124–125
Hume, David, on sensible knaves, 73–75,
    83–84, 172nn16–18

IEEE (Institute for Electrical and
    Electronics Engineers), code of
    ethics, 142, 178n11
Imagination
    morality and, 137, 153
    professionals and, 133, 140–141,
      144–145, 164
Immorality, 24, 29
Impartiality, 27–28, 168n30
Indifference, 167n25
Institute for Electrical and Electronics
    Engineers (IEEE), code of ethics,
    142, 178n11
Integrity, 57, 67–84, 137
    characteristics of, 67–68
    compromise and, 122, 125, 177n17,
      177nn27–28
    conscience and, 75–79, 81–82

meaningful work and, 82–84
professionals and, 68–69, 83, 84, 96,
116–117, 177nn3–5
Ring of Gyges and, 69–71
trading, and knaves sensible or not,
73–75, 83–84

Jaksa, James, 136–138, 178n4
Janis, Irving, 127–130, 178n30
Johnson & Johnson (firm), 149
Jonsen, Albert, work by, 7, 12, 89, 166n16,
174n12
Josephson Institute of Ethics, Los
Angeles, 179n2
Journalists as professionals, 44, 169n30
Judgment, 51–66, 153
bribery and, 56–60, 133
good, and professionals, 51–54, 66, 133,
164
moral norms and, 50, 98
universalizability in, 27–28
Justification, 23, 26–28, 55, 119–120, 164

Kaidman, Stephen, on standards for
journalists, 44–45, 169nn30–31
Kant, Immanuel, 72, 156–157, 172n15
Kelsey, Dr. Fran, 142, 144, 145
Kipnis, Kenneth, 40–41
Kohlberg, Lawrence
on moral development, 152, 154–157,
163, 180nn7–8, 180nn10–13
moral dilemma approach of, 152,
168n30
moral schemas and Kohlberg's stages,
157–159, 161–162
Kurosawa, Akira, 83, 173n42

La Caze, Marguerite, on integrity, 68–69,
171nn7–11
Ladd, John, 108–109, 175nn15–21
Landers, Charles, 52, 54, 170n2
Law-breaking, justification and, 23
Le Chambon, France, good works in,
102–104
LeMessurier, William, 138–141

Lest Innocent Blood By Shed (Hallie),
102–104, 175nn4–6
Levine, Michael P., on integrity, 68–69,
171nn7–11
Lewis, Norm, 75–77, 172n22
Love Canal, New York State, good works
and, 105, 109
Luck, professional responsibility and,
141–145
Lying, 17, 31, 40, 43–44, 168n35

Martin, Mike
on meaningful work, 82–83, 172n30
on wrongdoing, 79–81, 172nn30–32
May, William F.
professional responsibility and, 3,
133–134, 135, 165n7, 178nn2–3
test of character and, 69–70, 134,
164
McEwan, Ian, on group vs. individual
goals, 118–122, 177nn8–15
Meaningful Work (Martin), 82, 172n30
Methods of Ethics (Sidgwick), 8, 12,
166nn17–18, 167n28
Methods of inquiry
Aristotle, 13, 166n36
casuistry and, 91, 94–95, 174n22
John Dewey, 40, 41, 153–154, 179n4
Socrates, 16–18
Middle axioms
casuistry as test of, 11–12
morality and, 8–9, 163, 166n19
utility to resolve, 10–11
Millikan, Robert A., 53–54
Minnesota Mining and Manufacturing
(firm), 80–81
Misconduct, 52, 53, 64, 76–77
Modesty, 137
Moral development, 151–164
becoming a responsible professional,
151–152
implications for professional ethics,
160–164, 180nn17–19
Kohlberg's approach to, 154–157
moral education, 152–154, 179nn1–3

Moral development, *continued*
   moral schemas and professional ethics
     in, 157–159
   schema application problems,
     159–160, 180nn15–16
Moral education
   children and, 25, 38, 39–40, 43, 152,
     163–164
   goals for, 2, 5–6, 165n6
   moral development in, 152–154,
     179nn1–3
   practical ethics in, 1–3
Moralists, 173n7
Morality. *See* Practical ethics
Moral norms
   critique of, for professionals,
     42–43
   generality of, 38–40, 41, 169nn17–19
   professional preparation and, 40–42,
     48–49
   reasonableness in following, 49–50
Moral perception, professional
   responsibility and, 145–149, 150,
     164, 179nn16–19
Moral pluralism, 123
Moral reasoning
   arguments in, 18–19
   Aristotle and, 13, 166n36
   ordinary people and, 98, 154–156, 163
   top-down approach to, 7–8, 12
Moral schemas
   application of, 159–160
   conventional as maintaining norms,
     157–158, 162
   Kohlberg's stages and, 157–159,
     161–162
   personal interest, 157
   postconventional as critical thinking,
     158, 162
Moral system, 10, 12, 22
Moral vices, 24, 25, 167n25
Moral virtues, 153
   first- and third-person perspective on,
     103, 175n5
   Gert's moral rules and, 24–25

professional responsibility and,
   133–135, 136–138, 178nn2–3
truthfulness among, 48–49
Morgenstern, Joseph, 138–140, 178nn5–8

Narvaez, Darcia, 156–157, 159, 180n14,
   180n16
National Commission for the Protection
   of Human Subjects of Biomedical
   and Behavioral Research, 89,
   174nn14–15
National Society for Professional
   Engineers (NSPE)
   service-learning and, 110–111
   shifting priorities of, 92–93, 94–95,
     135–136, 174n23
Neglectfulness, 16, 23, 25
NSPE (National Society for Professional
   Engineers), 92–93, 94–95, 110–111,
   135–136, 174n23
Nurses as professionals, 69, 85, 173n1

Objectivity, 137
Openness, 53, 137

Parnas, David, 81–82, 173nn36–41
Perception. *See* Moral perception
Perseverance, 137
Philosophical reflection
   assumptions of, 1, 5–6
   contributions of, to practical ethics,
     7–13, 19, 153
Physicians. *See* Doctors as professionals
Piaget, Jean, 154, 180n9, 180n12
Piety, Socratic inquiry and, 16–18
Plato, 15–20, 70–71, 166n1, 171nn12–13
Plumbers as professionals, 33–35
Pluralism
   as moral, 123
   as reasonable, 125, 126, 177n22, 177n26,
     177nn19–20
Plural subjects, working together as,
   116–118, 176–177n2, 176n1,
   177nn3–7
Police officers as professionals, 85, 173n1

Practical ethics
  collaborative work and (*see* Working
    together)
  enduring issue of, 1, 14–15, 165n3
  Golden Rule in, 28–31, 168nn31–35
  judgment and, 9–10, 11, 21, 24–25, 27,
    55–56, 98
  justification in, 23, 26–28, 55
  morally significant good works (*see*
    Good works)
  philosophical contributions to, 7–13
  reasonableness as goal of, 6–7, 116,
    165n14
  teaching of, 1–3, 5–6, 136–138, 141, 154,
    165n6, 173n7, 178n4, 178n10
  theory and practice, 20–21
  See also titles of this same name
Practical Ethics (Reid), 11, 12, 166n34,
    166nn31–32
Practical Ethics (Sidgwick)
  critical thinking and, 163–164, 180n20
  morality of common sense in, 8–11,
    166n19 (see also *Common Morality*
    (Gert))
  science or theory of right and, 9–10,
    166n23
Problem ownership, working together
  and, 113–114
Professional ethics
  moral development and, 157–159,
    160–164, 180nn17–19
  problems in, 161–162
Professional persons
  conflicts of interest and, 60–66
  criteria for, 4, 35, 51, 68, 104, 175n9 (*see
    also* Integrity)
  good judgment of, 51–54, 66, 133
  moral norms and preparation of,
    40–42, 48–49, 83, 109–112, 160–161
    (*see also* Codes of ethics)
  postconventional thinking and, 158, 162
  as prudent stewards, 72–73, 133
  sensible knaves as, 74–75
  trust and expectations of, 32–33, 36, 43,
    57, 74, 168nn7–8, 172n20

truthfulness in, 43–45
  See also specifics, e.g., Doctors as
    professionals; Engineers as
    professionals
Professional responsibility, 33
  being lucky and, 141–145
  betrayals of, 52–54
  ethics and, 1–3, 14, 20, 81–82, 157–159,
    160–164
  good works in, 104–107
  imagination and, 133, 140–141, 144–145
  individual *vs.* collective, 4, 69, 88,
    96–97, 106–107 (*see also* Working
    together)
  moral perception and, 145–149, 150,
    179nn16–19
  preparation for (*see* Moral
    development)
  settled dispositions as virtues and,
    133–135, 136–138, 163, 164, 178nn2–3
  test of character in, 3–4, 69–71, 80–81
Promise-keeping, 8, 23, 25, 33
Prudent stewards, 72–73, 84, 133
  See also Sensible knaves
Public welfare
  as engineering priority, 91–92, 94–95,
    111, 133, 135–136, 138–141
  perception and, 148–149
  sustainable development in, 111, 176n26

Randolph, Isham, 90
Rawls, John, 123, 177n19
Reasonableness
  in following moral norms, 49–50, 123
  goal of practical ethics as, 6–7, 116
  promoted in children, 6, 153,
    165nn12–13, 179n3
  public justification and, 26–27
  uncertainty in, 7, 165n15
Reciprocity, 29–30, 154
Reflection. *See* Philosophical reflection
Reid, Thomas
  moral system and, 10, 162, 166nn27–30
  practical ethics and, 2, 11, 13, 165n4,
    166nn31–32

Reid, Thomas, *continued*
    on universalizability, 27, 167n28
    on veracity and credulity, 37–38,
        168nn12–16
    works by, 165n4, 166n31, 168n10
Respect, 153
Responsibility, 2, 3, 5, 153
    See also Professional responsibility
Rest, James
    DIT of, 163, 180nn14,16
    on moral thinking, 156–157, 159,
        180n14, 180n16
Review boards
    ABET, 109, 175nn22–23
    BER, 92–93, 94–95, 174n23
    HSIRBs, 89, 113, 174nn12–15
Rightdoing
    by scientists, 81–82, 173nn36–41
    vs. wrongdoing, 79–81, 172nn30–32
Righteousness. *See* Piety
Ring of Gyges, integrity and, 69–71,
    171–172n14

Safety. *See* Public welfare
Science
    systems of morality as, 12, 166n34
    teaching of, 153–154, 179n5
    as theory of right, 9–10, 166n23
    truthfulness and, 45–49, 53, 64, 137
Scientists
    code of ethics for, 89, 173n5,
        174nn12–15
    moral vs. technical standards for,
        46–48, 169–170n46
    professional responsibility betrayals
        by, 52–54, 170nn3–5
    professional responsibility exemplified
        by, 142–143, 179nn12–13
    rightdoing by, 81–82, 173nn36–41
Self-sacrifice, 137
Sensible knaves, 73–75, 76–77, 83–84,
    172n19
    See also Prudent stewards
Service-learning, good works and,
    109–112, 175–176n24, 175nn22–23,
    176nn25–30

Sharp, Ann Margaret, 6, 165nn12–13
Sibley, W. H., 6–7, 165n14
Sidgwick, Henry
    dissatisfaction with Whewell by, 12,
        166n33
    philosophical vs. practical and, 1, 165n1
    practical ethics and, 2, 9–10, 13, 83,
        165n4
    top-down approach to ethics by, 8,
        162–163, 166nn17–18
    on universalizability, 167n28
    works by, 8, 165n1, 166n18
Singer, Marcus G., 29–30, 31, 168n34
Smith, Adam, 33, 168n1
Social explanation, wrongdoing and,
    79–81
Socrates
    in Plato's *Apology,* 19–20, 167nn9–11
    in Plato's *Crito,* 18–19, 54–55, 97–98, 115
    in Plato's *Euthyphro,* 15–18, 115
Splitter, Lawrence, 6, 165nn12–13
Sunstein, Cass
    on agreement despite differences,
        88–90, 173nn8–9, 174n16
    on theoretical ambitions, 28–35,
        97–99, 174n
Supererogatory behavior, 100
Sustainable development, 111, 176n26

Taeusch, Carl, 91, 174n21
Teachers. *See* Educators as professionals
Thalidomide, 142
Thoma, Stephen
    on ethical problems in professional
        life, 161–162, 180nn17–19
    on moral thinking, 156–157, 159,
        180n14, 180n16
Thompson, Dennis, 88, 173n10, 174n11
Tipping, bribery compared to, 56–57
Toulmin, Stephen, work by, 7, 12, 89,
    166n16, 174n12
Trocme, Andre, 102–103, 175n5
Trocme, Magda, 102–103, 175nn5–6
Trustworthiness, 57, 153
    as earned trait, 76, 172n23
    need for, 33–35

professionals and, 32–33, 36, 52, 74–75, 151, 168nn7–8, 172n20
prudent stewards and, 72–73
truthfulness as part of, 35–37
untrustworthiness vs., 23, 40, 167n21
voluntary agreements and, 33–35, 168n2
Truthfulness, 8
honesty and trust in, 35–37, 40
morality and, 25, 38–40, 48–49
professionals and, 40–42, 43–45
science and, 45–48
veracity and credulity in, 37–38
Turow, Scott, on bribery, 57, 59, 170nn12–14, 171n17

Uncertainty, 7, 124–125, 126, 165n15
Undependability, 25
Unfairness, 24, 25
U. S. Dept. of Health, Education, and Welfare, 174nn14–15
U. S. Food and Drug Administration, 143
U. S. Marshal Space Agency, 131
Universalizability, 27–29, 167n28
Untrustworthiness, 23, 40, 167n21
See also Trustworthiness
Urmson, J. O., 85, 100, 103, 173n1, 174n1
Utilitarianism, 9, 11, 156–157, 166n18
Sidgwick on, 8, 9, 10

Values clarification, 152
Veracity, 37–38
Vision, as moral virtue, 137

Voluntary agreements, 33–35, 154, 168n2

Wallace, James, 162
on moral norms, 38–44, 48–50, 169nn17–19, 169nn22–29
on science and truthfulness, 45–48
Warnock Committee, 124–125
Whately, Richard, 29, 30, 168nn33
Whewell, William, 2, 13, 21, 162, 165n4
Sidgwick's dissatisfaction with, 12, 166n33
Whistleblowing, 131–132, 178n34
Wilson, Jeane, 76, 172n23
Wisdom, possession of, 19–20
Working together, 113–132
compromise and, 122–125, 177n17, 177n28
dissent when, 130–132
Euthyphro and Crito again, 114–115
group decision making and, 124, 126–127
groupthink when, 127–130
group vs. individual goals when, 116–117, 118–122
problem ownership when, 113–114
uncertainty in, 124–125, 126
walking together and, 116–118
World Trade Center, New York City, disaster, 109
Worthwhile knowledge, 19–20
Wrongdoing, 79–81, 172nn30–32
vs. rightdoing, 81–82, 173nn36–41

DATE DUE